On Your Way
Rejoicing

DAILY READINGS
WITH THE BIBLE

LOUIS M.
TAMMINGA

PAIDEIA PRESS
St. Catharines, Ontario, Canada

Most of the material in this book appeared in an earlier form in *The Family Altar* or *Today*, which are publications of the Back to God Hour. Each page has been rewritten and expanded. The material is used here with the permission of the original publisher.

ISBN 0-88815-039-3 (cloth)
ISBN 0-88815-038-5 (paper)
Printed in the United States of America.

On Your Way
Rejoicing

On Your Way Rejoicing

And he replied, "I believe that Jesus Christ is the Son of God." [And he] went on his way rejoicing (Acts 8:37, 39).

Some of the finest timberlands on the North American continent are found in British Columbia. In the springtime thousands of logs can be seen shooting down the rivers, the rich harvest of a winter season's cutting. Sometimes a jam occurs and the entire flow comes to a standstill. But lumberjacks with expert eyes soon detect the one log that holds the wooden tide. They pry it loose, no matter how tough the job, and the flow moves on once more.

Have you ever had the feeling that your life was stuck, that you just couldn't move anymore? A terrible feeling, wasn't it?

The Bible tells us that the jam in our life is ultimately caused by one log—*sin*. It takes an expert eye to detect the log of sin. Only when you have been trained in the school of the Spirit and the Word can you recognize it. Then you will also know where to go for help. Christ will come to your rescue when you ask Him. He will remove sin. Once you have accepted Him, you can move again and get somewhere. What joy!

Ethiopia's Minister of Finance couldn't go on anymore either. One day he just ran away from it all. But God arranged a meeting with Philip, who led him to Christ. His sins were forgiven, and he could live again, live to the full!

"He went on his way rejoicing . . ."

That's what God has in store for you!

You can be *on your way rejoicing*!

Let's read more about it in the Bible.

God of heaven and earth, we confess that we have come to a standstill because of unforgiven sin. Lead us to repentance and to acceptance of Christ. Help us to walk and run and skip on life's road rejoicing. Your name be praised forever. Amen.

The Grand Design

And God blessed them, and God said to them, "Be fruitful and multiply, and fill the earth and subdue it; and have dominion over . . . every living thing . . ." The Lord God took the man and put him in the garden of Eden to till it and keep it . . . Then the Lord God said, "It is not good that the man should be alone; I will make him a helper fit for him." . . . The man gave names . . . to every beast . . . (Gen. 1:28; 2:15, 18, 20).

Our world has many critics. They agree that this is a bad world. But where, exactly, has the world gone wrong? We must go to the Bible for the answer, for the Bible tells us of the great design God had for the world. When man rejected that design, misery and death were the result.

When God created the earth, He intended to keep in touch with it. God appointed our first parents, Adam and Eve, to be His representatives here. They were to rule and develop the earth for His sake. Their everyday work and life was service to God, an expression of their relationship of love with God.

Note that God designed life for man on earth according to a definite *pattern*, a *structure*. Genesis 1 and 2 imply that.

God established *marriage*. God gave Eve to be Adam's wife. God established the *home*. God told Adam and Eve to have children. God established *work*. Adam had to till the soil and dress the garden. God established *learning*. Adam observed the animals, then gave them names. God established *government*. Adam must "keep" the garden of Eden and have dominion over the earth. God established *worship*. On the sabbath day Adam and Eve might sit down with God and reflect on their relationship with Him. Man had everything to live for in close company with his God.

Is God interested in our personal little world? The sober words of Genesis 1 are our marching orders! It all makes sense. God delights in our faithfulness and a job well done.

Father, see my life as I manage my daily affairs in this small corner of Your vineyard. Through Christ my Lord. Amen.

The Great Breakaway

*Then the eyes of both were opened and they knew that they were naked.
And [Adam] and his wife hid themselves from the presence of the Lord God
. . . And to Adam he said, ". . . cursed is the ground because of you . . .
thorns and thistles it shall bring forth" (Gen. 3:7, 8, 17-18).*

Because of that one reckless moment of sin, three tragic things
happened to Adam and Eve, our first parents.

They cut themselves loose from God: *fear* lingered between
them and God.

They became estranged from each other: *shame* entered their
marriage.

They lost touch with God's good earth: the earth was *cursed*
for the sake of man's sin.

We will never be able to imagine the tragedy of sin, no matter
how much we are part of it and how many of its results we see
around us. This is its pathetic burden: when God entered Paradise,
His royal children cowered as slaves behind the trees of the garden.
Never again would they meet their God in joyful worship, never
again own each other in carefree love, never again delight in Eden's
groves. In the sweat of his brow, man would wrest a living from the
stubborn soil. Storms and floods would batter the land, and strife
and hatred would claim their many victims. Man had become a
lonely vagabond in a forsaken world.

Your problems and sufferings stem from that great
breakaway. It blocks every shortcut toward happiness and
fulfillment. All human solutions fall short here.

Not a very comforting thought, is it?

But when all our ways run dead, God comes with a new way.
His Spirit leads you to Christ, God's Son, who alone can unlock
Eden's gate.

*Holy God, we thank You for the painful diagnosis of our malady; lead us
on the way of healing and restoration. In Jesus Christ our Lord. Amen.*

Restoration in Christ

Now in putting everything in subjection to him, he left nothing outside his control. As it is, we do not yet see everything in subjection to him. But we see Jesus . . . crowned with glory and honor because of the suffering of death, so that by the grace of God he might taste death for every one (Heb. 2:8-9).

The work of Christ is richer than we can ever imagine.

Today's Bible verse tells us that He *suffered death* for us. He did this to pay for Adam's sins and the sins of Adam's children. Those who believe in Christ as Savior are freed from the burden of guilt. Jesus tasted death for them. God accepts such people as His own children. Have you confessed your sins? Don't delay it. Without forgiveness there is no hope.

But Jesus did more than pay for the sins of believers: there was still that *unfinished task* of Adam and his children. Christ took over where Adam left off. The Bible calls Him, therefore, the "last Adam" (I Cor. 15:45). During His whole life on earth, Christ wholeheartedly met the demands of the Kingdom of God by doing the will of God in loving obedience. He did this also for His followers. Because of His life's work, the Son was crowned with glory and honor by the Father.

Believers share that bliss with the Master. The forgiven sinner can go to Christ every day for new courage, new vision, and new energy. This gives him the power and desire to do God's will in every part of life. Thus Christians today can begin to do what Adam was created to do.

But, you say, we see so little of it.

Are you sure? Look again. Today's text tells us that Jesus Christ is crowned with glory and honor because of His suffering. You own that with Him. And the world will see that glory and honor through you when you reach out toward those in distress.

Lord Jesus, take possession of us, fill us with the beauty of Your redemption, and help us to share it with people in our life. Amen.

Angel of Darkness

"Be sober, be watchful. Your adversary the devil prowls around like a roaring lion, seeking some one to devour (I Pet. 5:8).
And no wonder, for even Satan disguises himself as an angel of light (II Cor. 11:14).

Satan fools you. He is the most self-effacing creature you will ever meet. The more he is minimized and ignored, the better he feels. In fact, he has convinced many people that he doesn't exist at all. They think that only the things we can see and touch are real, and they smile good-naturedly about the Christian notion of real devils and demons.

A frequent character in mystery movies is the fiendish scientist who dreams of making himself invisible in order to dominate the world. Satan has achieved much more than that. He is not only invisible, he is also a master of disguise, appearing as an angel of light, even though he is bloodthirsty as a lion. If it weren't for the restraining hand of God, there would be no limit to the havoc he could cause. Even at that, he is the chief cause of today's hopelessness. He sows suspicion, he causes conflict, he corrupts morals, he mars beauty, and he distorts truth.

How can we ever hope to restore meaning and harmony to our world if we ignore satan and his hordes of demons? We must first acknowledge that we are no match for him. Our leaders in society must do that too. Next, we must call for help. The only helper is Christ. He defeated satan when He died on the cross for the sins of His believers. A society that makes room for the rule of Christ is no longer at the mercy of satan.

Christ sent satan away by speaking to him from the Word of God. We must read that Word daily, study it, pray about it, and live it. Only then will we become strong people for the Lord. The world needs such people.

Thank You, Lord Jesus, for having defeated the devil. Holy Spirit, open our eyes that we may recognize the workings of the prince of darkness. Amen.

Yes, There Is Hope

For in him all things were created, in heaven and on earth, visible and invisible, whether thrones or dominions or principalities or authorities—all things were created through him and for him. He is before all things, and in him all things hold together (Col. 1:16-17).

A Christian magazine reported the graduation speech of Stephanie Mills given at Mills College, Oakland, California. The title of her address was: "The Future Is a Hoax." She said that she saw ahead only an overpopulated world doomed to cannibalism, a horribly disfigured planet with mankind continuing to spread "like an unfeeling, unthinking cancer across the earth." She felt that the most humane thing to do would be to have no children and to establish some form of population control.

Though Stephanie's words of despair disturb us, they express a fear we all sense. What is so distressing about the problems of our world is that no one seems to be in control. The future is shrouded in the ugly clouds of conflict, poverty, alienation, and enslavement.

Is there no hope left?

Yes, there is! Today's Bible passage tells us that Christ is in control. Every power on earth is dependent on Him, we read. All things were created in Him and hold together in Him. We cannot understand that, but we accept it by faith. Because of Christ, we can have hope and joy even in this dark world.

The future is not a hoax.

We enter upon it confidently, though not lightly.

Two conditions must be met in order for us to experience hope and power.

There must be a personal tie between Christ and us. We the saved, He the Savior; we the members of the Body, He the Head.

And, secondly, we must bring His healing grace to this very sick world. We will read more about that.

Lord, let us not perish in hopelessness. Reach the distressed through Your followers. Amen.

Through Darkness to Light

And I will have pity on Not Pitied, and I will say to Not my People, "You are my people"; and he shall say, "Thou art my God" (Hos. 2:23).

There is one question that comes up over and over: *Why did God permit sin to enter the world?*

As we search for an answer in the Word of God, we are led to a confession rather than a simple answer. *God displayed His love most abundantly in Christ's triumph over sin.*

In our text God's people Israel are compared to an unfaithful wife who forsakes her husband. But when Israel confesses this terrible unfaithfulness, God forgives His people, and they embrace in a newfound unity. God's people then call out in great astonishment, "Thou art my God!"

On the one hand we say: "If only Israel had not committed those vulgar sins!"

On the other hand we must say: "God showed the riches of His grace more abundantly than before."

Another example.

The prodigal son should have known better than to leave his father's house and waste his goods with the Jezebels abroad. Of course! Yet, in the end the wastrel boy held more riches in his hands than before: a deeper dimension of the Father's love and grace.

Our generation seems to be confronted with more grinding problems than ever before. The foundations begin to crumble. We say: "If only the fall in Paradise had not happened . . ." But today's doom may become God's occasion to blaze a trail of grace more brightly than ever before.

And we will say in holy amazement: "Thou art my God!"

Merciful loving God, show us ever more clearly Your compassion. May it be the fuel in our lamps so that we can let them shine. Amen.

Hope Because of the Spirit

We know that the whole creation has been groaning in travail together until now . . . Likewise the Spirit helps us in our weakness; for we do not know how to pray as we ought, but the Spirit himself intercedes for us with sighs too deep for words (Rom. 8:22, 26).

The young of our day are not the only ones who express fear for the future. The older and wiser have expressed the futility of life before. In 1939 the great thinker Albert Einstein conducted a sober ceremony at the New York World's Fair at which a tube was buried 50 feet below the site of the fair. Provision had been made for the tube to be unearthed by anthropologists in the year 6939. The tube contained, among other documents, a brief message from Einstein. It said: "Everyone lives in fear of being eliminated from the economic cycle. We live in fear and terror for the future . . . We live in the dark and we die in the dark."

It has now become fashionable to analyze the meaninglessness of life and make dire predictions.

Today's Bible passage uses a far more positive and hopeful approach. It speaks of the Holy Spirit and of prayer. Yes, says Romans 8, we are weak and we don't know how to pray. But the Holy Spirit comes to our rescue. He prays for us, and His prayer is very intense.

Now, all that is a mystery beyond our understanding, but Romans 8 adds *two results* which we can observe. This work of the Spirit completes the ties which bind us to God as His children. And that leads to the next thing: God's creation is being relieved of its burden of damnation.

The divine order is beautifully simple. Man's fall into sin saddled creation with this anguished curse; through man's salvation, this curse is lifted away and life is possible once more.

Thank You, Holy Spirit, for Your mighty works in Christ's children. May all of life experience Your healing through us. For Christ's sake. Amen.

Monumental Misunderstanding

Then they said, "Come, let us build ourselves a city, and a tower . . . and let us make a name for ourselves . . ." And the Lord said, . . . "Come, let us go down and there confuse their language, that they may not understand one another . . ." (Gen. 11:4, 7).

One of the most baffling mysteries about today's crisis is that it shouldn't have happened. We possess all the knowledge to analyze the distress of our civilization, we have the means to remedy it, and yet, somehow we can't understand what ails us, much less find a cure. How is it that with our fabulous resources we can't create a little happiness and security?

The story of the tower of Babel provides a clue. There was a deep longing for unity and harmony among the people who lived just after the great flood, so they built a great society and an ambitious culture. But there was one thing lacking. *God* had no place in that society. *Therefore God did not bless that society.* Soon everything went wrong. The people just didn't understand each other anymore, they couldn't get along, and their commonwealth fell apart. The tower of Babel, deserted and unfinished, stood as a monumental reminder of human failure.

Our modern civilization has all the means to bring about the abundant life. But it has not given God's precepts a place in public life, in welfare, in education, in industry, in labor. *Now God withholds His blessings.* Social scientists may dismiss this factor, since it cannot be measured, but in the meantime our society continues to crumble. Let there be found among Christians everywhere earnest prayer for the indispensable blessings of God, the Creator and Upholder of life.

We, personally, should take stock of our gifts, our resources, our opportunities, and our time, and ask ourselves: How do we serve God with them all?

We must admit, Lord, that building towers is in the marrow of our bones. Help us now to restore Your honor to life. Amen.

The Quest for Relief

There are many who say, "Oh that we might see some good! Lift up the light of thy countenance upon us, O Lord!" (Ps. 4:6).

Demonstrators assembled before the royal palace in Jerusalem. They demanded better times from King David. "Come, show us something good," they shouted.

David did what more heads of state should have done in later centuries: he went to the Lord. His request to God was very specific. He said, "Lord, lift up the light of thy countenance upon us!"

That prayer had a wonderful meaning.

David was thinking of a mother who bent over a sick child, her face filled with pity and understanding. God will do that to people, even to nations, when they call on Him. He will do that to us too.

An old doctor who belonged to the generation of physicians who made house calls once observed that some of the most urgent requests for his services had come in the late evening. He suggested that there is something fearsome about the midnight hour, and that many sick cannot go on.

Perhaps people and nations see in today's problems the gathering darkness of the midnight hour, the ominous feeling Churchill expressed in his farewell speech: "Our problems are too great for us to solve."

In that midnight hour, we must go to our heavenly physician. He will lift the light of His countenance upon us. He can do that because in Christ Jesus He came so close to us that He assumed our flesh. Christ lived our life and died our death. All things are now in Christ's hand. He will help us and lead us. With Him we can go on.

Heavenly Father, You know the times in which we live. For a moment we thought it was no use anymore. But we saw Christ, and now we know better. Amen.

A Great Challenge for the Church

Always be prepared to make a defense to any one who calls you to account for the hope that is in you, yet do it with gentleness and reverence (I Pet. 3:15).

This dark world will not receive the light of hope if we hide it. The apostle Peter wrote to Christians who were persecuted, and it must have been very hard for them to evangelize. But Peter urges them, nevertheless, to speak up for Christ.

Most of us are free citizens. Nothing keeps us from telling others about the Christian faith except ourselves. Nearly everybody agrees that the churches today have no message for life, and modern society ignores the churches.

Is the church ignored because the real Christian hope of which Peter speaks is absent from so many churches? Ronald Knox tells of a guided tour he took through the mighty St. Paul's Cathedral in London and then comments, "Never had I been so conscious of the real absence." Churches are empty when the hearts of the members are empty, and they become alive when Christ fills hearts with hope. Hope is that vision which knows Christ as the Redeemer and Restorer of life before the face of God.

Do you have that hope? Then you personally should get it out into the open, for *you are the church!* There is no other way for the church to reach the hopeless than through you. Those Christians of Peter's day felt so rich with Christ in their hearts that their outlook on life changed radically and they simply had to do something about it. That's how hope conquered the dark world then. It can do the same thing again! The world needs it! And you have it, if you believe in Jesus!

Holy Spirit, set us afire, remove the barriers in us that hinder the free reign of Christ, and help us to give account of our hope. May a great revival come to the churches through us all. For Jesus' sake. Amen.

Restoration Through Offense

They dragged Jason and some of the brethren before the city authorities, crying, "These men who have turned the world upside down have come here also . . ." (Acts. 17:6).

When the hope of Christ is brought to the world, it encounters much resistance. Paul and Silas brought the gospel of Christ to the people of Thessalonica for about three weeks. Some were saved, but many rejected the gospel and aroused the citizens to hate Christians.

The argument which Paul's enemies used before the city council is very noteworthy: "These that have turned *the world upside down* are come hither also; and these all do contrary to the decrees of Ceasar, saying that there is another king, one Jesus." That was a lie, but one thing they had observed correctly: the preaching of Christ shook life to its foundations.

Are you prepared to be a representative of Christ, at any time, at any place, at the risk of being rejected and abused? The Kingdom of Christ cannot come any other way. It will not leave people uncommitted. Those who will not submit their ways to Christ will become haters of Him. The test of Christian faithfulness, then, is to continue in loving kingdom service in spite of rejection.

When Bernard and his Cistercian monks moved into Wormwood Valley in France, around the beginning of the twelfth century, they were met with hatred and bitterness. But years of preaching and exemplifying the gospel of Christ chased away the darkness and suffering from Wormwood Valley. People turned to Christ, and their lives unfolded in love and understanding. Later that region became known as the Valley of Clairvaux, the valley of clear vision. Hence the name, Bernard of Clairvaux. Does that name suit us? Then we will turn the world *right side up!*

Spirit of Light, help us to express the kingdom vision of our Lord at the risk of being reviled. For Jesus' sake. Amen.

Vision for Youth

Your sons and daughters shall prophesy, and your young men shall see visions (Acts 2:17).

There once was a time when Christianity was attacked in big universities; then there came a time that it was ridiculed; after that it was ignored. A professor said, "The suffering of Biafran children shows that it is immoral to suppose there is a God."

But history didn't stand still. Scholars have begun to feel increasingly uneasy about the causes of world conditions. Both the free West and the Communist world face problems that are totally the making of the secular mind. There is widespread fear that the nations just can't continue on their own.

God may well use this spirit of chastening to open many doors for the gospel. He can use the distemper of our times to let His Word have access to council chambers, halls of learning, and board rooms.

All that would then embody a great challenge for a new generation of Christians. They will be prepared for that challenge when they *see* more in this world than meets the eye. That's what today's Scripture text says. Our sons and daughters will see *visions* and will prophesy accordingly. It all began at Pentecost. There the Holy Spirit was given to the church of the New Testament. He takes several steps with young Christians. First He introduces them to Christ so that they are saved, then He makes them grow in the knowledge of Christ, and from there He leads them in understanding what Christ means for society.

May our young people be diligent students in the school of the Spirit, for their task is of strategic importance.

Holy Spirit, equip a new generation among us for a life of service in keeping with the needs of our age. Make them totally loyal to Christ. Amen.

Godly Detachment

And [Jesus] said to them, "Truly, I say to you, this poor widow has put in more than all those who are contributing to the treasury . . . her whole living" (Mark 12:43-4).

Who gives you health?
Who brings your children home every day?
Who makes the crops grow and provides for man and beast?
That's right—God!
And that makes us humble, for He doesn't owe it to us. It embarrasses us somewhat too. We worry and fret about our needs, and here we realize again that everything depends on the Lord.

Let me tell you how I picture this widow lady Jesus saw in the temple. She had loved her husband, she had needed him, and when he died it seemed to her that everything was over. But then, amazingly, she made a discovery. It seemed as if God moved right in with her. He spoke to her, He supplied her daily needs, He listened to her, and, as time went on, He meant everything to her.

The rest is simple.

One day she gave all her holdings to the Lord—two coppers.

It was a wonderful gesture. Not really all that heroic from her point of view. It was an expression of *godly detachment* in earthly concerns. Every day was a joint venture with God, whose storehouse was never depleted.

Now, you must conduct your affairs in keeping with the demands of our day and age. There are no two lives alike. But there is one virtue we all must develop: *godly detachment*. It means that we have the right estimate of life. Our relationship with God is the hub around which everything turns. As a spin-off, we get courage to go on, to do our work responsibly, and we find our table decked with food. Nothing can intimidate us.

Thank You, heavenly Father, for taking care of us and being our Partner. We count on You. Through Christ. Amen.

Humility

I thank him . . . Christ Jesus our Lord, because he judged me faithful by appointing me to his service, though I formerly . . . persecuted . . . him (I Tim. 1:12-13).

Paul had been called to service by Christ. He considered that an exceptional honor—the more so since he had been guilty of great evil before.

Paul stresses the sinfulness of his early life very strongly here. He tells his young friend Timothy that he had persecuted the Christ. In the original language Paul actually states, "I was a persecutor." That is a very strong expression. A man who goes fishing for a day is not yet a fisherman. He who fails is not yet a failure. But Paul says in effect, "I was a persecutor; it was in the marrow of my bones; I was Mr. Persecutor himself."

Why this display of humility? Because it was in the way of humility that Paul could honestly see the reality of his misery, and the greatness of Christ's mercy over him. Humility was for Paul the gateway to freedom from sin, freedom to let go of himself and serve Christ. In verse 14 Paul states, "The grace of our Lord overflowed for me." In humility Paul had become nothing in himself but everything in Christ.

Paul had good reason to share this with Timothy. Timothy faced many problems in the ministry. He felt unworthy and inferior. In Christian humility Timothy could frankly acknowledge his weaknesses, but he could also see Christ Jesus. "Look what He did for me!" Paul says. "He will do that for you too, Timothy!"

Hallelujah! What a Savior!

May humility be your outstanding gift. It will enable you to assess yourself honestly. Free from pretense, you can make Christ central in your life. Only then can you be truly your own person.

You have given us the honor of serving You, dear Savior; may we freely go to You for help and direction. Purge away, Holy Spirit, all our negative feelings and motives. May we truly understand ourselves. Through Your mercy. Amen.

Happiness

And all Judah rejoiced . . . (II Chron. 15:15).

The Russian poet Maxim Gorki, who died in 1936, once visited Coney Island's amusement park. Observing the huge framework of high rides filled with screaming people, he remarked to his host, "What a sad people they must be."

Much has been written, especially in these last few years, about depression and sadness. It has been said that we have more riches than our fathers and mothers but are less happy. Perhaps that is true. So many people today labor furiously to afford things and build a little estate, only to find life slipping through their fingers. Sadder still is the realization that we have lost the capacity to be happy. For some reason, we can't shake the feeling of being disgruntled with ourselves and with people in our lives.

But here in the book of Chronicles we read of genuinely happy people. All Judah rejoiced. How did they do it? The remarkable thing was that they lived during hard times: ". . . great disturbances afflicted all the inhabitants of the lands. They were broken in pieces" (vs. 5-6).

What was the cause? "For a long time Israel was without the true God" (vs. 3).

And how did they get happiness? "But when in their distress they turned to the Lord . . . and sought him, he was found by them" (vs. 4).

Deeply felt happiness doesn't often spring from agreeable circumstances. Where people have been reconciled to God, there happiness begins to flow. Wander away from God, and cheer will soon shrivel up. True fulfillment is rooted in harmony with God and people. This explains why fortunate people are not always happy people. It also explains why the Lord expects *you* to have happiness in *your* heart.

Lord, You have created us for a life of happy service in this world. Safeguard us in Christ's redemption. Lift the burden of heaviness from our shoulders. Because of our Mediator. Amen.

Dependence Is Strength

For [the harlot] said, "I will go after my lovers, who give me my bread and my water, my wool and my flax, my oil and my drink" (Hos. 2:5).
I will betroth you to me in faithfulness . . . "And in that day, says the Lord, I will answer the heavens and they shall answer the earth; and the earth shall answer the grain, the wine, and the oil, and they shall answer Jezreel" (Hos. 2:20-22).

The two texts above this meditation embody two lifestyles. The first one is *man-centered*; the second is *God-centered*.

The first one is a very cramped style, a very small world. Just me myself—*my* bread, *my* water, *my* wool . . . my . . . my . . . Hosea compares this lifestyle to that of an immoral woman who has left her husband. From here on life is only self-seeking and self-serving.

The God-centered lifestyle has endless possibilities. Hosea portrays it most interestingly. He shows the majestic interdependence of life. It all begins with reconciliation: God and His people are reunited in forgiveness and love. That leads to a chain reaction. Heaven and earth are connected. God blesses the skies. The clouds "answer" the fields, rain falls in abundance, the fields "answer" the eager roots of grain and vine-trees, and there is goodly yield of fruits to "answer" the need of the people. They, in turn, "answer" their God (vs. 23): they live for Him and commune with Him. All in all, an amazing chain reaction of blessedness. When you love God and serve Him, one good thing leads to another.

Could you ever imagine a richer life? Christians who have this relationship with God recognize every gift in life as a token of His love. They become very *strong* people because they know they can depend on God. They are also very *generous* people: because they received freely, they give freely.

Loving God, we praise You for making covenant with Your people. Thank You for providing us with everything we need. Help us to bless others. For Jesus' sake. Amen.

The Blessings of Love

*Now there was at Joppa a disciple named Tabitha, which means Dorcas
[gazelle]. She was full of good works and acts of charity. In those days she
fell sick and died . . . All the widows stood beside [Peter] . . . showing tunics
and other garments which Dorcas made (Acts 9:36-7, 39).*

Dorcas was a blessing. But she would be the first to give credit
to Christ, who had saved her and lived in her heart ever since.

She had a special arrangement with the Lord. The more she
gave in Jesus' name, the more He gave her and the more joyful her
life became. Her helpfulness to people was no burden to her; it was
part of the resurrection life of Christ through her.

Her service of love found an ever widening echo in Joppa. The
people around her grew in appreciation, and that lit up their lives,
from which others, in turn, were blessed. When Dorcas died, the
people came out in great numbers, exhibiting the things Dorcas had
made for them. Through their sorrow, those Christians experienced the joy of Christ. Dorcas had done more for the people than
she realized. She had not only enriched them with her goods, she
had also enriched them in their persons. She had made them better
people.

You should take stock of your life. What have you made of it?
Have you noticed how swiftly life passes by once you settle into a
certain routine? Dorcas came to terms with her Lord and herself,
and she lived for others. She discovered real joy. It gave her peace
and fulfillment. What a life! You may have to overcome some
resistance in your heart to develop such a life, but you can do it in
the Master's power. Ask Him to open your eyes to people who need
you. And the people with whom you deal will, in turn, become that
way themselves. A great undercurrent of Christian joy will be
generated in the world.

*Lord Jesus, show us the ongoing power of Your goodness in this world.
Help us not only to see ideals but to weave them into the routine of the day.
Through us have mercy on this world. Amen.*

Hope in Sorrow

Blessed are those who mourn, for they shall be comforted (Matt. 5:4).

The ideal: on your way rejoicing.

The reality: mourning and sadness.

Isn't that a correct assessment?

Well, it is true that you know moments of loneliness, failure, and frustration. And many around you suffer pain, mental anguish, and feel hopeless under the pressure of problems. Among the nations there is starvation, poverty and oppression.

Is the way of rejoicing forever blocked?

Hear the words of Christ. In the Sermon on the Mount, which we read today, He singles out those who are sad and says that they will be comforted. The word *comfort* means *intense power*. He promises you that today.

Did you say that you haven't felt it?

Then perhaps you haven't followed the right road to that comfort. You see, *Jesus Christ Himself is that comfort.* He traveled a long way to become our comfort. He was born in our human flesh. He took our sin and guilt upon Himself. He bore all our griefs and sorrows. He bids you now to accept Him as Savior. Then you, too, will be a forgiven person. You, too, can then lay your sorrow at His feet. Don't think for a moment that He doesn't understand what you go through: He has gone through it Himself. Don't think that He has no time for you: He has bought you at the price of His life. And don't think that He is unable to supply your needs in your particular situation: He triumphed over death and hell. All power has been given to our Christ on earth and in heaven. He offers you His comfort, His *intense power*, because He offers Himself.

With Him you can go your way rejoicing.

Dear Savior, give that power to all who are mourning today. We confess again that You are a perfect Savior and that Your promises will not fail. Holy Spirit, make it true for us. Amen.

Courage

At the end of forty days they returned from spying out the land. But Caleb quieted the people before Moses, and said, "Let us go up at once, and occupy it; for we are well able to overcome it" (Num. 13:25, 30).

Twelve spies returned from surveying the land of Canaan. Ten brought a bad report: they were afraid and predicted that the land could not be taken. Two spies (Joshua and Caleb) brought a good report: they were courageous and urged the people of Israel to go up and possess the land.

What makes some people courageous and others cowardly? Is courage an inborn gift which some people have and others don't?

It is not that simple.

Courage basically has to do with what we *see.*

The ten spies saw with their physical eyes. And, indeed, their eyes didn't lie! The inhabitants of Canaan were heavily armed giants. The two spies saw them too, but they saw more; with their spiritual eyes they saw *God.* And that gave them courage. With God they were indeed in the majority, even though they brought out a minority report.

We are surrounded by grim realities. Disasters strike everywhere. How long can society continue? But we also see spiritual dimensions. God is in charge. In His company we are *not* grasshoppers! We trace our ancestry to Paradise. We were meant to rule—a race of kings and queens. God will see us through. Since He will multiply our puny efforts to bring relief to the suffering, we take courage and march on. It's not who you are but who you know.

Perhaps you face circumstances that fill you with the heavy feeling of anxiety. But do you believe that the God who bought you in Christ's blood will also protect you? Then you have courage!

Help us to continue life's journey with courage, dear God, for Your strength will possess our hearts. Holy Spirit, keep our eyes directed toward God. Amen.

Restoration Through Moderation

Rejoice in the Lord always; again I will say, Rejoice. Let all men know your forbearance (Phil. 4:4-5).

It is one thing to confess the rule of Christ as the only hope for our day, it is another to *live* it. The Kingdom of Christ will ultimately bring its blessings to the nations if believers everywhere personally follow their Lord. Paul tells us that our *moderation* or *forbearance* must be shown to everybody. By *moderation* or *forbearance* Paul means: *live the life of victorious friendliness.*

Believers do not have to put up a grim fight for their rights and place. They strive for the administration of justice, of course, also for themselves, but they don't do so with grim despair. In Christ they are elevated to the status of *royalty.* Believers are therefore filled with the power and compassion of the *King,* ready to save and to bless. This attitude is so strong because its origin is in Christ and believers are one with Christ. They are able to look at things somewhat from a distance, and it becomes their second nature to seek the well-being of God's creatures and creation.

It once happened that the disciples engaged in an absurd debate as to who among them was the greatest. Jesus then stooped down and washed their feet. He told the baffled disciples to do the same for each other. John Calvin once urged believers to show forbearance before judges, even when condemned to death and led to the scaffold.

It is striking here in the Letter to the Philippians that Paul links this patient kindness with *rejoicing.* Apparently this self-effacement doesn't drain you. It relaxes you, it relaxes people in your life, and it creates the kind of atmosphere where energy and wisdom can steadily multiply.

Dear Lord, how patient You are with us every day again. Holy Spirit, show us how strong our Savior is so that we never feel threatened. Fill us with kindness. Amen.

Diligence

The sluggard buries his hand in the dish . . . (Prov. 19:24).
The hand of the diligent will rule . . . (Prov. 12:24).

In each of these texts we notice the word *hand*.

The first hand belongs to the *sluggard*, the second to the *diligent*.

We might conclude that the first one is slow and lazy, and the second one quick and industrious. But that is not so much the point of these two texts. We read that the hand of the sluggard is "buried in the dish." He is busy in his own way. He is feeding himself; he makes *consumption* a full-time concern. The hand of the diligent, we read, "rules," which means that he arranges things, that he is a real *provider*.

The two hands, then, stand for two basic views of life and work.

The *sluggard* lives and works under a big umbrella that removes God and heaven from his view. God has nothing to do with his life. He is his own purpose in his work. His work makes it possible for him to have big or small pleasures, depending on good or bad fortunes and a variety of tastes.

The *diligent* man of our text knows God's company in his daily work. He is God's representative and seeks the well-being of his fellow man, and the improvement of his Father's world. He may reach this ideal only partially and his job may be grim, but deep down he had contact with God whom he serves.

Do you know God as your partner in life and work? John Calvin said, "If work is to find its original meaning, if work is to give satisfaction to the worker, man must associate himself with God. He must let himself be possessed of God and turn the management of his work to God."

We lay the burdens of our toil before You, Father, and we ask for courage to do a good and honest job in Your world. For Jesus' sake. Amen.

A Wallet Full of Holes

You have sown much, and harvested little; you eat, but you never have enough; you drink, but you never have your fill; you clothe yourselves, but no one is warm; and he who earns wages earns wages to put them into a bag with holes. Thus says the Lord of hosts . . . Go up to the hills and bring wood and build the house . . . (Hag. 1:6-8).

Money is very frustrating. You get your paycheck, and you pay a little debt here and an overdue bill there. The car needs repair, and mother announces that another child has outgrown his clothes. The paycheck is gone and you hope there will be some relief next time. But you know better.

It's an old story. It plagued the people of Haggai's day. The people toiled and scraped and worried, but they never got ahead. It seemed as if they put their wages in a bag with holes.

Haggai doesn't come with a solution for that frustrating problem. But Haggai does show them what is behind their problem. You see, the people had come back from Babylon, where they had spent seventy years in exile. Then God commanded them to rebuild the temple in Jerusalem because it was through the temple that God was present among the people. But the people had other plans. They used all their money and time to build their homes and farms. Since God was not part of their enterprise, they never got ahead, no matter how hard they worked. Haggai preached the only possible remedy: build the temple! Then everything else would prosper, and the holes in their bags would be plugged!

Haggai's message has profound meaning for us today. Our hearts are God's temple; Christ wants to live there. If He is not in charge, our life will be a rat race and our finest achievements will bring nothing but frustration.

Ultimately the choice is up to us: own things for Christ's sake or be owned by things for the devil's sake.

Father, help us to keep in step with Christ, and to make You the partner in all our affairs. Amen.

On the Go

Now the word of the Lord came to Jonah . . . saying, "Arise, go to Nineveh, that great city, and cry against it; for their wickedness has come up before me." But Jonah rose to flee to Tarshish from the presence of the Lord (Jon. 1:1-3).

The moving industry has become big business. One fourth of the population moves every year. People are on the go. Why? Some are like Jonah booking passage to Tarshish: they can't face their obligations, so they leave. Some are like Jacob on his way to Paddan-aram running away from his mistakes. Some are like Moses taking up ranching in Midian to be safe from hostile forces. Some are like Elimelech and Naomi emigrating to Moab to escape a depression at home.

To be sure, not everybody escapes by moving. There are other escape routes. Some take to drinking, some to a whirl of social activities, some to accumulating money, and some gulp down pills.

What is really back of it all?

Dag Hammarskjöld once wrote, "The longest journey is the journey inward." Quite true. But there is a longer journey—the journey to God. Yet God is not far away. He came to this broken world in Christ, His Son. Christ became like us in our restlessness. He once said, "Foxes have holes and birds of the air have nests; but the Son of man has nowhere to lay his head" (Matt. 8:20). Go to Him. Give Him your burdens. Confess your sins. Accept Him as Savior. Then you will find God. Then you will find yourself. Then life will be different. Then you will have power to face hostility, setbacks and mistakes. Then you can dedicate your life to God.

You and your God! Have you realized the power of that partnership? You could do great things for God and His people. Why don't you? See whether you are traveling with Him!

Lord, keep my eyes firmly directed upon the one goal of service and growth. Holy Spirit, teach me how to come to terms with myself and my God. Amen.

Hope in the Valley of Death

Even though I walk through the valley of the shadow of death, I fear no evil; for thou art with me; thy rod and thy staff, they comfort me (Ps. 23:4).

The Bible never glosses over life's grim problems. And it never promises that becoming a Christian will end or solve all problems. Yet the Bible brings good news. It tells us that the powers of darkness will never prevail against God's children.

Psalm 23 teaches us more details about that promise. The poet sings of green pastures, of still waters, and of peace of mind. Good! Let's not overlook the multitude of wonderful blessings God gives us daily. But now the poet digs a bit deeper. He tells us that his happiness does not really depend on the good moments of life. His joy has a deeper source. He depends on the *Giver* of those good moments. His love-relationship with God is the source of his peace and contentment. Even when life brings sorrow, he will still know that joy. He trusts in his God. He even goes so far as to say that in the face of *death* he will not be afraid.

That's no small matter. Are you afraid that grief could strike suddenly? Are you hurting under a painful situation right now? Psalm 23 offers you one special promise: "For thou art with me." You may say that too. God will make that profession true.

Have you noticed that problem-solving has become second nature to us? We are out to change disagreeable situations. These meditations are probably a poor manual for that sort of thing. But as Christian believers we must ever point each other to the faithfulness of our God. The Old Testament believers knew that they were part of the "Am Olam," the eternal people, the children of the covenant who had experienced the corporate connection and faced both life and death with poise.

Lord, be our Shepherd. Help us to notice Your presence; give us light in the valley; steel our resolve in the face of despair. Through Jesus Christ our Lord. Amen.

Hope for the Crippled Home

But if you forsake [God], he will forsake you. For a long time Israel was without the true God . . . In those times there was no peace . . . for great disturbances afflicted all the inhabitants of the lands. They were broken in pieces . . . (II Chron. 15:2-3, 5-6).

People weren't quite so smart in 1880 as in 1980, but they knew more about the art of living than we do. The *Encyclopaedia Britannica* reports that in 1880 one in every 20 marriages ended in divorce. In 1915 it was one in every twelve. In 1950 it was one in four. Now divorces run at a rate approaching one in every three marriages.

What has gone wrong with our homes? What has gone wrong with our world? The prophet Oded gave the answer: "If you forsake God, he will forsake you." Thus the people of Judah became a desperately unhappy nation. Everybody was scared. Everything the people undertook ended in frustration. "Great disturbances afflicted all the inhabitants of the lands. They were broken in pieces" (vs. 5-6).

Isn't that an accurate description of our day? Psychologists have called it "massive neurosis." It's a self-perpetuating thing. Children are afflicted with it, and they carry it into their families.

But let us understand one thing clearly: *it doesn't have to be that way*. We have a Father in heaven who is very concerned about the well-being of our homes and families. He wants to show us the way to happiness and harmony. Hasn't He promised us the mind of Christ? Christ gave Himself; His joy was the well-being of others. We can share that mind of Christ. Within one family we can accept each other in mutual understanding and care. Thank God that there are still many such homes left. They are the nation's hope.

Lord, may many people come to You with their grief and problems. Will You mend hearts and situations, and may we experience peace and joy in our homes. Amen.

The Restoration of Our Environment

The fields are laid waste, the ground mourns . . . Be confounded, O tillers of the soil, wail, O vinedressers, for the wheat and the barley; because the harvest of the field has perished (Joel 1:10-11).

Driven by unbridled greed, we have nearly succeeded in wrecking God's creation. We have polluted the air, exhausted the soil, and poisoned our water. "Mankind has emerged as the great pollutant of the universe," said a Back-to-God Hour broadcast. "The spacemen circling our world's great cities saw the brown gasses lying like a scab over the deep blue of our planet. On the surface of the earth the corrupted rivers, dying lakes, and assaulted oceans continued their horrifying deterioration." The irresponsible use of chemical fertilizers, weed-killers, and insecticides has ruined nature's life-giving cycles. The farmer's plow is no longer followed by circling birds, for worms have become scarce. In some midwestern states the pheasant population is only 20 percent of what it used to be because of chemical poisoning. One state reports that 70 percent of its farm wells were found to be polluted with nitrate and atrazene.

Is it any wonder that there is so much unhappiness, sickness and sadness in the land with our air, soil, water, and food infected with poison?

Christ came to restore us to being good custodians in the Father's world. We must take good care of His fields, His cities, His rivers, His atmosphere, and His creatures. What will become of our children and grandchildren if we keep on assaulting nature's own sources of life? What must they do if we keep on designing a style of life that demands more and more fossil fuel?

Work and prayer go together in the Bible. So do private and public efforts—and all of them include you!

God, You created the world in great wisdom. Forgive us where we soiled and abused it. Help us to restore Your handiwork to health and beauty. Amen.

Hope for the Starving?

. . . and there will be famines . . . in various places (Matt. 24:7).
Blessed are the merciful, for they shall obtain mercy (Matt. 5:7).

"Suppose," somebody wrote recently, "that all the world's starving people would come to your door for food. How long do you think the line would be?" Well, brace yourself. That line would go back over the horizon, across mountains and oceans, around the globe, until it would reach your door again, and that not once or twice, but it would circle the world five times. Two thirds of the human race lack the basic necessities of life.

The world's population is growing at the rate of 180,000 daily. If that rate continues, the population will double by the end of this century. The increase in food production is falling far behind the increase in people. The British statesman and author C. P. Snow wrote that famine conditions, which will become more widespread, will cause political upheavals that will further slow down food production, all of which will unavoidably bring a sea of hunger. Only if the nations combined their resources, applying them to food production and population control instead of weaponry and luxury goods, could this global disaster be prevented.

How can Christians be part of this great challenge? Only a grass-roots movement among citizens of the land can bring it about. Statesmen can ultimately do no more than the electorate will allow them. It is up to people like us. Christ said, "Blessed are the merciful, for they shall obtain mercy." Those who fail to show mercy forfeit mercy for themselves. Christ was mindful of the needs of sick and hungry people. With the gospel He brought relief. Relief actions, today, should have priority among the churches.

Merciful Savior, help us to be examples of responsible living. Open our hearts toward the needy, and show us the way to be part of the solution to the problems of our day. Through Christ. Amen.

Wars Come from the Heart

What causes wars, and what causes fightings among you? Is it not your passions that are at war in your members? . . . you covet and cannot obtain; so you fight and wage war (James 4:1-2).

The cause of war is as old as human history. We know the arguments to justify warfare. And indeed, there have been wars which restored freedom to many. But wars have brought few blessings and solved few problems. The price paid in human lives and money has been staggering.

All through history, people tried hard to avoid war and create a better world. Centuries ago Leonardo da Vinci designed a human flying machine. His pupil, Astro, looked on in great excitement and gasped, "Messere, imagine people seeing you fly. People will be as angels in higher spheres, the nations will unite, and never will there be any more war." Well, people learned to fly, and they promptly turned their flying machines into war machines. But hope springs eternal. The first world war was hailed by the leaders of that day as "the war to end all wars."

Is there no escape from the curse of war?

God's Word says that the cause of war lies in *man's heart. We* are selfish and greedy, and we demand greedy policies of our governments. Modern society is almost solely guided by the profit motive. If the cause of warfare lies in the human heart, then the solution must begin in the hearts of men too. Instead of demanding advantages for ourselves, we must repent, give, serve, bless, and heal. As Christians we must pray and work for peace and press for policies which seek to relieve tensions, help the suffering, and aid the weak toward honorable independence.

Father of all mercies, grant peace to the nations. May we learn the grace of self-denial and Christian generosity. Help us to be less concerned about ourselves and more about others. We plead for light. In Christ's name. Amen.

The Reformation of Labor

Then I saw another beast which rose out of the earth . . . it causes all . . . to be marked on the right hand or the forehead, so that no one can buy or sell unless he has the mark . . . (Rev. 13:11, 16-17).

The book of Revelation tells us that satan keeps a close eye on man's means of livelihood. In fact, he tries to keep his hand on it as well. You can readily understand why. Man's daily bread is very important to him. Take a man's living away, and he is at your mercy. If satan could control the economic process, he would control almost all of life. Today's text reveals that this is exactly satan's intention. But then, there is bound to be a big battle, for Jesus Christ is Lord of all of life. He also lays claim on man's daily work. Thus the battle between the regime of satan and the Kingdom of Christ is also fought where men do their daily work.

A prominent labor leader recently said in an address, "Don't call our unions neutral . . . These unions are committed to an ideology that embraces the total well-being of our workers . . . We can only win the battle when our members give their total loyalty." Yet, legislation often stipulates that only one union shall have the bargaining rights in one place of employment, and all workers shall be members of that union as a condition for employment!

This morning the radio reported on two more major strikes in industry. Union negotiators keep rejecting contract offers. The loss in man-hours is staggering. No one around the bargaining table seems to be one bit concerned about the well-being of the nation. Back of it lies the totally greedy notion of the class struggle between labor and management.

Christians come with the Biblical vision: workers and bosses accepting each other as partners in a very big job God gave them in His earth, to do good and to provide for life.

Lord, be present with Your Word and Spirit in the world of labor relations. Restore satisfaction and pride to our daily work. Bless the labors of our hands. Amen.

The Reformation of Enterprise

Come now, you who say, "Today or tomorrow we will go into such and such a town . . . and trade and get gain. Come now, you rich, weep and howl . . . Behold, the wages of the laborers . . . which you kept back by fraud, cry out . . . You have lived on the earth in luxury . . . You have condemned, you have killed the righteous man . . . (James 4:13; 5:1, 4, 6).

We have developed toughness into an art. Marketing skills and salesmanship utilize the findings of science aimed at turning prospective buyers into helpless victims. Courses are given to enable salesmen to hammer down sales resistance. But products become increasingly shoddy and fail to measure up to promises. A monstrously deceptive advertising industry spews its torrent of falsehoods upon the public. Ruthless, cut-throat competition smothers honorable intentions in business and industry. Greed, exploitation, and the desire for higher profits and wages rob daily work of joy.

In Arthur Miller's *Death of a Salesman*, Uncle Ben tells his nephew, Willy Loman, "Life is a jungle, Willy, be hard. Some go into the jungle and find the diamond. Some go and get caught by the tigers. Life is a jungle, Willy, be hard."

Do we realize what lies back of this greed and materialism? A false religion of life, a religion with its own gospel and its own prophets! The goal is simple but all-embracing: higher profits via the road of increased consumption.

Read the text above this meditation again. Strong language, isn't it? James calls the adherents of the religion of materialism to repentance. Have you heard that call? Good for you! Then you can accept a new kind of life from Christ. You can have real peace and fulfillment in your enterprise if your first goal is to serve mankind; you can have happiness in a product well made and a service well rendered. Yes, you will have problems too, but Christ will be there and will provide you with courage and wisdom.

Lord Jesus, we have obscured the purpose of life and have become slaves of things and goods. Set us free, dear Savior, and help us in our responsibilities. Amen.

"Where Are You?"

But the Lord God called to the man, and said to him, "Where are you?"
(Gen. 3:9).

Did it ever strike you that there are many questions in the
Bible? Some are simple, some are heart-rending, and some concern
deep matters of faith and eternal life. This month, let's pause with
some of the questions and see what we can learn from them and
from the answers.

The first question in the Bible is of dramatic importance. It
was asked by God when Adam and Eve had eaten from the forbid-
den fruit in Eden. In one reckless moment of pride, they had
broken their love-relationship with God. The King's children had
become slaves of sin. Afterward, when God looked for His
children, He couldn't find them. They had hid themselves. It was
then that God asked that anguished question: "Where are you?"

Ultimately God answered that question Himself. He kept
looking for Adam and Eve; He kept pursuing them. And He found
them. No, He did not disown them. He promised them salvation.
God's answer came in the life and death of His own Son, Jesus
Christ.

Have you felt the distress of being so far from God? He is
looking for you. There is no need to hide any longer. You also may
accept God's answer which He gave to you in His Son.

The way God looks for men is illustrated in C. S. Lewis's
record of his conversion. He wrote, "You must picture me alone in
that room in Magdelen, night after night feeling the steady unrelent-
ing approach of Him Whom I so earnestly desired not to meet.
That which I greatly feared at last came upon me. I knelt down in
prayer and admitted that God was God and became the most dejec-
ted and reluctant convert in all England."

Thank You, Lord, for coming and searching for us wayward sinners.
Father, keep us from fleeing from Your heavenly mercy, and surround us
with Your saving grace. In Christ. Amen.

"Am I My Brother's Keeper?"

Then the Lord said to Cain, "Where is Abel your brother?" He said, "I do not know; am I my brother's keeper?" (Gen. 4:9).

Sin multiplied in Adam's family. Cain developed bitter hatred against his younger brother Abel. One day, when they were in the field, he killed him.

Ours is a world of broken personal relationships. Eleven out of every twelve years of world history have witnessed open warfare.

Our homes are broken by divorce, juvenile courts cannot handle the increasing number of cases, and more and more people are considering suicide a respectable way out of their problems. Cutthroat competition has become the motto of business. Several labor unions have openly avowed the doctrine of the class struggle.

But more tragic than Cain's crime was the hardening of Cain's heart. He refused to confess his sins. When God called him to account for his brutal act, he retorted, "Am I my brother's keeper?"

When people, institutions and nations refuse to listen to the Word of God, the sin of Cain is duplicated. Without personal repentance and a return to God, there is no hope.

God did not forget Cain's sin, but neither did He withdraw His offer of salvation. Years later, the Letter to the Hebrews described the blood of Christ in terms that remind us of Cain and his sin. We read: "[Jesus' blood] speaks more graciously than the blood of Abel" (Heb. 12:24).

Those who believe in Christ are accepted by God. They receive brothers and sisters in Him. They delight in the restoration of life. An ancient Christian proverb says: "Nothing is more becoming than that love should be recompensed by love."

Lord Jesus, may Your love fill our hearts and may we love one another sincerely. May people everywhere listen to the Word of God. Amen.

"What Are You Doing Here, Elijah?"

. . . and behold, the word of the Lord came to him, and he said to him, "What are you doing here, Elijah?" (I Kings 19:9).

The outstanding German tank commander General Von Thoma, who led crack panzer divisions in Poland, Russia and North Africa, was asked to review the causes of German defeat. He answered: "In modern warfare the tactics are not the main thing; the important thing is the organization of one's resources to maintain the momentum."

How true this is for the Christian's warfare too.

The source of power at his disposal is infinite, but the battle is often too much. Elijah experienced that. He had done great things for God. Fearlessly he had stood alone at Mount Carmel facing 450 prophets of Baal. At his prayer, fire had rained from heaven. Yet, when wicked Queen Jezebel threatened his life, he fled into the desert. There an angel found him under the juniper tree ready to die because he was so discouraged. Elijah had taken his eyes off God; suddenly the powers of evil seemed unconquerably big.

The question the Lord now addresses to Elijah is a disconcerting one: "What are you doing here, Elijah?" Nothing, really. Once you get off the royal highway of faith, you can get bogged down on dozens of side roads. That's why God asks the question. Elijah has to recognize that he has gotten nowhere.

And that is how it has always been. If you do not replenish yourself, you grow tired and exhausted, and without realizing it you take your eyes away from God. The next moment you find yourself under the juniper tree, not knowing where to go—all of which goes to show how important regular prayer and Bible reading is.

Father in heaven, continually bring us back to the one source of power. Lead us back to Your living Word. May we be much in prayer. And use us then in Your service. Amen.

"Are Abana and Pharpar Better?"

But Naaman was angry, and went away, saying . . . "Are not Abana and Pharpar . . . better than all the waters of Israel?" (II Kings 5:11-12).

Naaman, the general, commands respect. He did things in a big way. He maintained his poise even when he had leprosy. He consented to consult Israel's prophet for healing, but when he went to see him, he traveled with an impressive retinue.

Naaman's reception in Israel, however, starkly contrasted with the general's bigness. The prophet sent his boy with the curt message: "Go and wash in the Jordan seven times." This was too much for the general to take. *He*—wash in that shallow, dirty Jordan? Never! If there was any washing to be done, it would be done in his own country's great rivers, Abana and Pharpar.

We all have things like Abana and Pharpar in our lives, don't we? These are things or ways of doing things that have become so precious that we are blind to help when it comes in another form.

Custom and ritual can become especially significant in our religious lives. Sometimes we can be so concerned about a specific liturgy or a certain form of preaching that we miss the central good news of the Bible.

Jesus said, "Repent . . . and believe" (Mark 1:15). With these words He asks us to do something that is simple and humbling. We must realize that our salvation can be won only through the suffering and death of the Lord Jesus Christ, and we must kneel at the cross, confess our sins, and acknowledge that Jesus alone is our Savior.

When he forgot his sacred rivers, Naaman was cleansed. When we forget everything else and trust in Jesus, we will be too.

Dear Jesus, teach us who we are. Reveal our smallness to us, for we have sinned. Help us to seek refuge with You before it is too late. Amen.

"Is All Well?"

So Gehazi followed Naaman. And when Naaman saw some one running after him, he alighted from the chariot to meet him, and said, "Is all well?" And he said, "All is well" (II Kings 5:21-2).

What a privileged man Gehazi was—servant of one of the greatest prophets of the Old Testament, Elisha, the man of God. He had heard the Word of God preached in power and conviction. He had witnessed a dozen or more spectacular miracles.

But Gehazi did not live up to these privileges. He lacked his master's integrity and childlike commitment. Gehazi was not an ungodly man, but he loved money. When Elisha had healed Naaman, the Syrian general, free of charge, Gehazi readily saw an opportunity for some easy cash. He quickly followed the general's procession, while his mind was busy fabricating a story about unexpected guests and the need for some entertainment money. In his innocence Naaman asked, "Is all well?" "All is well," said the liar.

We are a strange mixture of good and bad. We want to dedicate our lives to God, yet the seeds of greed are still there too. So our lives are not always consistent with the grace in us. We puzzle unbelievers around us. They ask questions about us. If only we would dare to let go of the securities of the flesh and rely on God completely! We cannot serve two masters.

The newspaper once reported a strange case of drowning near the city where we live. While the victim was yelling for help, a rope was thrown to him, but he would not grab it. Later it was found that his hands were clutching some slippery branches under water, which he had not dared let go.

If you are holding on to your own security, let go and take hold of Christ!

Lord Jesus, help us so that we will not be like Gehazi. Don't let us try to serve God and ourselves at the same time. By nature, this is the way we are. Deliver us. Amen.

"Is It Well?"

"Is it well with you? Is it well with your husband? Is it well with the child?"
And she answered, "It is well" (II Kings 4:26).

"How are you?" we ask. "Fine," we answer. But it's not always true. We may feel terrible and still say, "Fine."

"Is it well?" Elisha asks the Shunammite woman. "It is well," she answers.

Remember, that woman had just witnessed her young son die on her lap. But her answer was not just a thoughtless platitude! We read that she was "a great woman." Big people think big things of God. For years, she and her husband had hoped for a child, until there was no ground for hope left. Then they became acquainted with Elisha, the man of God. He had been their regular guest, and with him God's possibilities had entered that home. God had blessed their hospitality with the birth of a baby boy. Now, when that young lad suddenly died, this great woman went back to God. Watch her urge on the horses as they speed through the valley to Mount Carmel, where the man of God is.

"Is it well?"

"It is well!"

Of course it was well! It is always well with those who speed with their sorrows, pains and trials to God. When that heroic woman went to God with her grief, it was as great a miracle of grace as the miraculous raising of her son from the dead which occurred later. The moment she decided to flee to God, He gave her the victory.

How our souls can be burdened with a multitude of concerns! We must take all that is broken and dead and speed through the valley of confession to the mountain where God eagerly awaits us.

Father in heaven, help us bring all our need and distress before Your throne of grace. Don't let us turn inward with our sorrow and our misery, but gently cause us to surrender our anguish to You, our God. In Christ. Amen.

"Watchman, What of the Night?"

The oracle concerning Dumah. One is calling to me from Seir, "Watchman, what of the night? Watchman, what of the night?" (Is. 21:11).

Have you ever flown over a big city by night? What a fabulous sight! Millions of lights blend together into a carpet of glowing brightness.

But with all our light, darkness rules in the heart of mankind.

A sprawling welfare system, education, science, automation, technology—all these things were thought to provide answers and solutions to this benighted world, but the darkness only deepened.

George Bernard Shaw, in *Too True to Be Good*, penned this pathetic confession: "The science to which I pinned my faith is bankrupt. Its counsels which should have established the millennium led directly to the suicide of Europe. I believed them once. In their name I helped destroy the faith of millions of worshipers in the temples of a thousand creeds. And now they look at me and witness the tragedy of an atheist who has lost his faith."

"Watchman, what of the night?"

People of all generations have asked that question. Lord, show us light in this dark age.

Jesus heard that call for light. He summarized His life and ministry in one sentence: "I am the light of the world" (John 8:12). He brought the light of the world by taking all the ills and sin of people upon Himself. Yours too. Sin is darkness—still today. Fun and pleasure cannot take that away. Jesus still offers Himself today. He wants to be the Light in your life. Call out: "Watchman, what of the night?" He will answer: "This way; I am the light."

Lord Jesus, we are glad that You are the Light of the world. Fill us with Your light. Give us compassion for those who are in darkness. Use us to lead them to the light. Amen.

"Can Iron Break?"

Can one break iron, iron from the north, and bronze? (Jer. 15:12).

Much has been written about the problem of suffering. In its deepest essence it defies description. Paul Schutz writes about it in his *Letters to Young People*: "There was so much sorrow during the Nazi days, so much terrorism, raping, injustice, cruelties and bombing that some ministers could not take it anymore and committed suicide."

Jeremiah went through similar tragic experiences. He had to announce that the Israelites would lose a cruel war because of their sins. He was the one sent to tell the parents and wives of the death of their sons and husbands. He had to announce to one woman that her seven sons were killed in battle. Moved with compassion he wrote: "Her sun went down while it was yet day" (vs. 9).

Jeremiah did what God's children have always done: he brought his burden to God. God's answer may have seemed hard, but it was full of comfort: "Can one break iron?" God promised that the burdens would not outweigh the power He gave His prophet.

Have you suffered? God will not forsake those who seek refuge with Him. The Heidelberg Catechism summarizes that only comfort: "That I, with body and soul, both in life and in death, am not my own, but belong to my faithful Savior, Jesus Christ."

It's a good thing we don't know what the future holds for us. If we knew, we might lose courage and be incapable of enjoying the blessings of the day.

It's a better thing that we do know that God will make us equal to any situation we must face. He will gird us with His power. "Can one break iron?"

Lord Jesus, we know that You experienced suffering during Your life on earth. Be with all who now experience pain and distress. Keep us faithful even until death. Amen.

"What Good Is Vine Wood?"

Son of man, how does the wood of the vine surpass any wood, the vine branch which is among the trees of the forest? (Ezek. 15:2).

Vine tree wood is worthless. It is gnarled and crooked. Nevertheless, the vine tree is highly valued. You see, the vine tree produces grapes that are counted among the finest fruits. Because of these fruits, the vine tree is regarded as a noble tree. But when the vine tree bears no fruit, the vine dresser wastes no time taking it out and burning it, because it needlessly takes up valuable space and robs the soil of nutrition. The vine dresser certainly doesn't have to maintain the vine tree for the quality of its wood. "Does the wood of the vine surpass any wood?" Or, you could say; What good is vine wood?

The implication is clear.

Unless God's people bear fruits of good works, they are of no use to God. Christians are often concerned about evil and wickedness, but they should be equally concerned about the curse of a negative, sterile Christianity (which is no Christianity). Our salvation has one great purpose—fruitbearing.

"What good is vine wood?"

In John 15, Christ takes up Ezekiel's metaphor and reveals its deeper meaning. Christ compares Himself to the vine tree and the believers to the branches. The branches that abide in Him bear much fruit; the branches that bear no fruit will be cast into the fire. This parable shows the necessity and lofty nature of good works. Christ works them through the believer.

Throughout the centuries, true Christians have understood that they must serve Christ's Kingdom. The church father Tertullian said: "It is . . . the deeds of noble love that lead many to put a brand upon us."

Savior, impress us with our great calling. Help us to seek and find the many opportunities to be a blessing. For the Master's sake. Amen.

"Does Evil Befall a City . . . ?"

Does evil befall a city, unless the Lord has done it? (Amos 3:6).

Bathurst, New Brunswick, Canada, is your average small city with its 16,000 inhabitants. It is no worse than other cities that size —or so it seemed. Some time ago the police force of Bathurst went on strike and the city instantly turned into a Gehenna of lawlessness. Rubber-burning drag-races became a nightly affair, store windows were smashed in, and cars were set on fire. All that while scores of citizens stood watching. Some of them were even cheering.

The sobering question is: Is Bathurst really worse than our city? Are the people worse than we are? If all that can happen to Bathurst, then it potentially happens to us! What does the Lord tell us in that event? Amos asks, "Does evil befall a city, unless the Lord has done it?" No, of course God did not cause evil. What Amos means is: Doesn't God *speak* in these events? Yes, He does! He wants us to know how frail the moral fiber of our society is. We are empty people, and empty people seek continuous excitement.

A tough gospel? It sure is! Tough enough to bring relief! Tough enough to change sin-hardened people into loving, caring believers. Amos witnessed to that. His voice thundered judgment in Samaria, but with only one goal—that the people repent and be saved for the Lord, saved for a constructive, meaningful life.

"Does evil befall a city . . . ?"

Knowledgeable people tell us that self-esteem is based on honest self-understanding, without which personal growth is impossible. The idealist is foremost a realist.

Father in heaven, may the nations know that You are God. May the hope of mankind be in You. Lord, bring helpless wanderers, also the sophisticated ones, back to You. Amen.

"Where Is My Honor?"

A son honors his father, and a servant his master. If then I am a father, where is my honor? (Mal. 1:6).

Our day is characterized by its consistent efforts to rid society of every reference to the name of God. The U.S. Supreme Court, in quick succession, banned school prayers, Bible reading, and even such traditional rhymes as "God is great, God is good, and we thank Him for our food." A federal judge in California ordered the phrase "So help me God" deleted from the courtroom oath.

In other areas of life the same trend has become the order of the day. Many labor unions have not only stricken references to the Christian faith from their constitution but have also banned "sectarian teachings" from discussions at union meetings. Union leaders maintain that religion is fine for private life, but not for public affairs.

That idea of pushing the service of God from the public sector into the private one was illustrated by a statement of Randolph Churchill in the *London Evening News* upon the death of the American statesman John Foster Dulles: "The main weakness in Mr. Dulles' statesmanship was his religious conviction: religion can be a great solace to a man in his private life, but such devout convictions can be an inconvenience in the field of politics."

We, as a Christian community, must do everything in our power to restore the blessings of the Christian faith to our society. Separation of church and state is a good principle; separation of Christian convictions and society is a monstrous one. We must join hearts, heads and hands to restore the will of God to the affairs of our lands.

"If I am a father, where is my honor?"

Lord Jesus, we confess that all things exist in and through You. Make us faithful in responding to Your rule. O God, may the nations acknowledge You as Creator and Father. Amen.

"What Is Your Name?"

*And Jesus asked him, "What is your name?" He replied, "My name is
Legion: for we are many" (Mark 5:9).*

Sin never stands still. It always corrupts, divides, and
estranges.

Once Jesus and His disciples entered the land of the
Gadarenes. A terrible thing happened to them there. A man with an
"unclean spirit" ran up to them and yelled: "What have I to do
with thee, Jesus? I adjure thee, torment me not!"

What a pitiful man! A voice from the dark void of "Godfor-
sakenness." Sin had separated that man from God. But sin had
done more. This man was not only without God, he had also lost
his fellow man. At night he would roam the graveyards all alone.
And sin had not stopped there. This man had even lost his "self."
Inwardly he was shattered. "My name is Legion," he said, "for we
are many."

Ours are days of great confusion and baffling problems.
Someone said: "We are like frightened passengers strapped to their
seats in a mighty airliner flying through fog blindly." At the root of
today's fear and distress lies man's estrangement from God, his
fellow man, and himself.

Modern man, *what is your name*? "My name is Legion."

Christ reached the depths of the Gadarene man's hell with His
Word. He cast out the demons and redeemed that man. Through
Christ, he found himself. He dressed himself, we read, and sat
down "in his right mind." Through Christ he also found his fellow
man and his God. Our text says that he witnessed to his people of
the great things Jesus had done.

We sometimes have the feeling that we are going to pieces. We
just cannot cope anymore. But our Lord is very compassionate.
With His cords of love, He will bind our lives together. Then we are
whole!

*Jesus, Savior, descend with Your healing power into the depth of our
hearts. Restore us to God, we pray, through Christ. Amen.*

"What Does It Profit?"

For what does it profit a man, to gain the whole world and forfeit his life? (Mark 8:36).

It would be a frightening experience for many of us to have a "God's eye view" of our earthly lives. All our motives would suddenly be exposed before us!

Christ speaks of that here in Mark 8. What He sees in the hearts of His hearers is greed. They would all like to own the world. But Jesus warns them: they might get riches, but the price would be their own life, which would mean that in the end they would have nothing.

All that has profound reasons. God's original design with man and the world was that man would be God's covenant partner and so, with God, would own the world. When he deserted God, he could not hold property anymore, no matter how hard he tried. Without God life is pathetic. Hemingway, in his book *The Old Man and the Sea*, tells the symbolical story of an old fisherman, Santiago, who goes farther out to sea than all the other fishermen, because he has not caught anything for 84 days. After a long struggle he finally catches a big fish which he ties alongside his boat. But when the old man enters the harbor, he discovers that a shark has eaten the fish; he only drags a skeleton along.

"What does it profit a man?"

To those who will hear, Christ offers a new blueprint for living, a blueprint which will stand the test of time and eternity. It involves denying ourselves and following Christ. That blueprint restores us to God, which in turn restores us to full ownership of His creation. It's just what Revelation 21:7 already predicted: he that overcomes shall inherit all things.

Thank You, Lord Jesus, for adding great riches to our salvation. Make us faithful stewards in Your service. May our lives glorify You. In Your name we pray. Amen.

"Do You Want to Be Healed?"

When Jesus saw him . . . he said to him, "Do you want to be healed?" The sick man answered him, "Sir, I have no man . . ." (John 5:6-7).

Loneliness is the terrible curse that clings to modern living.

The nuclear physicist J. Robert Oppenheimer sighed: "The vastness of life, the greatness of the globe, the otherness of people, the otherness of ways, and the all-encompassing dark . . ."

Immense efforts have been put forth to glue life together again. Governments have encouraged community centers. People have become great joiners of clubs, cliques, and brotherhoods. But one psychiatrist said: "The lonely have taken to pack-running in mindless organizations." David Riesman published his study of modern man under the title *The Lonely Crowd.*

Christians can identify with the lonely because Christ did. And Christ did because He suffered more loneliness than any human being. He was forsaken by God and man because of our sins; He underwent hell.

That is why He went to Bethesda's pool on that feast day to visit the sick. He talked with a man who had been there for 38 years. "Do you want to be healed?" Jesus asked. What a question! But Christ meant more than getting the use of his legs back; He wanted him to be restored to a full life with his fellow men.

It is one thing, of course, to read about the many other people being liberated from loneliness, but quite another to experience that personally. It is said of Christ that He left the ninety-and-nine to find the one. You are not beyond His grasp! The loneliness of Bethesda drew Him irresistibly. Yours does too.

Lord Jesus, help us to remember that the lonely awakened Your compassion. Come to us in our loneliness, and use us to lead the lonely to You, our Savior. Amen.

"Will You Also Go Away?"

Jesus said to the twelve, "Do you also wish to go away?" Simon Peter answered him, "Lord, to whom shall we go? You have the words of eternal life; and we have believed . . ." (John 6:67-9).

Jesus' question "Do you also wish to go away?" comes at the end of some spectacular happenings. Jesus had preached to a large crowd and afterwards had miraculously provided them with bread and fish. The people were naturally very excited, and the next day they came out in full force to hear Him again. But that day had a sad ending. Christ explained that bread for the stomach was of no benefit if there was not first bread for the soul. He meant that life has no foundation unless the people confess their sin and helplessness and turn to Him as their Redeemer. What bothered the people was that Jesus implied that their noblest efforts could not earn them God's forgiveness and favor—in other words, that they were a total write-off. And so, in spite of the wonderful free meal, they became angry with Jesus and left Him. Even people who had called themselves "disciples" left Him (vs. 66); only the twelve stayed.

You have known the weight of certain very important moments in your life. Such a moment has now come in the lives of the disciples. It is quiet for a while. Then Jesus asks this momentous question: "Will you also go away?" They must choose; they stand at the crossroad of two destinies. The choice is theirs, and it is totally voluntary.

The disciple Peter gives an answer to the question. He puts it in the form of an exclamation: "Lord, to whom shall we go? You have the words of eternal life!" He means to say that there is only one way. Christ is the way!

Have you made that choice? Do not lean on the Christianity of your family or on your church membership. Let Him be your personal Savior.

Thank You, Holy Spirit, for showing us the right questions and the right answers. Bring us face to face with Christ our Savior. Amen.

"Are There Few That Be Saved?"

And some one said to him, "Lord, will those who are saved be few?" And he said to them, "Strive to enter by the narrow door . . ." (Luke 13:23-4).

Do you think that there are many people who will go to heaven? That question has troubled a lot of people. Will I be saved? How about my wife, my children? Long ago, when Jesus was on earth, people were anxious about it. Once when Jesus was preaching, someone called out from the audience: "Lord, are there few that be saved?"

Jesus' answer is surprising. He does not answer the question because He finds it unacceptable. He says instead, "Strive to enter in!"

That word *strive* has a unique meaning here. Yes, it means that you must heed the call to conversion. You must deny yourself and weep over your sins. But it is a striving that does not arise out of human determination alone. It must be a striving that is rooted in the sovereign grace of God. No one is saved just because *he* tried so hard.

Salvation is by grace alone. It is the free gift of God to unworthy sinners. The Holy Spirit puts life into a dead sinner's heart. This means that we must give up on ourselves and put all our hope in Christ. In a way, that is not as painless as it sounds. When we give up on ourselves, we die a bit inside. Paul said that we must die unto ourselves. "Strive to enter in" means that we come running to God with our distress and let Him do it all in us and for us.

Someone used a little parable to describe it. As we approach the narrow gate we see the superscription: "Strive to enter in;" once we are through the gate we look back and see the superscription on the other side: "By sovereign grace alone."

Only those who know this secret by faith can be entrusted with further information about heaven. God told Abraham that the number of the saved may be compared to the sand on the seashore. John confirmed this later, when he saw the heavens opened. Then he saw "a great multitude which no one can number, clothed with white robes and palms in their hands" (Rev. 7:9).

Almighty God, Your works of salvation are great! Have mercy upon us and help us strive to enter in so that we will be a part of the multitude that no man can number. Amen.

"How Often?"

"Lord, how often shall my brother sin against me, and I forgive him? As many as seven times?" (Matt. 18:21).

To be in Jesus' company is no easy matter.

Peter experienced that. He followed Jesus and soon learned that Jesus' love, compassion and concern knew no bounds. It soon became apparent, too, that Jesus expected the same of His disciples. "If any one strikes you on the right cheek, turn to him the other also," He said (Matt. 5:39).

That bothered Peter. Peter was an honest man; he knew his limitations, and so he came with a proposal. "Lord, I am willing to forgive seven times. Would that be an acceptable limit?"

There is something appealing about Peter's question. Wouldn't it be convenient if the Christian life could be described as a definite assignment? Then we would have the possibility of saying sometimes, "Mission accomplished; time out for a rest."

Listen to Christ's answer. "You must forgive seventy times seven times." But that's an endless number of times, you say. Yes, that's just what Jesus meant: there is no limit. There is no end to forgiving others, no end to being compassionate, no end to giving yourself, no end to doing the Lord's bidding, no end to living for Him.

Impossible?

No! For, if you have been born again, Christ Himself will live in you. You live through Christ. Whatever you do is done out of His great power. The life of the Christian is rooted in the endless grace of Christ. Our Savior provides what He demands. The believer is not only saved by grace; he also lives by that grace.

Lord Jesus, fill us with Your grace. Give us Your Holy Spirit so that we may fight the good fight of faith in Your power. Use us mightily in Your service. Amen.

"Is Divorce Lawful?"

And Pharisees came up to him and tested him by asking, "Is it lawful to divorce one's wife for any cause?" (Matt. 19:3).

A wave of divorces has swept over the world. Learned men have studied the problem, but the epidemic has not been halted.

Could the reason be that modern man has closed his heart to the Word of God?

The Bible tells us that marriage must include a third partner—God. Marriage is such a sacred union that Christ called it a picture of the union between Himself and the Church. Husband and wife do not enter marriage to receive, but to give. They do not seek themselves; they enrich each other's life. They serve each other. And father and mother devote themselves to the well-being of the children. God blesses such homes. He adorns them with His presence and shields them with His love. Such homes are a blessing to the church and to society.

The Bible also has much to say about the cause of present day marital distress. God's Word tells us about sin. Modern marriage counselors have often ignored the reality of sin. Sin turns things upside down. It suggests that getting a lot of things makes a person happy. Husband and wife begin to quarrel because they seek their own selfish gain. Only through conversion in Christ will Christian love enter a home, a love that seeks to give, to commune and to bless.

Do you strive to live that Christian love in your home?

In his biography of the Duke of Marlborough, Churchill tells about the duke's lifelong devotion to his wife. He concludes: "Such a story of married love makes all the sizzling pictures of purple passion, served up on the newsstand, taste like ten cents worth of cold potatoes."

O God in heaven, save our homes. May husbands and wives and children go to You with their burdens. In Jesus' name we pray. Amen.

"What Is Truth?"

Jesus answered . . . "Every one who is of the truth hears my voice." Pilate said to him, "What is truth?" (John 18:37-8).

Pilate didn't care much about truth. As far as he was concerned, truth was a hazy thing and quite useless anyway. He shrugged his shoulders and asked. "What is truth?"

There have been people like Pilate throughout history. They said that no one can really pinpoint truth. In fact, people purposely shied away from the certainty of truth. Gotthold Lessing, a deep thinker, said: "If God had truth in His right hand and the search for truth in His left, I would choose the left."

Do you wonder how man became a truth-doubter? It is because man closed the Bible. The Bible says something very beautiful about truth. Truth, according to the Bible, is much more than stating that two plus two equals four. Truth has something to do with life. In fact, the Bible tells us that a human life is either truth or a lie. An example of a true life is found in Paradise. Adam loved God; he responded with his whole existence to the love of God. Adam's life was truth. A life of love to God is a true life. When sin entered the world, man became a stranger to God. His life became a lie. He may still say that two plus two equals four, but his life is no longer truth.

Sometimes it seems as if little children have a sixth sense that enables them to discern whether a man's life is wholesome, sincere and properly related to God. They are attracted to those whose lives are *true* in the deepest sense of the word, and they shy away from those who are living a lie. We need that ability too, so that we can know ourselves better, and others better as well.

That is why Christ said of Himself, "I am the way, the truth, and the life" (John 14:6). He came to this world to bring us back to God as His children. Now we can be true to God, true to people, and true to ourselves. And from that truth we create a new atmosphere. We spread cheer, we give help, we return love, and we express hope. We live the truth!

Holy Spirit, we confess that falsehood has a strong grip on our soul. Forgive us for serving ourselves. Cleanse us in Christ's blood. May our love for God and our neighbor be genuine. Through Christ. Amen.

"Why Hast Thou Forsaken Me?"

And about the ninth hour Jesus cried with a loud voice, "My God, my God, why hast thou forsaken me?" (Matt. 27:46).

Do you want to understand something of the suffering of Christ? Come, then, to the hill of crucifixion. See how lonely Jesus is. Judas has sold Him. Peter has denied Him. The disciples have fled in panic. He is all alone on Golgotha's hill, hanging in His wounds on the cross. The minutes tick away. High overhead the sun burns down upon His naked body. His tongue is parched with thirst. And then, suddenly, night envelops the hill as if a huge hand, invisible, had scooped away the light of the sun. Time presses heavily on Golgotha. One hour, two hours, three hours. "And about the ninth hour Jesus cried with a loud voice, 'My God, my God, why hast thou forsaken me?' "

No, not even when we stand near the cross can we understand what Jesus went through. The Father withdrew His love from His Son. Satanic forces of hell stormed upon Him. The psalmist groped for words to describe it: "Many bulls have compassed me." "The ploughers plowed upon my back" (Ps. 22:12; 129:3). The Son of God suffered hell for us. We can only kneel and confess from the Word of God that God's wrath over our sins was poured out upon Him.

Because He has borne that wrath, there is now forgiveness for sinners. We may feel forsaken sometimes, but we really never are. Our fellowship with God has a strong foundation. Slaves of sin have become free children of God.

Hallelujah! All praise and adoration to the Lamb of God!

My God, my God, why hast Thou accepted me?

Lord Jesus, give us grace that we may accept the complete redemption which You wrought for us when You were forsaken by the Father. Father, we thank You that we may be Your children forever. Through Jesus Christ our Lord. Amen.

"Whom Do You Seek?"

Jesus said to her, "Woman, why are you weeping? Whom do you seek?" (John 20:15).

"Whom do you seek?"

Mary Magdalene did not recognize Jesus that early morning in the garden of Joseph of Arimathea. We may wonder why she didn't. Was it because of the tears in her eyes? Some have suggested that Jesus Himself had changed after the resurrection: He was now the glorified Lord. But that could not be so. He looked earthly enough to be mistaken for the gardener. We often have the same notion. We think that the risen, glorified Lord was "out of this world," but the Bible portrays Him with His own human body: Thomas could feel the holes in His hands and in His side, and He ate a piece of fish.

Whom do you seek?

Do you think you have a Savior who is not really part of your daily life? The only thing that is foreign to your glorified Lord is sin. But His glorified body is a human body. He partakes of your world, your personal world, and He wants to set it aglow with His presence and His grace. You can take all your needs to Him; your life is special to Him. The disciples on their way to Emmaus found Him normally human; what they also found was that their hearts were burning within them.

This is a sad world. But let no one say that there is no hope. Jesus lifted the curse from the earth, and we can live with vigor because of His presence among us. It all depends on one question: Whom do you seek—Christ or yourself? The farmer may welcome Him and plow a straight furrow in His company. The dentist may do some fine dentistry in the presence of this interested Spectator. Yes, this risen Lord "fits in" here on earth with His blessed nearness. "It is no longer I that live but Christ Jesus in me," Paul exclaimed.

Lord Jesus, open our eyes that we may be deeply aware of Your constant presence. May we serve You in the fullness of everyday life. We pray in Your name. Amen.

"Have You Any Fish?"

Just as day was breaking, Jesus stood on the beach; yet the disciples did not know that it was Jesus. Jesus said to them, "Children, have you any fish?" (John 21:4-5).

There appears to be something relaxing about John 21. Jesus has risen from the dead, He has appeared to several disciples, His work on earth is nearly finished, and in a few more days He will ascend into heaven.

The disciples also took some time out and returned to their vocation as fishermen. Now, normal life has its ups and downs; that night was a disappointing one, for they caught nothing. And it was then that Jesus appeared on the shore with that very simple question: "Do you have any fish?"

But simple questions can be profound. Jesus understood the situation the disciples were in. A night without a catch of fish would not bring ruin to the disciples, but it was an annoying experience nevertheless. With this one brief question, Jesus enters that mood: "Do you have any fish?" He finds their disappointment important enough to make it His concern.

Imagine that—Christ entering with His resurrection beauty into our daily problems! Notice how honest His approach is. Not overly tactful on the one hand, and not rude on the other. He simply zeroes in on their predicament: "What about your fishing this past night?"

He asks us about the car that broke down, a bill that has to be paid, a headache that recurs, a sale that fell through, a bad mark in school, a visit that went poorly, a person who ignores you, the colleague you can't get along with, your husband's temper, your son's stubbornness, the leaky roof—everything. If it concerns you, it concerns Christ.

Help us, risen Lord, to share our daily concerns with You. Thanks, Lord, for Your goodness. Amen.

"Do You Love Me?"

Jesus said to Simon Peter, "Simon, son of John, do you love me?" (John 21:15).

We recognize this as a very important question: "Do you love me?" Our eternal life depends on the answer to that question. If we don't love Christ, we cannot be children of God.

But in John 21 this question has a concrete occasion—for two reasons.

Jesus asks the question three times. Jesus did that—and Peter knew it—because Peter had denied Him three times. Christ wanted to clear that matter away, so He put it on the table. Do you remember, Peter? What about it?

Love is never abstract. It is embodied in very practical situations, actual events, and real relationships. How do our everyday affairs affect our love for Christ? When we tolerate wrong situations, we may well wonder about our love for Christ. When we fail to make amends to those who suffered damage from our mistakes, the question about our love to Him is very real. Love must harmonize with our daily practices.

Christ had a second purpose with this question. He wanted Peter to accept a special task of leadership in the church. That task could only be accomplished if Peter really loved his Lord. Peter had to understand that clearly. Christ meant serious business; there was much at stake. The only source from which Peter could do it was love to Christ.

We often assume that we can do with our lives as we please. Not Christ. He wants us to serve as responsible members of His church. We can, if we daily seek His love.

Holy Spirit, renew Christ's love in us daily. May it be the substance of our devotion and service to the Master. Amen.

"Why Do You Stand Looking Up?"

Men of Galilee, why do you stand looking into heaven? (Acts 1:11).

No wonder the disciples stood gazing up into heaven. Their Master had just told them to evangelize the whole world, and then, suddenly, He ascended into heaven and left them behind alone. The general, so to speak, set the attack for 12 noon and then left at 11:45.

Many Christians, of all ages, have stood gazing toward heaven. They withdrew from life with its earthly relationships. For them, only spiritual things counted. Francis of Assissi called his body "my brother donkey."

But Christ never meant it to be that way. With His own earthly body, He is our representative in heaven. Now there is hope for that which is earthly. His redemptive work continues in heaven today. He is busy in heaven establishing His Kingdom on earth. Christians must apply the authority of that Kingdom to every earthly relationship, every institution, every area of life.

High up in the Andes mountains, at the border of Chile and Argentina, there is a huge statue of Christ. It was poured from the iron of cannons used in the war between those two countries. A visitor once remarked: "What a beautiful thought: the nearness of Christ is the only guarantee for peace." Now that *is* a beautiful thought, undoubtedly, but the church of Christ knows that in His person He has to be in heaven to complete His work for us *there*. And knowing that, we work with Him *here*.

One day Christ will return from heaven in much the same way as He left. He will then unite heaven and earth. A renewed creation will mirror the glories of God's presence in every part.

Lord Jesus, we are grateful that You have taken our flesh to heaven. Bless Your Kingdom here on earth, Lord. Help us to be faithful to the end. May Your church pray for Your return. Amen.

"What Must I Do to Be Saved?"

. . . and brought them out and said, "Men, what must I do to be saved?"
And they said, "Believe in the Lord Jesus, and you will be saved, and your
household" (Acts 16:30-1).

Appearances are deceptive. Things are not what they seem to
be.

Paul and Silas, beaten and flogged, thrown into jail, seemed so
weak. And the warden, master of the situation, seemed so strong as
he retired for the night.

But watch God uncover reality.

Paul and Silas sing psalms in the night. The power of God sets
all the prisoners free. And the warden, in desperation, wants to
take his own life. That's God's reality. Faith is strong; unbelief is
pitifully weak.

Once the gospel has opened human eyes to that reality, there is
hope. Trembling, the warden asks what he must do to be saved.
The answer is as simple as it is majestic. "Believe in the Lord Jesus
Christ." That's the heart of the gospel. Jesus! He fulfilled the law
of love in our stead. He died for all our sins. Believe in Him, accept
Him, give yourself to Him.

That salvation gives us the right evaluation of life. Faith in
Christ changes our outlook and transforms our values. In the final
analysis, the unbeliever puts a wrong estimate on everything. "He
trembles at a straw, because he thought it was a falling beam; he
topples by a beam, because he thought it was a straw," Thielicke
once said.

Indeed. Instead of being interested first of all in running a jail
and sleeping quietly at night, the jailer washed the wounds of Paul
and Silas, took them into his house, and gave them a meal.

Reality had become reality through salvation in Christ.

Thank You, Lord and Redeemer, for salvation full and free. May we live
out of Your forgiving grace. Teach us how all things have become new in
Christ. In Your name we pray. Amen.

"Hear Without a Preacher?"

How are they to believe in him of whom they have never heard? And how are they to hear without a preacher? (Rom. 10:14).

You are that preacher!

What a distinction to be appointed a bearer of the good tidings of salvation!

But the task is tremendously big.

It is a seesaw battle.

For some time Mohammedanism grew much faster in Africa than Christianity. It became a formidable threat. Now that trend seems to have been reversed. For this we thank God.

But there are other disturbing situations. Nine percent of the world's people live in English-speaking countries. Those nine percent have the benefit of the services of ninety percent of the world's ordained preachers. Mission authorities also point out that although more missionaries are being sent out every year, this increase does not keep pace with population growth.

These last several years have witnessed mass evangelism with new techniques and new communication skills. It will take more time to assess the integrity and lasting results of the new approaches. Some very prominent people in politics and show business have testified to their conversion. Freelance evangelism has become popular.

What we do know with absolute certainty is that a worldwide mission outburst must be borne up by revival among God's people. History has known two such outbursts. The first was during the early Christian era. The second came with the great Reformation of the sixteenth century. People in those days were on fire for the Lord. They talked about Him, sang about Him, and witnessed of Him. A third outburst will come when God's ordinary people will take His Word to heart, live it, apply it to life, and bring it to their fellow men.

Cause us to become deeply involved in spreading the gospel, Lord, in our hopes, our prayers, our speaking, our giving. Bless the young churches. Protect Your missionaries. Bless the Word of God around the world today. Amen.

"Are They Not Ministering Spirits?"

Are they not all ministering spirits sent forth to serve, for the sake of those who are to obtain salvation? (Heb. 1:14).

Have we shut up the angels within the pages of the Bible? Have we confined them to heaven? Have we limited their presence to the past? If we have, we have been blind! They are very busy, here on earth, for believers today! They moved right through the forbidding gate of concentration camps to protect and console God's children. They accompany children on their way to school. Jesus said: "In heaven their angels always behold the face of my Father" (Matt. 18:10).

Many missionaries have testified to the wondrous deeds of rescue performed by angels. Without the ministry of angels, the church would not be what it is today. Many of our fears would be allayed if we would think more of the presence and power of these tireless workers of God. Milton once said: "Millions of spiritual creatures walk the earth unseen, both when we sleep and when we wake."

The most wonderful thing about angels' work is that it is always related to the redemption of God's people. While Daniel prayed, Michael and his angel warriors fought a fierce battle against satan and his demons at the court of Persia's king. An angel guided Philip to the Gaza road to explain the gospel to Candace's prime minister. And John tells us in Revelation that an angel took the prayers of God's people, put them on the golden altar, and thereupon cast them upon the earth unleashing judgments and plagues (Rev. 8:3-5).

No, we don't worship angels, for we are children of God and they are only servants of God. But don't underestimate the power and concern of these great spirits of God in your life!

Great God in heaven, thank You for sending down Your angels to minister to us. May this, too, take our fears away. Amen.

"Who Shall Stand?"

For the great day of their wrath has come, and who can stand before it? (Rev. 6:17).

The historian Toynbee has said that all arms build-ups have ended in war. We don't know what our present arms race will lead to, in spite of the SALT talks. The build-up already began soon after the second world war.

Underlying the conflicts of our age is a far more embracing conflict of far longer standing, and it is heading, unavoidably, to its ultimate showdown. It is the struggle between Christ's forces and satan's forces. That struggle affects everything that exists; everybody is drawn into it.

Here, in Revelation 6, we read something of the final judgment day. No one can imagine the terror in the hearts of those who have fought on the wrong side of the battle of the kingdoms. In the verses just before today's text, John gives us a glimpse: "Then the kings of the earth and the great men and the generals and the rich and the strong, and every one, slave and free, hid in the caves and among the rocks of the mountains, calling to the mountains and rocks, 'Fall on us and hide us from the face of him who is seated on the throne and from the wrath of the Lamb.' "

It is at this point that John directs a question to readers of all centuries: The day of wrath has come; *who can stand before it*?

Blessed are those who can say: "Yes, I can stand before that wrath." They can say that because their Lord stood there for them when He died on the cross. If you confess Him as your Savior, you can also say that—by His grace! Christianity is at once very serious and very joyful.

Lord Jesus, we pray that Your coming may be hastened. Help us to aim and direct our lives toward that great day. Hallelujah. Thine the glory! Hallelujah, amen!

"As Nothing?"

Who is left among you that saw this house in its former glory? How do you see it now? Is it not in your sight as nothing? . . . and I will fill this house with splendor, says the Lord of hosts (Hag. 2:3, 7).

Older people tend to think that standards of conduct erode through the years. They feel secure in the established patterns of virtue and are a bit suspicious of ever changing lifestyles.

Life, however, comes with many challenges. We need the seasoned wisdom of the old, but also the fresh initiatives of the young. Not only the young but also the old can fail. Today's text is an example.

The people had returned from exile in Babylon and had found Jerusalem and the temple in ruins. The prophet Haggai and other great leaders led the people in an ambitious building program. But the problems were many. There were times when the weary builders became discouraged and wanted to quit. That's when the older people should have encouraged the younger ones, but they didn't. Instead they belittled the work of the builders. They said, "You should have seen Solomon's temple which we knew as children."

Haggai rebuked the discouragers. He told them that they should not go by appearance but by substance. The new temple, though modest in size, would be filled with the glory of the Lord. In the end the temple was completed, and through the temple service Jesus Christ was born. He is the substance of all that Christianity stands for.

We are eager to maintain the sound quality of life. We want to safeguard ourselves against the evils of our day. That's good; that's our God-given duty. But be careful. In our concern to safeguard what is good, we are tempted to package life in a soil-proof wrapper. As time goes on, we focus our attention on the wrapper—not on life itself anymore. Thus our concern is self-defeating, since evil latches on to the heart. To young and old comes God's promise: let Me fill your heart with My holiness.

Help us, Lord, not to lean on our own opinions, but to open our eyes to see new demands and better ways to meet them. We pray for the unity of all Your people. Amen.

Enoch

Enoch walked with God; and he was not, for God took him (Gen. 5:24).

This month we will visit some people in the Old Testament. Many of those people knew the pain of failure, but also the forgiving grace of God. They all played a role in God's plans for mankind in the coming of the Messiah, Jesus Christ.

Our first visit brings us to a wonderful person named Enoch. Of him the Bible says that he *walked with God*.

Walking with God . . .

Now, that seems simple enough. You move in God's company, you commune with God. But isn't it remarkable that we do so little of it? Maybe walking with God is not as simple as it sounds.

Let's look at some implications.

In order to walk with God you have to have *peace* with God. "Do two people walk together if they are not agreed?" Amos asked (Amos 3:3). This means that we must be serious about finding salvation in Christ. Enoch's relationship with God reached out for the cross of Christ.

There is another thing we must consider in Enoch's walk with God—*separation*. Enoch lived in a period of widespread evil, and he testified against that evil. You can read all about that in the little epistle of Jude. Walking with God means that you do not walk with His enemies. Walking with God takes courage. But without the struggle, there can be no victory. Enoch knew that victory. One day God brought Enoch straight to heaven; he did not taste death. Amazing. In his walk with God, Enoch reached out not only for the Christ's crucifixion but also for His resurrection.

We praise You, God of our fathers, for the greatness of Enoch's faith. Help us to live in the power of the Savior's death and life. Amen.

Lamech

When Lamech had lived a hundred and eighty-two years, he became the father of a son, and called his name Noah, saying, "Out of the ground which the Lord has cursed this one shall bring us relief from our work and from the toil of our hands" (Gen. 5:28-9).

Our next visit is with Lamech. But we must make sure to go to the right address. There is another Lamech whom we do not want to see, the one with the two wives, the one who swore so terribly. He is the seventh generation from Adam in the line of Cain. Our Lamech is the ninth generation from Adam in the line of Seth.

We are intrigued by Lamech. Being nine generations removed from Adam, would he know the details of the fall of Paradise? Yes, he does. Lamech, it turns out, is impressed with the *hardship* of daily work. He does not want to complain, but what bothers him is the *cause* of that hardship—the curse which the Lord pronounced upon the earth when He visited Adam and Eve in Paradise. After nine generations, then, that was still a live issue with practical implications.

Another reason why a visit to Lamech is special is that at the age of 182 he has just become a father. The baby's name is *Noah*. On that special occasion, Lamech announces that he believes Noah will bring relief from the hardships of daily work. That also goes back to Paradise, where God had promised that rescue from the affliction of sin would come from the descendants of Eve. Lamech banks on that. *Noah is the one!* Alas, Noah was not the Messiah. It took many more generations before the Redeemer would be born. But Lamech's confession stands: God's promise of grace has everything to do with the struggles of making a daily living. That alone makes Lamech a special man.

Lord, we live in a sophisticated age. But may people see again that sin is the cause of all our problems. Send us Your grace in Christ. Amen.

Noah

Then Noah built an altar to the Lord . . . and [Noah] drank of the wine,
and became drunk, and lay uncovered in his tent (Gen. 8:20; 9:21).

Noah was a man of spiritual stature. Of him we read in
Genesis 6:9: "Noah was a righteous man, blameless in his
generation; Noah walked with God."

But one day this great man fell. He drank, became drunk, and
made a spectacle of himself, which in turn brought out the worst in
his son Ham, whose behavior led to further grief and suffering.

Have you known your moment of shame? As a criminal returns to the site of his crime, so people who fail tend to turn in upon
their failure. Christians should not do that. Note what the Bible
tells us about Noah. There was an altar in Noah's life upon
which he burned sacrifices to the Lord. Through those sacrifices
God gave Noah forgiveness of sins. And as a forgiven man, Noah
could face God, his children and himself. Forgiveness restores
esteem and acceptance. Without those, no one can fully live.

As people who read the New Testament, we know that the
altar in Noah's life pointed forward to the sacrifice Christ made on
the cross. His sacrifice takes the bitter regrets of believers and empties them of their shame.

Many centuries later, the Letter to the Hebrews calls Noah "an
heir of the righteousness which comes by faith" (11:7). That is a
striking statement. An "heir" receives treasures for which he has
not worked. It is a free gift to which he is entitled because the
testator has so ordered. There is something joyful about being an
heir, especially when the inheritance is "the righteousness of
faith." It dispels all shame and regret.

Lord, You have called us to walk in righteousness. Supply us daily with
Your grace, and cause us to do much for You. Amen.

Melchizedek

Melchizedek [was] king of Salem . . .
And Abram gave him a tenth of everything (Gen. 14:18, 20).

Melchizedek is one of the most remarkable men in the Bible. During Abraham's days he was king and priest of Salem, which later became Jerusalem. When Abraham returned from defeating the "kings of the North," Melchizedek blessed Abraham and Abraham gave a tenth of his goods to Melchizedek.

This gives us something to think about. Abraham had been separated from mankind so that Jesus Christ could be born from his generations. The Old Testament confines itself, to a large extent, to recording the history of the Israelites, Abraham's descendants. Abraham represented God's program of salvation.

But we must not forget that God's concerns all along remained much broader than the nation of Israel (Gen. 12:3). His great aim was to bring salvation to the entire human race. Melchizedek personified that broader concern; he represented all mankind before God's face.

Hebrews 7 tells us more about the importance of Melchizedek. We are told that Melchizedek was superior to Abraham, and that Christ's priesthood was after the likeness of Melchizedek, not after Aaron, who was of Abraham's generations. Christ was born through Abraham's ministry. But when He finished His work, He restored His own to the priesthood of Melchizedek. They became prophets, priests and kings "of God Most High" (vs. 18)—Adam's children of peace ("Salem," vs. 18).

As we study some people of the Old Testament this month, be sure to look beyond the horizons of their lives to see God's yearning to save mankind, to save you, to restore you to true humanhood.

Almighty God, how wondrous Your great acts of salvation, Your counsel of peace. Help us to walk in the path of service. Amen.

Abraham

And Abraham said of Sarah his wife, "She is my sister." And Abimelech king of Gerar sent and took Sarah (Gen. 20:2).

Even Abraham, the "father of all believers," was not above failure caused by fear. Traveling through Gerar, Abraham faced a delicate problem. He was afraid that the king of Gerar would kill him so that he would be free to marry Sarah. So Abraham pretended that Sarah was his sister. And sure enough, the king's servants brought Sarah to the king without paying attention to Abraham.

Though Abraham had saved his skin, he now also found himself in a hopeless situation. At this point God took over. He told the king of Gerar to restore Sarah to Abraham. The king quickly obeyed, but not without a severe rebuke to Abraham, whom he acidly addressed as "Sarah's brother."

It's not necessary to analyze Abraham's feelings at this point. His heart must have been filled with embarrassment, guilt and humiliation. Here is one instance where a believer compares unfavorably with an unbeliever—at least, if we go by first impressions. But don't go by first impressions. God's Word never does; it goes by God's promises. God sees Abraham as the father of believers, even though he fell lamentably below that high distinction.

We learn two things here. Our hope is in God's grace toward us in Christ, not in our high moral standards or the excellence of our conduct. But we must also live up to our high calling to bring honor to God's name. Micah 6:8 sums it up: "What does the Lord require of you but to do justice, and to love kindness, and to walk humbly with your God?"

Dear Lord, may those who do not know You as Father be drawn to inquire about You because of our godliness. Help us never to give offense. Amen.

Sarah

And Sarah said, "God has made laughter for me . . ." (Gen. 21:6).

Sarah was a woman of dignity, but as human as any of us. One day she showed her weakness in a painful way. Abraham entertained visitors, and Sarah could hear their conversation while preparing the meal in her tent. One of the visitors, who was no less than God Himself, told Abraham that Sarah would have a son. Then Sarah, already 89, laughed, not realizing that the visitor could hear her clearly. When the visitor asked, "Why did Sarah laugh?", Sarah, overcome by embarrassment, brazenly denied it.

Amazing, isn't it, how simply the Bible relates these typically human situations. We have all known similar situations. But make no mistake, this is not just an unimportant incident in the life of average people. God is busy here preparing redemption for all mankind. Great things are at stake. God tells these old people that they will have a son who will be one of the forefathers of Christ.

A year later Abraham and Sarah had their baby boy, and Sarah laughed again. This time her laughter was not of unbelief but of spiritual happiness. The elated parents had no problem choosing a name for the little boy: *Isaac*, for Isaac means *laughter*.

The redeemed in Christ are important people to God. He rates their acts of faithful service very highly. His Kingdom comes through their obedience. Those who have the mind of Christ become more and more aware of the importance of their involvement in God's plans. They have abiding joy; they know the secret of holy laughter.

Come, Lord, use us as You unfold Your program among people and nations. May we be found ready to give ourselves. Give us the vision to recognize our calling. Amen.

Lot

Then the Lord rained on Sodom and Gomorrah brimstone and fire (Gen. 19:24).

Sometimes failure comes at a great price.

Take the case of Lot, Abraham's nephew.

When Abraham moved into Canaan from Ur of the Chaldees, he took Lot with him. God had blessed Abraham richly, both spiritually and materially. Abraham was a generous man, and he let Lot share fully in the abundance. But Lot wanted more, at least in terms of material goods. So one day Lot surveyed the land, told his uncle Abraham that he had found greener pastures yonder, and took leave.

We next hear of Lot in connection with the destruction of the evil cities of Sodom and Gomorrah. Very unfortunately, this was the area where Lot had been farming so prosperously. As fire rained from the sky, Lot escaped the inferno, but at a tragic cost. His wife died and he lost all his goods. But that was not all. In a sad way, Lot became the father of his daughters' sons, who became two nations, the *Moabites* and the *Ammonites*, who fought against Israel for centuries and obstructed the coming of Christ the Messiah.

Yes, as far as Lot himself is concerned, he was saved. In II Peter 2:7-8 we read: "[God] rescued righteous Lot . . . vexed in his righteous soul day after day with their lawless deeds." He objected to the evil of Sodom, but he stayed, and so he died as a lonely man who made no contribution toward God's program.

What a man sows, that will he reap. How true that is also for us. Use your gifts; life is short.

Holy Spirit, remove selfishness from our motives and equip us to make the will of Christ known in the world. In Jesus' name. Amen.

Rebekah

Then Rebekah took the best garments of Esau . . . and put them on Jacob her younger son; and the skins of the kids she put upon his hands and upon the smooth part of the neck. [Isaac] said, "Are you really my son Esau?" Now Esau hated Jacob because of the blessing with which his father had blessed him (Gen. 27:15-16, 24, 41).

Fire has a way of dying down when it is not tended, and so does spiritual fervor. It has happened to many people. It happened to Isaac and Rebekah. They were a godly couple and wanted nothing more than to serve the Lord, but when you read the Biblical record about their lives, you unavoidably get the feeling that they lost their early enthusiasm. The result was that they became more and more absorbed in the daily routine of life. Small vices began to enter family life to do their pernicious work.

One of those vices was *favoritism.*

The father sided with one son, the mother with the other. One thing led to another. Mother and son cheated the ailing father and stole the other son's birthright. Lasting hatred between the two brothers was the result.

History's record speaks clear language. The younger son barely saved his life by escaping hastily to his uncle's place. The descendants of the older son, the *Edomites* became bitter enemies of the descendents of the younger son, the *Israelites*. Herod the Edomite sought to kill the Christ child in Bethlehem.

Disturbing, isn't it, that human failures have such forbidding consequences in the Bible? They still do today. God is very serious when He asks obedience from us. But there is also comfort. Christ was born from Rebekah's flesh. That brings Him close to us. He knows our ways. In the way of forgiveness He will try it again and again with us.

Lord, set us free from the tyranny of our vices. Help us to love and guide our children with fairness and honesty. Give us the vision of a life of service. Amen.

Jacob

Esau said, "Is he not rightly named Jacob? For he has supplanted me these two times." But Jacob said, "I will not let you go, unless you bless me" (Gen. 27:36; 32:26).

His name meant *swindler*, and a swindler he was. Jacob cheated his older brother out of his birthright, and later, by hook and crook, he became a wealthy man.

But his wealth did not bring him happiness. His marriage went bad, and his children caused him much grief. He never really felt at home anywhere.

One night, facing a host of problems, he went to the river Jabbok where he met God face to face. There he realized that a man is nothing if he doesn't have God. In that moment of deep agony, he begged God to *bless* him. That moment became the turning point in his life. He confessed his total dependence on God and admitted that in his hunger for riches he had been a slave of greed and fear.

That's where real life began for Jacob. God gave him a new name—*Israel*, which means *prince of God*. A nation was named after him, a nation of princely people to whom the Messiah Christ was born. That nation had to learn the same painful but glorious lesson: real life begins with the fear of God because to live apart from God is death.

We have to learn that lesson too. We scratch for a "better" life while the Father has already given us the best life—life in Christ.

Again the apostle Peter sums it up for us: "But you are a chosen race, a royal priesthood, a holy nation, God's own people, that you may declare the wonderful deeds of him who called you out of darkness into his marvelous light. Once you were no people but now you are God's people" (I Pet. 2:9).

What a life!

Father, we pray for total salvation. Give us the freedom in Christ to live the abundant life. Holy Spirit, create in us a new spirit. Renew God's promises to us every day. For Jesus sake. Amen.

Reuben

Among the clans of Reuben there were great searchings of heart. Why did you tarry among the sheepfolds, to hear the piping for the flocks? (Judges 5:15-16).

You have met those people who like to talk about religion but do not get around doing much for the Lord; they like to discuss theology, but they do not do much for the church and the spread of the gospel. At mission rallies they sing, "Like a mighty army moves the church of God," and then it's back to the rocking chairs again.

Reuben, Jacob's oldest son, had been that way. He talked about saving Joseph from his angry brothers, but he lacked the courage to take drastic action. He was never an example of godliness to the rest of the family.

The tribe of Reuben showed the same characteristics. All talk, no action.

One day Deborah, the judge who functioned as head of state, summoned Israel's able-bodied men to fight against Jabin, the Canaanite king who had oppressed them for years. Immediately the people of Reuben engaged in a lively discussion. "There were great searchings of heart." But in the meantime a war was being fought without Reuben showing up. When the war was over, the Reubenites were still talking. But Deborah, who was not only a great judge but also a gifted poet, lashed Reuben with the whip of her words, "Why did you tarry, Reuben?"

Note that Deborah faulted Reuben not for having had searchings of heart, but for not having acted upon them. It is necessary for the churches to do confessional work, to be involved in theology, to have workshops in evangelism, to survey world hunger and refugee needs, to publish bulletins. But the best insights are futile if they are not translated into work and action. The job must get done.

Thy will be done on earth as it is in heaven. May we do it in deed. For Jesus' sake. Amen.

Judah

Now therefore, let your servant, I pray you, remain instead of the lad as a slave to my lord; and let the lad go back with his brothers (Gen. 44:33).

Sometimes believers rise to great heights of service and do things they thought themselves totally incapable of.

It happened to Judah, the son of Jacob.

The Bible reveals a lot of sins Judah committed, the worst probably being that he suggested to the other brothers that they sell Joseph as a slave to Egypt. He dearly wished later that he had not. When there was a famine in Canaan, Judah and his brothers traveled to Egypt for a load of grain, and that gave Joseph, who in the meantime had become governor of Egypt, the opportunity to put quite a bit of pressure on his brothers. He demanded that they bring their youngest brother Benjamin, who had remained behind with their father, and when Benjamin arrived Joseph refused to let him return. The brothers realized that this would be the breaking point for father Jacob, and it was in this painful impasse that Judah stood up and became great in spiritual self-denial. He offered to *take Benjamin's place* and become Joseph's slave. In a very moving address, he portrayed the sorrow of father Jacob and his love for Benjamin.

How could Judah reach the level of such spiritual excellence? We give the glory to God, who did it by His grace. That grace did greater things. From the generations of Judah, Jesus Christ was born. Christ made that His mission—to *take the place* of those whom the Father had given Him. Judah pre-figured his great Son.

There will be moments when your strength will be tested beyond endurance. See then your Savior, who took your place and offers you His power.

Thank You, dear Lord, for Your promise to stand with us in the hour of trial. Help us to accept every challenge in Your strength. For Christ's sake. Amen.

Jochebed

. . . she hid him three months . . . she took for him a basket . . . and placed it among the reeds at the river's brink (Ex. 2:2-3).

Jochebed will be remembered with honor for the ingenuity and courage with which she saved the life of her little boy Moses.

Now, of course all mothers display heroism when it comes to the safety of their children, but there is a spiritual dimension in what Jochebed did that must not be overlooked. Acts 7:20 tells us that Moses was beautiful *before God*. In Hebrews 11:23 we read that it was *by faith* that Moses was hid. Jochebed must have seen behind Pharaoh's cruel action an attack by satan himself, seeking to destroy the people of Israel so that the promised Messiah of God would not be born.

Satan's dealings with mankind are marked by a great deal of consistency. He is out to get the new generation. If he could create a mood of indifference or skepticism among our youth, the future would be his. As parents and churches we cannot pay enough attention to our children and young people. The temptations surrounding them are so many and so pernicious! It is not enough that we teach them the tenets of the Christian faith; we must also display that faith in our own lives as a model for them. And as a Christian community we must be concerned about the application of our faith to daily life. Our prayers must go up daily for the well-being of a new generation.

Deep runs the Nile . . . But as a mother's love and spiritual vision saved the day for the Kingdom in ancient Egypt, so God will bless the faithfulness of parents today. To Him be the glory.

Please safeguard our children, heavenly Father. Keep them close to You, and make them grow in faith and conviction. Amen.

Moses

. . . and [Moses] said to them, "Hear now, you rebels . . ." And Moses lifted up his hand and struck the rock with his rod twice (Num. 20:10-11).

We now visit Moses, the leader of God's people as they traveled through the desert to the promised land. Hear what the Bible tells us about Moses: "And there has not arisen a prophet since in Israel like Moses, whom the Lord knew face to face, none like him for all the signs and the wonders which the Lord sent him to do in the land of Egypt, to Pharaoh and to all his servants and to all his land, and for all the mighty power and all the great and terrible deeds which Moses wrought in the sight of all Israel" (Deut. 34:10-12).

Of this great man, too, we read that he missed the mark.

One day, standing before the assembled congregation, Moses lost his temper and brought dishonor to God. True, Moses had good reasons. The people had blamed him for all their misery and demanded instant solutions for their problems. God, however, had supported Moses and promised water from the rock for the thirsty people. Even so, Moses could not restrain his anger. He yelled at the people and struck the rock with his rod.

Moses' disobedience had two consequences—one sad, one glad. God forbade Moses to enter the promised land with the people. Nevertheless, just before Moses died, God took him to the top of Mount Nebo and showed him the land (Deut. 34:1-3). That last event in Moses' life was also the greatest: he saw the future salvation of the world which Christ would work in the land of promise beyond the Jordan.

Perhaps you have known your moment of shame. Perhaps the pain still lingers. Come, climb the mountain of God's grace and take in the panorama of salvation. Then, with Moses, you will have your greatest moment.

O God, how great the promises of forgiveness and renewal. Keep us from dwelling on old regrets. Through Christ we pray. Amen.

Rahab

And Joshua . . . sent two men . . . as spies . . . and [they] came into the house of a harlot whose name was Rahab, and lodged there . . . and [Rahab] said to the men . . . "The Lord your God is he who is God in heaven and on earth . . ." (Josh. 2:1, 9, 11).

We follow the people of Israel as they enter the promised land. The great adventure of conquering the nations of Canaan has begun. Now and then we read of individual people among those nations who surrendered to the God of Israel and became loyal to His people.

One such person was Rahab.

Actually, Rahab was not a likely candidate for membership in the Old Testament church. She had made a mess of her life, she had lost her respect, and the future offered only further degradation. The end would be despair.

But her contact with the Israelites caused an amazing turn of events in her life. Rahab lived in the city of Jericho, which was the key fortification in Canaan's defense system. One day two secret agents of Israel found their way into the city to survey its layout. In danger of being apprehended by the Jericho security forces, they quickly took refuge in Rahab's house. All of a sudden Rahab was drawn into the battle for Israel's survival. Her choice was a difficult one: be loyal to her own people, or join the cause of Israel's God. Who can fathom the mystery of God's grace which made her choose for the Lord?

From that choice, followed a beautiful new chapter in Rahab's life. When Israel's army took over the city, she was accepted as a member of the people. From Matthew 1:5, we learn that she married a man named Salmon, and they became the parents of Boaz, who was the great-grandfather of King David. Thus she became one of the foremothers of Christ.

Now we understand anew why Christians shouldn't use the word *hopeless* easily. God still gives new possibilities and a new challenge.

Lord, give us hope. Break the shackles which tie us to a sinful past. Amen.

Naomi

She said to them, "Do not call me Naomi, call me Mara, for the Almighty has dealt very bitterly with me" (Ruth 1:20).

When she was born, her parents and neighbors agreed that they had never seen such a beautiful baby. They called her Naomi, which means *pleasantness, delight.*

Years later she returned to her hometown, old and disillusioned. The people said wonderingly, "Is that the lovely Naomi?" Her cynical answer came quickly, "Call me *Mara, bitterness*, for the Almighty has dealt bitterly with me!"

We can sympathize with Naomi. Her life had been extremely hard. She and her family had suffered poverty, their emigration to Moab had been a failure, and her husband and boys had died in a foreign land. She returned to Bethlehem, a poor, grief-stricken widow, all alone, to face acquaintances of long ago. "Call me Mara . . ."

But that down-and-out woman became living proof that God can turn a sad ending into a new beginning. Read all about it in the little book of Ruth. Her daughter-in-law Ruth married the rich landowner Boaz, and they had a son called Obed who was the grandfather of David, who was one of the forefathers of Jesus Christ.

What a wonderful God we have!

Sometimes our hearts are filled with a mixture of disappointment and anger. We punish ourselves by deciding that there is no future for people such as us and that we are born for misfortune. What's the use? But God will have none of that! He has invested too much in us for such defeatism. He invites us to come to Christ and exchange our bitterness for the sweetness of Christ's grace. Jesus said, "Him who comes to me I will not cast out" (John 6:37).

That's right, the name is *Naomi*, the delightful one.

Lord, we are grateful for the hope about which the Bible speaks. Turn our defeat into victory. Bring us back to full participation in the program of salvation. Amen.

Ruth

But Ruth said, ". . . where you go I will go, and where you lodge I will lodge; your people shall be my people, and your God my God" (Ruth 1:16-17).

Ruth's life had known several unexpected turns. Having grown up in Moab, she met and married a young man, Chilion, the son of Jewish immigrants who had left the Judean hill country because of repeated crop failures. Several tragedies befell the young woman; in a short time her father-in-law, her brother-in-law and her husband died. Since there was not much to live for in Moab, Ruth's mother-in-law decided to return to Judea. Ruth announced that she would go along.

The picture which emerges is that Ruth was a woman of love, faithfulness and firm resolve. Her decision to stay with her mother-in-law in a foreign land took a lot of courage and self-denial. The Bible makes it plain that the source of that courage lay in God Himself. We read of a wonderful confession Ruth made: "Your people shall be my people, and your God my God." The God of that confession saw her through during the difficult months ahead. And that same God used her in His plans as we saw yesterday. All was well that ended well.

The center of our attention, then, is not first of all the person of Ruth and her splendid character, though undeniably inspiring, but rather God Himself and the way He works. We see that over and over again: God plans His program sovereignly, recruiting people in the most unexpected manner, providing for them carefully all the while, yet requiring of them all their energy and devotion.

The early New Testament Christians made a deep impact on the world because they didn't just confess Christ as Savior, they also confessed Him as Lord.

Thank You, Lord, for giving us a role in Your program and caring for us in all our daily needs. For Jesus' sake. Amen.

Deborah

[Deborah] sent and summoned Barak . . . and said to him, "The Lord, the God of Israel, commands you, 'Go, gather your men at Mount Tabor.'" Barak said to her, "If you will go with me, I will go" (Judges 4:6, 8).

Has your church stagnated? Have you? People who stagnate accept things as they are; they adjust to disagreeable situations and are content with what they have. They advise us to go easy on new programs that cost money and effort. Stagnation blocks progress and breeds complacency.

Stagnation can only be broken through by a blast from the Word of God. In Judges 4 that happened through a woman called Deborah. Once God's Word took hold of Deborah, there was no stopping. She summoned Barak, who appears to have been his own military high command, and told him to attack the Canaanites who had dominated the country for twenty years. That was a tall order. The Canaanite army was comprised of a large infantry and 900 chariots, the ancient version of modern tanks.

Barak scratched his head, for the mission seemed impossible, but he consented to go if Deborah would go along herself. That was almost ironic: the commanding general seeking the company of a woman. But it was a wise move! Deborah was God's prophetess, the bearer of His Word. When you go in the power of the Word, you cannot lose!

And they didn't. Israel did the impossible—well, actually *God* did. We read, "The Lord routed Sisera and all his chariots and all his army" (vs. 15). The nation was free! The people could live again to the full and serve the Lord with gladness.

Shall we pray for a mighty outburst of God's Word? That would rid us of a genteel form of Christianity to which the world has never objected. It would mean sacrifices, but things would get done.

Lord, You gave us a job to do, but we have become slow of heart. Help us to become industrious Christians and to love Your ways. In the power of Christ. Amen.

Jael

But Jael the wife of Heber took a tent peg, and took a hammer in her hand, and went softly to him and drove the peg into his temple . . . So he died (Judges 4:21).

Something in us likes a fence—a fence to sit on. The fence-sitter in us keeps us from making a choice either for God or against Him. While others toil, we avoid uncomfortable involvement by staying on the fence.

Heber and Jael were in that situation. They were descendents of *Hobab*, the father-in-law of Moses, whose family had agreed to join Israel on the long journey to Canaan. Those families, the Kenites, had remained with Israel without having become an actual part of the nation. They had found this a convenient arrangement, managing to stay clear of Israel's struggles, while profiting from its protection. We read that while Israel suffered from the oppression of the Canaanites during Deborah's days, the Kenites negotiated a separate peace.

But God has a way of troubling the fence-sitter. That afternoon while Jael, Heber's wife, was puttering around in her tent, there, suddenly, the commander of the Canaanite army stood before her in a desperate search for refuge from the pursuing Israelites. Jael then had to choose. A choice for Sisera would be a choice against Israel. There was no way in between. And Jael made the right choice. In her tent she killed him and made a contribution to Israel's survival. The fence-sitter had tumbled down, right on God's bandwagon, so to speak. In her song Deborah called Jael a "most blessed woman."

Through the years God has often brought sudden crises to fence-sitters and forced them to make a choice. Blessed are those who choose for God and join the ranks of His followers.

Lord, if we have not made up our mind about You, forgive us and lead us to wholehearted commitment. Fill our hearts with enthusiasm, and use us. Amen.

Gideon

Then Gideon said to God, "If thou wilt deliver Israel by my hand, as thou hast said, behold, I am laying a fleece of wool on the threshing floor; if there is dew on the fleece alone, and it is dry on all the ground, then I shall know that thou wilt deliver Israel by my hand, as thou hast said" (Judges 6:36-7).

Doubt is a strange thing. The word *doubt* is related to the word *double;* the doubter cannot make up his mind which of two courses to take. Sometimes doubt can be prompted by unbelief and ends in death. But it can also happen that sincere believers just do not have the courage to accept all the consequences of their commitment to God. Such doubters may go to God for courage and reassurance.

Who can fail to sympathize with Gideon? The times were hard with the Midianites firmly in control, looting, burning, and killing. Gideon had no ambition to be a savior; he was only a young man helping his father store some grain so that the Midianites would not find it. To that young man God came with the announcement that he would be the commander of the troops and fight the Midianites.

Gideon was a godly man, but this was just too much for him. He took his doubts to God with the proposition of the fleece of wool: if left outside that night, let it only be wet with dew while the ground around it stayed dry. God accepted that, did as Gideon asked, and helped him over his doubts. In God's power Gideon did defeat the Midianites and led the nation to a period of spiritual growth.

Christ knew that New Testament believers would also know the pain of doubt. He made permanent provision for them—the Bible and the sacraments. Those who steep themselves in the Scriptures and use the sacraments faithfully will grow strong in faith. The certainty of salvation will dissolve their doubt.

Lord, give us strong convictions to do Your will in courage and faithfulness. Fill us every time again, Holy Spirit, with grace from above. Through Christ. Amen.

Samson

Then [Samson] bowed with all his might; and the house fell upon the lords and upon all the people that were in it (Judges 16:30).

What a tragedy, the life of Samson! God had given him a very special office, and with that office great power and gifts. Samson's calling was to safeguard the nation of Israel from the attacks of its many enemies and to lead it to a deeper understanding of its spiritual redemption. But he constantly lost sight of the challenge of his office and became entangled in countless questionable affairs. God had hardly rescued him from the one fiasco when he was already entangled in the next. In the end his enemies captured him, deprived him of his strength, humiliated him, gouged out his eyes, and put him to work in the prison mill. The end seemed inevitable.

But when we have come to the end, God blazes His own trails.

In that dark hour, God opened Samson's spiritual eyes, and he discovered again the faithfulness of his God. He confessed his sins, God forgave him, and He restored him to his office. In God's power, Samson avenged the anger of God's enemies, afflicted an enormous loss on them, and thus broke their stranglehold on Israel. The coming of the Messiah had been safeguarded once more. In his death Samson still took part in preparing redemption for the world.

Samson's life and death bring out two basic laws in God's Kingdom. Responsible service to God and His cause is not optional; God holds us accountable for what we have done with our talents and opportunities. But God is also very gracious. He will forgive His erring people when they come to Him in repentance. He will rescue them when they cry to Him for relief, and in many cases He will restore them to service once more. Don't give up.

Father, open our eyes to our waywardness, but show us also Your boundless grace. Bring us back and put us to work. Because of Jesus we dare ask this. Amen.

Job and His Wife

Then his wife said to him, "Do you still hold fast your integrity? Curse God, and die" (Job 2:9).

Job's suffering came swiftly and ruthlessly: first his possessions stolen, then his children killed, and finally the terrible illness.

But that was only part of Job's affliction.

Job suffered a lot of spiritual distress. His friends came over and implied that his sins were the cause of his misfortunes. In his own soul Job struggled to understand God's ways. How could God permit satan to bring so much harm upon him? Added to all came the bitterness that had grown in the heart of Job's wife. Overcome by anger and grief, she spat it out: "Why don't you face it, Job? God is through with you. Why don't you give up?"

At the end of the book of Job, some of the mysteries of suffering are explained. There we also read of healing and restoration. All is well that ends well—for Job's wife too. But looking back, she most likely wished that she had never spoken the angry words that added to her husband's grief.

Suffering can be a severe strain on a marriage. Just when husband and wife need each other most, they can sometimes drift apart, not knowing how to find the way back to each other. It is often not the suffering itself that is our greatest burden, it is the *way* we cope with it that is our problem. We are our own greatest problem. It takes self-denial to go with our burdens to our heavenly Father. Before His throne we will also find our loved ones and our fellow believers. Reading the book of Job impresses us again with frailty of life and our great need of each other and of sound counseling.

Sometimes, dear Lord, we fail in comforting one another in moments of distress. Sometimes our marriages have lost their intimacy. Give us restoration and hope. Amen.

Samuel

And Samuel said, "Speak, for thy servant hears." And Samuel grew, and the Lord was with him and let none of his words fall to the ground (I Samuel 3:10, 19).

Suppose you were Samuel's biographer. What factor would you single out that accounted most for his greatness? You would be hard-pressed to do that because Samuel was a rich personality who lived an eventful life.

You may remember that it has been said by experts that the first few years of a person's life are determinative for the rest of his life. The first three chapters of the book of Samuel underscore this in the case of Samuel. His mother could give him only a few years of Christian nurture, but its fruits remained for a lifetime. Reading the third chapter of this Bible book, there emerges the theme for Samuel's life, the secret of his greatness—*his excellent hearing!* He heard everything the Lord told him: "Speak, Lord, for thy servant hears." Samuel was foremost a spokesman for God. That was his life's mission. It was really the Lord's own doing. We read: "The Lord let none of his words fall to the ground." Samuel was a perfect funnel. He always kept his ears tuned to heaven, and the Lord could be sure that whatever Samuel heard was faithfully reported to the nation. Truly, the mark of a great prophet!

That's how Samuel will be remembered. That's how the nation had many years of peace. The Word was heard among the people.

As for us, we may have interesting ideas and argue them cogently, but what good does it do if we don't echo God's Word? We go through life surrounded by a cloud of noise. Let's withdraw, then, hear our God speak to us, apply His Word, and experience peace.

Lord, we talk much and hear little. Open our hearts to Your Word. May we dwell on it always. We pray in Christ. Amen.

Jonathan

. . . the soul of Jonathan was knit to the soul of David, and Jonathan loved him as his own soul. Then Jonathan made a covenant with David (I Sam. 18:1, 3).

Friendship—what is it? By what mysterious forces were Jonathan, the prince of Israel, and David, then a young shepherd, drawn to one another? We will not understand that fully, but we can see from Scripture some beautiful fruits of that friendship.

David was brought into the palace in order to play the lyre for King Saul, Jonathan's father, who suffered from an evil spirit. That's when Jonathan and David met. The future looked grim for Saul and indeed for all Israel. A battle was shaping up between Israel and Philistia, with the chances of Israel winning practically nil. At that critical moment, David stepped forward, killed the giant Goliath, and led Israel to victory. It was then that Jonathan pledged his friendship to David. In the course of that friendship, it became clear to Jonathan that not he, but David, would be Israel's next king. What was Jonathan's reaction? He gave David his robe and his armor, a symbolic gesture that he recognized him as the crown prince.

Now we see the hand of God. He filled Jonathan's heart with the peace of friendship instead of the spirit of jealousy. That peace enabled him to recognize the Word of God which was behind it all. By that Word David had been chosen king, and by that Word he had slain Goliath. In order to let that Word have its free course in Israel, Jonathan stepped aside in David's favor. In the way of that friendship, Jonathan greatly strengthened David personally, enabling him to become a king whose rule would restore God's Word to the nation.

All friendship that enables people to live more richly out of God's Word is God-given friendship that leaves a heritage of precious fruit.

Dear God, we stand in awe before the wisdom of Your ways with people. May we taste the peace of Christ and be a blessing to many around us. Teach us the secret of godly friendship. Amen.

David

It happened, late one afternoon, when David arose from his couch and was walking upon the roof of the king's house, that he saw from the roof a woman bathing; and the woman was very beautiful (II Sam. 11:2).
Have mercy on me, O God (Ps. 51:1).

We wonder about ourselves. We love the Lord, we do His bidding, and then, all of a sudden, there come those moments of real doubt and emptiness. Or, to go a step further, sin overtakes us and we ask why were we not stronger. How could David, who had walked so closely with the Lord, fall into such sin? And, worse, how could he continue in it? The record is grim. First he committed adultery and then, in cold blood, he devised the murder of the woman's husband, a man who was an example of godly virtue. Who will fathom sin's inscrutable ways?

One reason, undoubtedly, was that David had grown sluggish in office. He no longer was a field commander with his troops; his generals had taken over while the king relaxed in his luxurious palace. Instead of rendering humble service to God's people as befitted a king by the grace of God, David had become a typical Oriental monarch. He had lost his sense of calling. People without a mission are helpless when satan attacks.

We must ask ourselves: What do we really live for? Do we feel a burden for people in distress? Do we hear the cry of the hungry? Are we concerned about the moral integrity of the society of which we are a part? Do we care about the spread of the gospel? Do we live out of Christ?

David did not go to complete ruin. God saw to that. The Holy Spirit led David to repentance and forgiveness and, through many tears, to joy. The Lord even restored him to service (Ps. 51).

You can escape evil's grip by fleeing to your God in repentance and trust. And you will discover that the pattern God used for David still holds for you today.

Have mercy on us, O God. Blot out our transgressions. Our tongues will sing of deliverance, and our mouths shall show forth praise. Amen.

Elijah

And he lay down and slept under a broom tree. He said, "I have been very jealous for the Lord . . . and I, even I only, am left; and they seek my life." And [the angel] said, "Arise and eat . . ." And the Lord said to him, "Go . . ." (I Kings 19:5, 10, 7, 15).

God has a way with people. He is wise and patient, like a good parent who knows the character weaknesses of his children.

The chapter we read today illustrates this. Elijah had done great things for God, he had witnessed for his God fearlessly before the assembled nation, and he had slain the cruel priests of Baal on Mount Carmel. Then he learned that Queen Jezebel had ordered his execution. All of a sudden, overcome by fear and discouragement, Elijah took refuge in hasty flight. To be sure, Jezebel's order was no empty threat. The danger was very real. But in that particular situation Elijah's capitulation was unexpected, since earlier that day he had faced greater threats in the power of God.

Today's text tells us of the remarkable ministry of God to His weary servant.

His eye was never away from Elijah as he wandered on and on into the wilderness of Beersheba. God let him sleep under a juniper tree for some time, and then told an angel to arouse Elijah. The angel did two things. First he fixed the prophet a meal. That was important: Elijah was exhausted, he had probably neglected himself, and his spiritual fatigue was connected with his physical fatigue. The meal strengthened his body and his soul.

Next, the angel outlined further tasks for Elijah. Kings had to be appointed, and another prophet had to be added to strengthen the Word-ministry among the people. There is something very recuperative about receiving new marching orders.

Amid all the complications of life, God provides in a unique way for His servants.

Holy Spirit, open our eyes and show us the mighty acts of God. Help us to believe in the critical hour that our Father will take care of us. Help us to be strong in the Word. Amen.

Jehoshaphat

*[Jehoshaphat] made a marriage alliance with Ahab (II Chron. 18:1).
Jehoshaphat made ships of Tarshish to go to Ophir for gold; but they did
not go, for the ships were wrecked at Ezion-geber. Then Ahaziah the son of
Ahab said to Jehoshaphat, "Let my servants go with your servants in the
ships," but Jehoshaphat was not willing (I Kings 22:48-9).*

In Jehoshaphat we meet a fairly unknown person in the Old
Testament. Yet, we must become acquainted with him, if only
because of the intriguing situation in which he found himself.

Jehoshaphat was a godly king, but in one respect he went
wrong. He married into the family of King Ahab, a man of great
evil. In spite of his good intentions, this association remained an
albatross around Jehoshaphat's neck. God warned the young king
to end the unholy socializing with his ungodly in-laws (II Chron.
19:2), but he just was not able to cut the ties.

Today's chapter tells us of an unfortunate development that
resulted from these visits. The two royal houses agreed to embark
on a combined business venture. At the wharves of Tarshish,
possibly on the Persian Gulf, a merchant marine was outfitted to
go to Ophir for gold. Governments always need money, and
Jehoshaphat probably figured this would be the answer to many
problems. But it was not to be so. It only created more difficulties.
God could not bless the venture. He blew upon the ships, and they
perished. Ahab and his associates promptly proposed another ex-
pedition, but Jehoshaphat recognized God's hand and was now
wise enough to refuse.

Are you involved in a lot of socializing in circles where God is
not respected and served? Then you are sailing on the wrong ship.
You had better get off before the Lord deals with that ship as He
did with Jehoshaphat's navy.

*Father, give us the grace and honesty to examine our relationships. May
our allegiance with our covenant God be true and strong, our only source
of power. Let Jesus Christ be Lord. Amen.*

Naaman

And Elisha sent a messenger to him, saying, "Go and wash in the Jordan seven times, and your flesh shall be restored, and you shall be clean" (II Kings 5:10).

Achievement means a lot to us. We are willing to work hard, but then we want something to show for it in the end. We cherish the admiration and esteem of others. A little monument of recognition here and there on our life's pathway suits us fine.

All that, of course, is not necessarily wrong in itself, but it is not without danger either. Achievement can easily become the foundation of our peace of mind rather than the results of faithfulness. Following the crash of the stock market which marked the beginning of the Depression of the 1930s, many people committed suicide because their life's savings were wiped out.

The Syrian general Naaman had that kind of a shattering experience. One day he discovered the beginnings of leprosy. He realized he was finished. Naaman traveled to Israel to consult a prophet there as a last resort for healing. The prophet accorded him none of the honors he was used to, but simply instructed him to wash seven times in the river Jordan. That implied total humility before God and complete submission to His commandments. No explanation was added. A proud man was reduced to the actuality of his naked self before his Creator. But when Naaman did as he was told and bowed before God, he was healed. In his healing he found himself: he praised God and was free from the worship of his self-made idols.

The joy of personal achievement can only be true and lasting when we realize that God gave it all, that He alone deserves praise, and that we seek to serve Him in all our ambitions.

Lord, we like to build our own stronghold. Pride marks so many of our endeavors. Make us humble; we totally depend on Your love to us. For Jesus' sake. Amen.

Jeremiah (I)

*Behold, O Lord, for I am in distress, my soul is in tumult . . . because I
have been very rebellious (Lam. 1:20).*
Thou didst invite as to the day of an appointed feast (Lam. 2:22).

God's Word leads us to think of the prophet Jeremiah today.

We learn something unexpected about him. We had thought of
him as of one of the great prophets of the Old Testament, a holy
man of God. And, to be sure, he was that. But today's text pictures
him in great fear. The reason was the wrath and power of an
enemy army ready to pounce on God's people. But it was not the
only reason. Jeremiah was upset about himself. "My soul, O Lord,
is in great tumult because I have been very rebellious." So there you
have it—a great prophet of God confessing sin that has bothered
him very much.

One chapter further we see the sun shining in Jeremiah's life
again. He tells us that the Lord has appointed a feast, and he,
Jeremiah, has been invited. What a wonderful turn of events! The
forgiving grace of the Lord leads not only to forgiveness but also to
joyful reunion. The feast is an occasion of great rejoicing. There is
recuperative power in celebration. Fear is banished from
Jeremiah's soul. His contribution to the Bible is an indication of a
very industrious life.

Those who are in Christ can experience the tremendous power
of peace. The great Canadian physician Sir William Osler, who was
a blessing to thousands, described a lifelong habit: "At night as I
lay off my clothes, I undress my soul too, laying aside its sins. In
the presence of God I lie down to rest, to awaken a free man with a
new life, and I begin each day with Christ in prayer."

*Dear Lord, if I am sometimes overcome by fear, cleanse me, support me,
and help me onward. By Your gospel remove fear from many lives. Amen.*

Jeremiah (II)

And I bought the field at Anathoth from Hanamel my cousin (Jer. 32:9).

A preacher must put his money where his mouth is.

Jeremiah was one preacher who passed the test.

It all came about in a very strange situation. Politically, times were hopeless: the army of the king of Babylon had surrounded Jerusalem. Personally, times were bad for Jeremiah: he had been imprisoned by the king of Judah for preaching a gospel not to the king's liking. In that dark hour, Jeremiah received a visitor—his cousin Hanamel, who came with the request that Jeremiah buy the family field in Anathoth in accordance with God's laws of redemption. Jeremiah could have objected: Anathoth was located in the territory occupied by the Babylonians. Moreover, he needed every bit of cash for his own survival. But we read that he bought the field and had the deed safely tucked away.

That was not only an example of obedience, it was foremost an act of *hope*. In the presence of the people, Jeremiah declared that the future looked good for houses, fields and vineyards. That was the gospel Jeremiah had preached, and that was the gospel he practiced. In spite of all the tragic events, he remained a prophet of hope.

Christianity generates a lot of words. We talk, we explain, we preach—words, words, words. Well, Jeremiah did too, but he lived what he said; he personified hope. In this dark world we must not only speak of hope but also put it into deeds of love and kindness. The tone of our voice, the look in our eyes, and the gestures of our hands must reflect the hope Christ restored among us.

Thank You, Lord, for bringing the hope of eternal life into our hearts. Help us to live up to our great calling. Amen.

Daniel

. . . he went to his house where he had windows in his upper chamber open toward Jerusalem; and he got down upon his knees three times a day and prayed and gave thanks before his God, as he had done previously (Dan. 6:10).

Daniel—what a man! For years on end, he was the first ruler under a number of famous emperors. Few human beings have had such a illustrious career.

But when we study the Biblical record, we realize that the outstanding feature of Daniel's life was not his success as a statesman but his humble dependence upon his God.

We read in today's text that Daniel was a man of *prayer*. That was the secret of his humility and courage. Three things are mentioned here about his prayer.

First, Daniel prayed *regularly*. Every day he secluded himself three times with God. Yes, he made it a custom. Good customs are the mainstay of spiritual health. Let's pray regularly.

Second, Daniel prayed with *reverence*. "He got down upon his knees . . ." God is very great and holy, and Daniel knew it. What could he do without God's help? Such respect for God will restore luster to our lives.

Third, Daniel prayed with his face toward *Jerusalem*. He expected redemption from God for the people of Israel. Through his prayers, he represented the nation in exile before God in heaven. God's grace was the foundation of his life.

Has God blessed you? Have you made some headway in the world? Do you hope for a successful career? Remember, Daniel never sought that. He only cared for God's people; he struggled hard to serve his God. God granted his wish and allowed him to serve abundantly. His shining career was incidental.

Thank You, Lord, for having used the great saints of old for Your cause on earth. Continue to mobilize Your children. Use me too. Amen.

Nehemiah

Then I replied to them, "The God of heaven will make us prosper, and we his servants will arise and build" (Neh. 2:20).

More than the generations before us have we become seekers of personal comfort. Powerful advertising pounds it into us: the goal of life is security and enjoyment. Churches can only count on marginal involvement of their members. Economic independence comes first; the struggles of bringing Christ to the nations runs a distant second. That's probably also why the energy crisis and the refugee problem disturb us. Our life of ease just cannot last in the face of so much suffering and the reality of dwindling resources.

President Carter said in the summer of 1979 that we must stop lamenting our inconveniences and contribute more toward finding solutions for society's problems. In a much deeper spiritual sense, the Bible has always told us that. Nehemiah had a splendid career at the court of King Artaxerxes, but word reached him that the Jews were not doing well in rebuilding the city of Jerusalem. That's when true greatness broke through in Nehemiah's soul. He traveled to Jerusalem and assumed leadership in the building project. Seldom has a mortal faced such difficulties. There were moments when the people just did not want to continue any longer; sometimes his very life was threatened. But Nehemiah never gave up. He kept urging the people, and in the end the city and the temple were rebuilt.

How did he do it? Mostly by prayer. Some of the most moving prayers in the Bible are found in the book of Nehemiah. The power of God was able to crush every problem, as it were, and from the debris new roads were built.

Fulfillment lies in being co-workers with God—not in personal convenience.

Touch our hearts, Holy Spirit. Draw us from self-seeking and lead us to the joy of representing the Lord among people. For His name's sake. Amen.

Disaster Course

They are darkened in their understanding . . . due to their hardness of heart (Eph. 4:18).

Newspapers reported a curious incident a few years ago at Niagara Falls. A large flock of geese on their annual southern flight settled down on the waters of the upper Niagara River for a rest. Several minutes later the strong currents swept flock after flock to the crest of the Horseshoe Falls. But the mighty roar of the falling water alarmed the birds, and by frantically flapping their wings, the birds rose up and saved themselves. The startling part of it all, however, was that the leading ganders guided their flocks so that they repeated these maneuvers over and over. Having risen from the angry waters, they would land on the river again, ride down the current once more, and repeat their escape. Before long many birds became exhausted and were swept to their death by the falling waters. Game officials were finally able to scare away the remaining birds by shooting in their direction.

This is a picture of what sin does to us.

Sin blinds us.

The Holy Spirit must open our eyes so that we will recognize sin for what it really is. He must show us the deadly consequences of sin. Only then will we flee to Christ, in whom there is true freedom.

This month we will follow Christ on His way of suffering and death. That's what our sins did to Him. But we will also witness His resurrection, His victory over the death of our sins. That's what He did for us. The more we read the Bible, the clearer we will see the wretched slavery from which Christ had to free us, and the more we will see the joys of Christian service. We have a great Savior!

Jesus, Savior and Lord, awaken us to salvation. Show us the evil power of sin, but show us also Your cleansing power. Forgive us, we pray. Help us to respond to Your love gladly and willingly. Always. Amen.

Like Us

For we have not a high priest who is unable to sympathize with our weaknesses, but one who in every respect has been tempted as we are, yet without sin (Heb. 4:15).

Are you able to enter into the suffering of others? It is a mark of greatness to forget yourself and enter into the experiences of your fellow man.

The painter Vincent van Gogh (1853-1890) worked in the infamous mines of Borinage and gained the confidence of the miners because he toiled and suffered alongside them. In his paintings he caught the hardships of those people.

But it is not easy.

Some priests in France followed Van Gogh's noble example. They hired themselves out to the same mines, working the regular shifts. But the miners soon resented their presence because they saw it as an *experiment*. They told the disconcerted priests, "You are not really part of us; you will soon leave us and forget us."

There is nothing new under the sun. The Spanish painter Pablo Picasso felt intensely drawn to human suffering, so he made it his calling to portray human woe. But in the course of time it brought him a fortune, and he bought himself a castle near the French Riviera, far from the misery of the world.

That sets Jesus Christ apart from all human saviors. He took all the ills and pain of the human race upon Himself, and then He died. That enabled Him to be our merciful High Priest who fully understands our plight.

Those who accept Christ become members of the body of which He is the Head. From there on they share life with Christ; they are in it together. That is the good news that comes to you today. No one can ever take it away.

Jesus, Lord and Savior, we thank You for Your suffering for us. You see and know all our needs. Help us to feel free to share our worries with You. Amen.

Fulfillment

Trust in the Lord . . . and enjoy security. Take delight in the Lord, and he will give you the desires of your heart (Ps. 37:3-4).

What is happiness and fulfillment? Does a picture appear before your mind's eye? Something like an oasis with fountains and fruit trees surrounded by the scorching desert sands? You will probably dismiss that as too obvious and contrived. But reconsider. You live on a planet that seems to be coursing through a dismally dark corner of the universe just now. Pretty near everything seems to go wrong. So what are you to do? You try your hardest to create a secure place and carve out a niche for yourself. So, you see, there is something in you that loves an oasis.

David, who wrote today's psalm, shares these feelings. With ecstasy he sings about the delights of having found security. And indeed, he has good reason to feel happy. He has been set free from cruel imprisonment. His enemies have fled, and David has come home to his people. Life, to David, is one beautiful oasis.

Ah, but wait, we overlooked a very important phrase in today's Bible verses. That phrase is "in the Lord." In fact, it occurs here twice. "In the Lord . . ." That means that David has come home *to his God*. He has confessed his mistakes; he has made up with his God. David and God have renewed their friendship; they have made covenant together. That is the only secure setting for fulfillment and happiness.

You, too, may have hope for a life of happiness. But don't reach for it as a child reaches for an apple on a tree. Be concerned about your relationship to God, and live for Him in thankfulness. Happiness follows in its wake.

Lord, we find it so hard to rejoice about living. We are afraid of unknown forces that threaten us. Bind our hearts to Yours, heavenly Father. Fill us with light, Holy Spirit. Amen.

Quest for Certainty

Behold, the Lord's hand is not shortened, that it cannot save . . . but your iniquities have made a separation between you and your God (Is. 59:1-2).

Many of us struggle with problems in our Christian faith. Can we know for sure that we are saved? How does it feel to be a Christian? What does our Christian faith do for us? What are the benefits of faithful church membership?

Ponder these questions for a while. You see, they tell us something about ourselves. By nature we seek our own advantage—not blatantly, to be sure, but we are adept at surrounding ourselves with agreeable circumstances. And, perhaps unawares, we look upon religion as an aid in building the beautiful life. There is something in us of the boy in Spurgeon's anecdote who was eager for his sister to be born again so that life would be easier for him. Why does this minister of the gospel toil so hard in his church? Could one small reason be that he longs for some visible results? As parents we urge our children to seek a good education. What are our motives? Do we want them to be great in God's service, or great in success?

Isaiah tells us here: "The hand of the Lord is not shortened, that it cannot save." With His grace He freely gives us all things. He provides in all our needs. His promises never fail. Why, then, should we still doubt, and have feelings of frustration and dissatisfaction? God calls a spade a spade: "But your iniquities have made a separation between you and your God."

Ultimately, our uncertainties and our discontent stem from our sinfulness. The way to happiness and vigor lies in confession and surrender. God made us for Himself. The one urgent question that remains for us is: "Lord, how can we serve You better?" That question must replace all others in importance. Someone reading Whitefield's *Journals*, with their amazing record of revival, was moved to pray: "Do it again, Lord, *beginning with me.*"

Lord, help us to see nothing but the perfection of Christ. Claim our undivided loyalty. For Your name's sake. Amen.

He Took My Place

Christ redeemed us from the curse of the law, having become a curse for us . . . (Gal. 3:13).

An interesting story is told about King Christian X of Denmark. After the German army had occupied Denmark in the spring of 1940, the king was given limited freedom and allowed to keep his bodyguard. One morning, while taking a ride through Copenhagen, the king saw a Nazi swastika flag waving over a public building in violation of the terms Hitler had imposed on Denmark. "Take it down!" the king ordered a German officer in front of the building. "Orders from Berlin," replied the officer. "Then I will send one of my soldiers to do it," the monarch declared. "The soldier will be shot," warned the Nazi officer. "Then I shall be that soldier," said the king. He entered the building and proceeded to take down the swastika himself.

Christ took our place!

He did it for us.

That's the heart of Christianity. We call it *substitutionary atonement*. We are all fallen sinners. God made us to be His princes on earth, but because of the fall into sin, we became rebels against God. Our relationship with God became so thoroughly poisoned that the Bible calls it *death*. We couldn't even sense our own misery; we didn't even *want* to seek salvation or return to God.

It was in this dismal context that Christ offered to take our place. He entered fully into our situation. He became guilty for us. In today's text we read that Christ *was made a curse for us*. He suffered hell for us: *He was forsaken by God.* By doing that He broke satan's hold on us. We are free!

> *Forbid it, Lord, that I should boast,*
> *Save in the death of Christ, my God!*
> *All the vain things that charm me most,*
> *I sacrifice them through His blood. Amen.*

The Acclaim of the People

The next day a great crowd who had come to the feast . . . went out to meet him, crying, "Hosanna! Blessed be . . . the King of Israel!" (John 12:12-13).

Does the way others think of you mean a lot to you? It is really a strange thing that we should be so sensitive to the approval of people. The newspapers make much of the popularity ratings of the President of the United States and the Prime Minister of Canada. But it should be clear to every sane mind that popularity is as shifting as the northern lights.

Shortly before the French Revolution (1789), the people of Paris rushed to Versailles to hang hated Queen Marie Antoinette. But the queen resolutely opened the door of the palace balcony and, standing straight with her children around her, calmly faced the crowd. The voices died down, and suddenly someone shouted, "Long live the queen!" Instantly the crowd chimed in.

Our Savior experienced how short-lived human approval really is. The people provided Him a royal welcome to Jerusalem. They sang, "Hosanna! Blessed be the King of Israel!" But only five days later the people of Jerusalem screamed, "Crucify Him! Crucify Him!" That became for Him a source of bitter suffering. His own people changed their minds that quickly.

Perhaps our happiness is based on the favor and approval of people around us. It is the most human thing to do, but it is also very foolish. It just won't last.

The Bible shows us a better way, a way that leads to Christ, who suffered bitter rejection for us. He restores us to God our Father, and we become part of the family of believers who love us for Jesus' sake in spite of our weaknesses. There is no sweeter peace, no greater security, than to love and be loved for the sake of Christ.

Lord, purify our loyalties. Help us to care for each other in Christian love. We thank You for the communion of the saints. Amen.

Jesus and the Jubilant Crowd

And the crowds that went before him and that followed him shouted,
"Hosanna to the Son of David! . . . Hosanna in the highest!" (Matt. 21:9).

Yesterday we saw what the acclaim of the people on Palm
Sunday meant to us. Today let's see what it meant to Christ. The
last week of suffering has now begun for the Savior. The disciples
obtained a donkey on which Jesus rode into Jerusalem via the
suburb Bethphage. A large crowd of people gave Him an en-
thusiastic welcome. They spread garments and palm branches on
the road in His honor. They sang from the Psalter: "Hosanna to
the Son of David! Behold, your king is coming to you. Hosanna in
the highest!"

Jesus' response to this course of events was mixed. On the one
hand He accepted this honor. When the Pharisees asked Him to
silence the crowd, He replied that the applause is necessary, lest the
stones cry out (Luke 19:40). On the other hand He was also deeply
aware of the blindness of the people. When Jerusalem appeared
before them in the valley below, He wept over it because He knew
its unbelief (Luke 19:41-2).

How selfish the singing crowd was! They saw in Jesus the
solution to the problems of the day. They thought His
revolutionary armies would drive out the hated Romans, and that
He would set up a glorious kingdom. That Jesus came to save them
from themselves and restore them to God was the farthest thing
from their minds. They expected Jesus to produce immediate
results. The crowds became very disappointed. Less than five days
later, these people shouted, "Crucify Him! Crucify Him!" Palm
Sunday was the entryway to the place of crucifixion.

We have the same problem with Christ, don't we? *We* want
Him to change our disagreeable *circumstances*. *He* wants to change
our disagreeable *hearts*.

You have suffered much for us, Lord Jesus. May our life be an expression
of gratitude for true forgiveness. Set us free from the shackles of
selfishness. Amen.

When We Failed

And Peter remembered the saying of Jesus, "Before the cock crows, you will deny me three times." And he went out and wept bitterly (Matt. 26:75). When Judas, his betrayer, saw that he was condemned, he repented and . . . throwing down the pieces of silver in the temple, he departed . . . and hanged himself (Matt. 27:3, 5).

Have you ever been betrayed by someone very dear to you? That was a bitter experience! But there is one experience still harder: that's when you yourself betray *someone who meant everything to you!*

You never did that, you say?

What about you and Christ?

Sin is a very personal thing. We have betrayed Christ, we have disowned Him, and we have scorned Him.

Consider what Peter and Judas did. Both were prominent in Christ's service. Peter was His spokesman, Judas His treasurer. At a crucial moment in Jesus' life, Peter denied Him and Judas sold Him. Both acknowledged their vile deeds; both were overwhelmed with regret. But note the big difference: Peter felt true *sorrow*, Judas felt *remorse*. In his sorrow Peter clung to Jesus; in his remorse Judas clung to nothing. That's why they ended in different worlds (John 2:15; Acts 1:20).

In the Lenten season it is not enough to believe in Christ's suffering. It is not even enough to weep about our sins. We must actually take our sins and brokenness *to the one Savior* and believe that He will forgive us. Peter did that. That was the beginning of a new life, a life of great courage, dignity and industry.

The way you evaluate God's Son ultimately determines how you evaluate yourself. If you acknowledge Him as Savior by grace, you will think well of yourself.

Holy Spirit, drive us out to Christ with all our shame. Create in us a noble spirit. Set us free in our Savior. Amen.

Jesus and Pilate

Pilate said to them, "Then what shall I do with Jesus who is called Christ?" They all said, "Let him be crucified" (Matt. 27:22).

Pilate wished he had never heard of Jesus. It brought him into a painful predicament. The crowd demanded the death sentence for Jesus even though Pilate knew He was innocent.

Pilate desperately tried to avoid making a decision. He had Jesus flogged to show the crowd that he considered Jesus nothing more than a slave, with no standing in a Roman court. Pilate bargained with the crowd and offered to release Jesus rather than the criminal Barabbas. Ultimately, however, Pilate could not avoid a choice: he delivered Jesus to be crucified.

Maybe you are like Pilate. You hate to make up your mind about Jesus. What a terrible predicament to be in! You cannot delay the choice forever. For you see, there will come a point of no return in your life, just as in Pilate's life. After that, the call to repentance will fall on deaf ears.

There is an old and very touching legend about Pilate. Years after Jesus' court case, when Pilate had returned to Rome, he was visited by a friend from Palestine. While reminiscing about the past, the friend asked, "Pilate, do you remember that rabbi of Nazareth whom you condemned to hanging, a man called Jesus?" Pilate searched his mind, but he could not recall the incident. His friend added details and Pilate tried frantically to remember, but he could not.

What a tragic thing when Christ is blotted from one's memory. But equally tragic is the attitude of many people who don't give Christ a second thought, being too busy with the concerns of life. And just as sad is the plight of people who call themselves Christians and believe what the Bible says about Jesus but don't really surrender to Him. To us all comes the call: Now is the hour of salvation!

Dear Lord, draw us with Your grace, take away our reluctance, remove our reservations. And save us. Amen.

Jesus and Simon

And as they went out, they came upon a man of Cyrene, Simon by name; this man they compelled to carry his cross (Matt. 27:32).

"Onward Christian soldiers" . . . "Christ shall have dominion" . . . "Stand up, stand up for Jesus" . . . Surely, you sing songs like these, but would you have carried the cross for Christ on His way to the hill of execution outside Jerusalem? Peter, who claimed so much, wasn't there. John, who loved so much, wasn't there.

That's why God made His own provisions. When Jesus collapsed under the weight of the cross, the soldiers forced an innocent passer-by, Simon of Cyrene, to carry Jesus' cross.

We don't know much about Simon. He wasn't the type who got involved much. While most of the people were in Jerusalem witnessing Jesus' trial, Simon spent the day in the field (Mark 15:21). But God had special plans for Simon. It was his destiny to carry the Savior's cross for every eye to see. We can see them move along in our imagination. They reach the top of Skull Hill. The soldiers take the cross from Simon. They put it on the ground and nail Jesus upon it. Then they lift up the cross. Simon is free again. Jesus hangs on Simon's cross.

Life wasn't the same for Simon after that. He and Jesus remained companions forever. In Mark 15:21, Simon is identified as the father of Alexander and Rufus, who were apparently well-known in early Christian circles. One of them became a helper of Paul in the spread of the Christian faith (Rom. 16:13).

And what about us? Are we willing to carry the cross of Christ in plain sight of all? When we are among friends and the conversation drifts in non-Christian directions, do we show our colors for the Lord? Are we willing to bear the cross of Christ in the practical areas of life—in politics, education, welfare, and labor?

Dear Jesus, You have borne all my sin and shame. I thank You. Quicken my heart and give me love and courage so that I will never be ashamed to testify about my allegiance to You. May Your name be praised forever. Amen.

Christ in the Agony of Thirst

And when they came to a place called Golgotha . . . they offered him wine to drink, mingled with gall; but when he tasted it, he would not drink it (Matt. 27:33-4).
And one of them at once ran and took a sponge, filled it with vinegar, and put it on a reed, and gave it to him to drink (Matt. 27:48).

Some years ago nine people crossed the North Mexican desert via "Devil's Highway." Halfway across, their truck stalled and they died in the infernal desert heat. Authorities commented, however, that fear was as much a factor in their death as thirst. Some had become so frantic that they had stuffed their mouths with sand.

Jesus, too, suffered agonizing thirst on the cross. But He didn't become frantic. He remained fully in control. How else could He be our Savior?

Note what the two verses above our meditation tell about His thirst. Just before Jesus was crucified, the soldiers offered Him wine drugged with myrrh, a drink given in merciful custom before execution to deaden pain. Jesus, however, declined, desiring to suffer fully and with a clear mind.

As the hours wore on, His strength ebbed away. Agonizing thirst threatened to overwhelm Him. With a loud voice He cried out for a drink. Someone reached up a sponge filled with vinegar. Having taken the liquid, His power returned. In full consciousness, the Savior faced the last items of the program set before Him—the mockery of the religious leaders and bystanders, and the actual moment of death itself, when He committed His spirit into the hands of the Father.

We stand in awe before such a Savior. How *victorious* His work, how *complete!* It is totally sufficient for you too, no matter how contemptible your sins. Don't try to make up for past failures. Receive this redemption as God's free gift. What a joy to live with Him forever!

Dear Savior, we thank You now for Your perfect sacrifice on the cross for our sin and guilt. Fill us with Your Spirit, that we may serve You gladly. Because of Calvary. Amen.

Since He Was Crucified

And when they had crucified him . . . (Matt. 27:35).

Crosses everywhere—ornamental crosses, crosses of applewood and chrome. Ah, someone said, but you must understand that they all point to the one great cross. But when I come to the Hill, there are three crosses. A Roman soldier shrugs his shoulders: "It's done everywhere—Gaul, Greece, Egypt. Today there are three." A bystander explains, "The pressure on the chest is terrible, the stretching of the arms . . ."

The sky darkens; the earth groans.

"Father, forgive them," He cries. "It is finished."

The people hurry back to Jerusalem. They don't want to miss the great feast of the lamb in the temple. They have important things to do. They hurry away from the cross.

"Jesus keep me near the cross," we sing. But are we prepared to face the cross at every winding of the road?

To own Christ as Savior is to let Him have His way with us.

It is a glorious thing to pledge allegiance to Christ. It is also a terrible thing.

Reconciliation is a big word. It means that we walk with the poor into the landlord's office. It means that we take the Christian vision to labor-management conflicts. It means that we refuse to accept, in word and practice, that business is business. It means that we don't glory in the national gross product breaking the trillion dollar barrier when children are starving around us. It means that our security is in Christ, and not in our safe careers. It means that we create evangelism opportunities.

Lives around the cross are radically new. The Lord of Good Friday said: "If anyone wants to follow Me, he must leave self behind. Day after day he must take up his cross, and come with Me."

Savior, we think of Your death for us. Holy Spirit lead us where we have to go. Break down every barrier between us and the Savior. Father, accept our lives as a love-offering to You. Through Christ our Lord. Amen.

For Me

Surely he has borne our griefs, and carried our sorrows . . . He was wounded for our transgressions, he was bruised for our iniquities (Is. 53:4-5).

We know it so well, we have heard it so often: Christ died for the sins of many.

But on Good Friday, let it grip our souls!

The reality of His suffering and death was ugly.

He was misunderstood, He was forsaken, He was betrayed, He was mocked, He was abused, He was slandered, He was classified with murderers, He was scourged, He was robbed of His clothes and His honor, He was physically pounded to the wood of the cross, He was left to hang in His wounds, He was deliberately surrendered to satan and hell.

And all the while, God did not come to His rescue, for He was the sin-laden substitute, forsaken of God and man.

We know it so well, we have heard it so often: Christ died for the sins of many. *But I did it all to Him—and you did.* Yet, amazingly, when we confess that, we share in His victory.

> Under an Eastern sky,
> Amidst a rabble's cry,
> A Man went forth to die
> For me.
>
> Thorn-crowned His blessed head,
> Blood-stained His every tread:
> Cross-laden, on He sped
> For me.
>
> Pierced were His hands and feet;
> Three hours o'er Him beat
> Fierce rays of noontide heat
> For me.
>
> Thus wert Thou made all mine;
> Lord, make me wholly Thine;
> Grant grace and strength divine
> To me.

Our sins, Lord Jesus, have been Your anguish. We praise You for the complete payment You have rendered for us. Make our life full and rich in You. Amen.

Buried for Our Sake

When it was evening, there came a rich man from Arimathea, named Joseph . . . And [he] took the body, and wrapped it in a clean linen shroud, and laid it in his own new tomb . . . and he rolled a great stone to the door of the tomb (Matt. 27:57, 59-60).

Jesus' body is now in Joseph's grave. The day is known as Holy Saturday. It is not known exactly why—perhaps for lack of a better name. For what shall we say of this day? Everything seems to have come to an uneasy standstill.

Yet this day, too, is part of God's program of salvation with man. The Son of man willingly and knowingly accepted the grave. The Bible calls Jesus the last Adam. Compare Him to the first. The first Adam was a man of great authority; he was God's custodian on earth. He was to develop and rule God's great world.

But after sin entered, the earth rebelled against Adam. Driven from the garden of Eden, he had to wrest a living from the stubborn soil. Soon he had to dig a grave for his son Abel. The memorials of passing civilizations have become graves—monuments of their desperate struggles.

Must the earth forever triumph over man?

No! For God gave us the last Adam, Jesus Christ. He is a complete Savior. The grave, too, He accepted for our sake. From that grave He rose victoriously. The earth trembled with joy. A new morning of hope dawned on mankind.

Those who accept Him as Lord are victorious with Him.

They are free to serve Him in a new mastery over life.

They follow the Lord in clearing the thorns and thistles.

They dry the tears of the weeping.

They right the wrong.

They feed the hungry.

They assist the poor.

They visit the prisoners.

They protest injustice.

And at each day's end, they lay their toil at the Master's feet.

Lord of life and death, we confess that You took the bitterness of the grave away. Thank You for preparing so much honor for us. Speed us with the light of hope into the darkness of this age. Amen.

Easter Confession

He is not here, for he has risen (Matt. 28:6).

On this Easter morning, we confess that Christ's resurrection affected all things, for we read that there was a great earthquake. We believe that His resurrection power, today, must be applied to every area of human existence.

On this Easter day, we confess that Christ was completely triumphant, for we read that the soldiers fled and that the angel sat upon the stone. He is victorious, today, over all His enemies—satan and sin included.

On this Easter Sunday, we confess that Christ gathers in His own with perfect care, for He sought out Mary in her sincere bewilderment. No sinner, today, is beyond the reach of His tender concern.

On this Easter, we confess that we rose with Him to newness of life, for He led Thomas to the confession, "My Lord and my God!" (John 20:28). We believe that this confession, today, binds believers together in Christ.

On this Easter day, we confess that we will rise with Christ on the last day, for we read, "Christ has been raised from the dead, the first fruits of those who have fallen asleep" (I Cor. 15:20).

We confess today with all Christians that the reality of Christian hope is firmly grounded in our Lord's resurrection, for, "If Christ has not been raised, then our preaching is in vain, and your faith is in vain" (I Cor. 15:14).

> "Alleluia!" now we cry
> to our King immortal.
> Who, triumphant, burst the bars
> of the tomb's dark portal;
> "Alleluia!" with the Son,
> God the Father praising;
> "Alleluia!" yet again
> to the Spirit raising.

Dear risen Savior, fill us anew with Your resurrection power. May it radiate from our hearts and faces. Use us to lead others to Your life. Amen.

Dying Without Fear

Death is swallowed up in victory. O death, where is thy victory? O death, where is thy sting? (I Cor. 15:53-4).

It is characteristic of our day that people are preoccupied with death without actually facing death. We talk and think about it, but we don't come to terms with it. It has been said that when we are not ready to die, we are not ready to live. There is some truth in that. We feel often fearful and helpless when death strikes in our immediate environment, and we don't know how to act. We stand at the bier of a loved one and say, "What a blessing that he didn't have to suffer much." Or with averted eyes we whisper, "She is better off now; we must not wish her back." These things are not untrue in themselves, but they scarcely hide the awkwardness which we sense and can do little about. And who can escape the reality of it all? The great poet Goethe, as he faced death, gasped, "More light, more light!" Tolstoy, who had radiated assurance as a social reformer, mumbled, "I do not understand what I must do." No, who understands death?

Even for the believer, death remains the last baffling riddle. But he is not alone. Christ entered death for him. Christ removed the sting of death—sin. Death has now lost its frightening power, says Paul in Corinthians. In fact, Christians can even rejoice with Paul. "O death where is thy victory?"

In the season of Lent, we thought of Christ's suffering and death. What a price He paid for our salvation. Now He will lead us through death's gate into the mansions of glory. Those who were relieved from the burden of sin through their Savior will then appear before God's throne. To their surprise, it will be without terror! That's a promise!

Lord Jesus, we confess now that You have taken our death upon Yourself completely. Also our fear. In the extreme hour, dear Lord, may we experience what You promised: Blessed are those who die in the Lord. Amen.

Why He Had to Rise

Remember how he told you . . . that [he must] be crucified, and on the third day rise (Luke 24:6-7).

Some people witnessed the events around Christ's resurrection; nobody witnessed the actual event itself. We accept the reality of the resurrection by faith.

It is striking that many people in the Bible misunderstood the resurrection. Why was that? Because Christ's victory over death was the outcome of His life's work, of His suffering and death for our sins. The people around Him had not understood that He had come to pay for their sins. Since they could not understand His *death*, they could not understand His *resurrection*.

Some examples will clarify this. Mary Magdalene saw Jesus that early Easter morning, but she didn't recognize Him, for she had misunderstood His suffering (John 20:11-18). The two disciples on their way to Emmaus didn't recognize Jesus either; only when He explained His suffering did their eyes open (Luke 24:13-35). For Thomas, Good Friday was a total defeat; hence he walked in darkness for over a week after Christ had risen (John 20:24-9). Peter had been in the empty tomb but failed to see that Christ had paid for his sin of betraying the Master, and so he did not taste Easter joy until Christ restored him in forgiveness (John 21:15-19).

So you see, we must view Christ's lifework as one total mandate from the Father, accomplished for us dead sinners. Only then can we believe that He rose from the dead. Those who have not repented of their sins would not believe the resurrection *even if they had seen it happen.* Those who share in His cross walk in the power of His resurrection victory forever.

Lord Jesus, risen Savior, we thank You that we may share in Your resurrection power over the death of our sins. Amen.

Easter Victory

. . . an angel of the Lord . . . rolled back the stone, and sat upon it. And for fear of him the guards trembled and became like dead men (Matt. 28:2, 4).

Love that angel of Easter morning! See him there, calmly sitting on the rolled away tombstone. Compare the angel to the soldiers who had guarded the grave. My, how high and mighty they had seemed! No one could stop them as they mocked Jesus, flogged Him, crucified Him, and sealed the gravestone with the imperial seal.

No one . . . ? One angel descended from heaven, and the soldiers ran like rabbits. They were frightened to death. "They became as dead men." And the angel sat upon the stone, in complete control of the situation. O heavenly humor!

Appearances are deceptive. Anti-Christian forces still seem so strong. Christians are still in jail. Believers are still mocked. The church still seems no match for the powers of this age. But after the resurrection, God's people have already gained the victory. Faith has overcome the world. Oh, to be sure, it took some time before the young church of Jerusalem saw that reality. Huddled together in a house, they were almost as afraid as the soldiers. Even after they had met the risen Lord, it took a lot of heavenly coaxing before they marched with the gospel. But once they did, they shook the foundations of the Roman empire.

And so it is today. What barriers we face! How the dangers of unbelief scare us! Fear is still the major obstacle for us today to carry the banner of Christ into the company of the unsaved, into the circle of sufferers, and before the forum of the rulers. But let Easter tear the veil away. Our risen Lord rules, and we rule with Him. He provides in every situation.

Do you doubt that He can do that for you? Well, if one angel-servant could be so gloriously in control, think what the Lord of that angel can do!

Lord of the heavenly hosts, show us anew that all situations are in Your hand. Dispel doubt from our hearts. Amen.

Fear and Joy at Easter

So they departed quickly from the tomb with fear and great joy (Matt. 28:8).

In 1559 the Scottish reformer John Knox wrote a letter to the queen's secretary that told of the misfortunes which had befallen the Reformation in Scotland. He summed up his plight by saying, "Disaster stares us in the face everywhere." Yet that same letter ended with hope. He wrote, "The cause of God never looked better, for we are now completely at His mercy."

How typical! The Christian experience is always one of *darkness* and *light*. Look at the faithful women near Jesus' grave on Easter morning. Having heard the angels' message of Christ's resurrection, they departed with *fear* and *joy*. Of course! For the women were worried about many things. They were bewildered, confused and afraid. The enemy was so strong, and the cause of the Master seemed hopeless. Hence they were filled with *fear*. But a great light blazed in their darkness too. Christ had conquered death! That gave them new hope, so they left with *joy*. And note that the text tells us that theirs was "fear and *great* joy." Their joy was bigger than their fear!

Christianity has plenty of reason for *fear*. Parts of the church are persecuted. Paganism grows faster than Christianity in North America and elsewhere. Materialism within the church obstructs the Christian way. Confusion and greed disrupt many homes. The Christian vision is banished from the affairs of society.

But Christians nevertheless have cause for *great joy*, for we have a Savior who broke the shackles of death. The Lord who gives us a task will also provide for us. The obedient will find out that when they run in the Master's power, their joy will be bigger than their fear!

Lord, we do not ask to be relieved from all trouble, but we do ask that as we share Easter joy with those in darkness, we may experience it ourselves. Amen.

Three Responses to Easter

Tell people, "His disciples came by night and stole him away" (Matt. 28:13).
And when they saw him they worshiped him . . . (Matt. 28:17).
. . . but some doubted (Matt. 28:17).

The soldiers who guarded Jesus' grave were entirely ignorant about the meaning of Easter. They became involved, nevertheless. As it was, they denied the reality of the resurrection and agreed to spread the lie that the friends of Jesus had stolen the body.

That was one response to Christ's victory over death. Many people still respond that way. Though they see death all around them, they don't seem to care about real life.

There is another way of responding to Easter. When the disciples saw the risen Lord, they worshiped Him. What a wonderful response! The first syllable of *worship* is related to *worth, value;* the second to *shape, create.* That is, the disciples gave expression to their immense esteem for Jesus. They wholeheartedly accepted Him; they staked all their happiness and security on Him.

But this Bible passage speaks of a third response to the risen Savior. We read: "Some doubted." The word *doubt* comes from a root from which our words *double* and *two* have been derived. Those disciples were inwardly divided. Though they did not reject the resurrection, they couldn't accept it either. Note that Jesus doesn't condemn the doubters. Rather, Jesus overcame their doubt in a twofold way. He gave them the reassuring promise of His power and authority, and He gave them the task of spreading the gospel. That is still the best remedy for doubt—back to the Word of Christ and back to our Christian task.

What is your response to the risen Savior?

Remember, faith faces the facts! Unbelief runs away from the reality of Christ's victory over the grave.

Lord of life, let Your Easter power break forth into our hearts. Dispel all doubts; create in us full commitment. Amen.

We Assume No Responsibility

For our sake he made him to be sin who knew no sin, so that in him we might become the righteousness of God (II Cor. 5:21).

It once happened that a student submitted an Easter poem to her high school paper for publication. The poem spoke of human failure and darkness, of Christ's suffering and dying, and of the victory of His resurrection. The poem somewhat embarrassed the editors of the school paper, but after some deliberation they decided to print it under this editorial note: "The Editors assume *no responsibility* for the contents expressed in the following."

Unwittingly the editors had underscored the heart of the gospel! We assumed *no responsibility* for what Adam and Eve did. We assumed *no responsibility* for the ocean of misery that deluged God's great world. We assumed *no responsibility* for the frightening chasm that separated man and God. We assumed *no responsibility* for the inexpressible weight of punishment that rested on the human race.

And because we assumed *no responsibility*, God gave His only begotten Son, whom He loved. *He assumed the responsibility*. He took our sins and guilt upon Himself. He paid the price. He paved the way from man's heart to God's heart. He conquered death, and now He rules heaven and earth. He did that all for us, and in our stead.

In today's chapter we read that He who knew no sin was actually made sin for us. But because He did that, the same chapter tells us, we have become a "new creation." That means that we share the newness of Christ in us. Through Him we can now assume responsibility for a new life, a new obedience and a new task. Life is good!

Help us, risen Lord, to live with vigor, to take on tasks, and to be obedient—all in Your power. Holy Spirit, keep the fire of love burning in our hearts. Amen.

Recognizing the Lord

But Mary stood weeping outside the tomb . . . Jesus said to her, "Mary."
She turned and said to him in Hebrew, "Rabonni!" (which means Teacher)
(John 20:11, 16).

Is Jesus close to us? We know the answer: He is always near.
But do we experience it that way? Do we readily turn to Him
because He is there? The words of the hymn are true:

> What a Friend we have in Jesus,
>   All our sins and griefs to bear!
> What a privilege to carry
>   Everything to God in prayer.
> O what peace we often forfeit,
>   O what needless pain we bear,
> All because we do not carry
>   Everything to God in prayer!

On Easter morning Mary Magdalene felt utterly forsaken. Her
Lord was not there anymore. He had been crucified and would
never return. All alone in the garden, she wept quietly. But all the
while the risen Lord was near. He heard her, He saw her, He ap-
proached her, and then He spoke to her. Even then Mary did not
sense His nearness. She mistook Him for the gardener. Her sorrow
was a wall between her and Jesus. But Christ would not allow that
wall to remain there. He addressed her again, more personally this
time. He mentioned her name: "Mary." And only then did she
recognize Him. But, hallelujah, what a recognition! What a
beautiful confession! "Rabonni—my Teacher!"

The risen Lord is that close to us. Through the daily exercise of
faith, we can cultivate the awareness of that closeness. While we
wait for a red light, we can talk to Him. When we see a need, we
alert Him to it. When we face problems, we ask Him for counsel.
When we feel afraid, we go to Him for courage. Easter blessings
are no less real than that.

Rabboni, bless us also with Your nearness in our lives. Fill us, Holy Spirit,
with great joy for belonging to our Savior. Amen.

In Christ

He who abides in me, and I in him, he it is that bears much fruit, for apart from me you can do nothing (John 15:5).

J. Hudson Taylor will be remembered for a long life of service as a pioneer missionary in the interior of China. He was a man of inexhaustible energy, gentle patience, and spiritual stature. What was the secret of his power? V. Raymond Edman tells of an Anglican pastor, H. B. Macartney of Melbourne, Australia, who visited Taylor in China and gave this description: "He was an object lesson in quietness. He drew from the Bank of Heaven every farthing of his daily income; whatever did not agitate the Savior or ruffle His spirit was not to agitate him. The serenity of the Lord Jesus concerning any matter at its most critical moment, this was his ideal and practical possession. He knew nothing of rush or hurry, of quivering nerves or vexation of spirit. He knew there was a peace passing all understanding, and that he could not do without it."

How can we, average mortals, hope to reach this ideal? The amazing thing is that this Christian serenity does not become ours by frantic effort or self-denial. The opposite is true. Christ *gives* it to His followers. He is the vine-tree; the believers are the branches. How do the branches bear fruit? Not by vain struggles for juices and sunshine, but rather, by simply abiding in the vine, in silent and undisturbed union. Blossoms and fruits then appear as spontaneous growth.

Amid all the confusion spawned by countless religious paperbacks, John 15 comes with profound simplicity: concentrate your thoughts and affections on Christ. Surrender your whole being to Him, and He will show you the way.

Thank You, Jesus, for making us one with You. Give us the confidence of faith to rely on You completely. And use us through Your grace. Amen.

Peace in the Church

I appeal to you . . . that all of you agree and that there be no dissensions among you (I Cor. 1:10).

Churches consist of people, and people, even Christian people, have differences. So it happens that those people, even Christian people, sometimes quarrel and disagree. Pastors will tell you that not all of it is an immediate threat to the survival of the church. Sometimes they are guilty of a bit of strife themselves. What is of more importance is what we do with our differences.

Arthur Mouw, a missionary to Dutch Borneo (now Kalimantan Barat) called his Dyak people together to discuss where to erect the new church building. On the jungle floor, the missionary drew a map of the villages of the immediate area. Then he invited the eleven heads of families to place a stone on the site of their choice. The first man put the stone close to his long-house. And so did the other ten—close to their own long-houses. No one meant malice, but no one wanted to walk far to church. Then the missionary took a larger stone and placed it as nearly as possible in the middle of those eleven stones. The men bowed their heads and hearts and asked for God's blessing.

We must always realize that believers are members of the one spiritual body of Christ. That unity must not only be confessed in faith, we must also work hard at giving it evidence in the life of the church. It is a mark of Christ's men and women that they resolve their differences in Christian self-denial.

What, exactly, are the motives that drive us in defending our position? Principles and doctrines can be very important, but they can also become little gods whom we revere with some passion. We agree that differences should be resolved at the foot of Christ's cross, but that means that we first esteem the other party in Christ.

Holy Spirit, bind us together in Christian love. May we express in deeds the unity we confess in words. For Christ's sake. Amen.

The Saint

So, whether you eat or drink, or whatever you do, do all to the glory of God (I Cor. 10:31).

Not all saintly people have understood what Biblical saintliness is. In the early Christian church there was a man called Demetrius who had an appointment with God Himself at a certain place. As he was hurrying along to get there, he met a peasant whose wagon had become stuck in the mud. Demetrius helped him. The mud was miry; the hole in the road was deep. It was necessary to struggle hard for an hour. When he was finished, Saint Demetrius rushed on to meet God, *but God was no longer there!*

This legend was meant to have a moral. The moral was that spiritual meditation is more important than the struggles of daily life. Demetrius should have known better than to help a peasant in his down-to-earth affairs.

This view of life lingers in disguised form among many Christians today. They intuitively rate so-called spiritual things higher than so-called material things. Take soul and body, for instance. A father may pray at suppertime, "Lord, bless this food to our bodies, and the reading of Your Word to our souls." He seems to imply that the soul needs the Bible, and the body the food. But what God has put together, let not Father put asunder. Both soul and body need food to survive, and both live through the Word. Elijah, under the juniper tree, needed a meal as one whole person, and he also needed the Word. The angel brought both to that one person Elijah.

Christ lifted the curse from His Father's handiwork. That person is spiritual who praises God in his daily affairs.

Father, we confess that the earth and its fullness is Yours. Help us to ascribe honor to You in the small and big things of daily life. Through Jesus Christ our Lord. Amen.

Rebelling Against Our Lot

We are afflicted in every way . . . so that the life of Jesus may be manifested in our mortal flesh (II Cor. 4:8, 11).

There are people who rebel against their lot in life. Thus they carry a double load. A widow who will not accept the road ahead becomes her own and others' burden. A man who refuses to abide an irreversible setback will consume himself in a nerve-racking emotional battle.

How, then, shall we cope with life's burdens? Shall we reach for shortcuts from misery? Is there an effective formula to relieve us from distress? Or must we just accept what comes our way?

The philosopher Nietzsche, a godless but careful observer of human ways, gave this advice: "Never rebel against fate. Give up your resistance, accept the inevitable, learn to love what you now hate, and mend your broken emotions, lest you bring yourself to ruin." Thielicke, Germany's great evangelical preacher, commented that such advice is like saying to a drowning person: "Stop the excitement, accept the water, learn to love your lot."

Let us hear what the apostle Paul has to say. He begins by acknowledging the reality of suffering: "We are troubled on every side . . ." But he then adds a precious promise: God will use suffering to bring the believer to a fuller experience of the resurrection life of Christ. That is a great mystery which no one can explain. But the fact remains: the way of trials leads to a richer sharing in the accomplished work of Christ. A faith so seasoned is no mean reward for tears shed in secret.

Dear God, draw us close to You in our trials. Help us to suffer with uplifted heads. Sustain all those who go through valleys of grief. For Jesus' sake. Amen.

To Live Is Christ

For me to live is Christ, and to die is gain (Phil. 1:21).

Some people don't take life very seriously—or death, for that matter. The writer Somerset Maugham was a keen observer of life and death, but he remained a cynic about both. He once remarked: "When my obituary at last appears in *The Times* and they say, 'What? I thought he died years ago!' my ghost will gently chuckle."

Some people are like *butterflies* in their life's outlook, fluttering from flower to flower. They live for their pleasures.

Some people are like *beavers* in constant toil. They never get done. They are always driven by some unfinished task.

Some people are like *sharks* always hunting for more. They are slaves of their greed, often at the expense of others.

But there was a young man, Paul, who was ready to embark on a most promising career. One day the Lord stopped him on his ambitious course and turned his life around. The cause of Christ gripped his heart. Paul's life did not just become *Christian*—no, it became *Christ Himself*. Christ was the Head of the Body of which Paul was a member. That was the secret of Paul's power. A life is not Christian by having some Christian aspects. A life is not Christian by adding a spiritual dimension.

Perhaps you are active in church matters, but you don't obey Christ in certain other areas of your life. Or perhaps you are concerned about sound doctrine and good morals, but you don't know intimate communion with Christ. To you comes the call today to repent and have a meeting with Christ. Let Him have His way in your heart; let Him tune your soul to His presence. Then, being grounded and rooted in Him, you will live with new joy and vigor. Only when to live is Christ can death be gain.

Savior, make us completely Yours. Cut the ties that bind us to secret idols. May we serve You in complete freedom. Amen

Eternal Life

Fight the good fight of the faith; take hold of the eternal life to which you were called when you made the good confession in the presence of many witnesses (I Tim. 6:12).

The little Sunday School incident which some ministers have even told from the pulpit is based on a misunderstanding. Here's what happened. The Sunday School teacher had told the story of the rich man and poor Lazarus. She then asked the children, "What would you rather be—the rich man or poor Lazarus?" Most were agreeable and said, "Lazarus"; some were realists and said, "The rich man." But one boy had the perfect combination. "Now the rich man," said he, "and in heaven poor Lazarus."

There is supposed to be a spiritual lesson here, but it's a mistaken one. Many people believe that eternal life lies in the far distant future beyond the vale of death. They figure that eternal life is connected with heaven, where they would all like to go. It's worth the price. Deny yourself much here, and reap the benefits with interest in the hereafter.

But here, in the first letter to Timothy, Paul has a different vision of eternity. Timothy is called to eternal life now, today. He made a "good confession," he accepted Christ, and therefore he may lay hold of eternal life in his present existence. The apostle John confirmed it. He said, "God gave us eternal life, and this life is in his Son" (I John 5:11).

What riches that we may own eternal life today! We are in Christ, and Christ is in us. He is in the driver's seat and governs our life. He supplies as He demands. Timothy had a lot of personal weaknesses; he had a lot of problems in the ministry. Paul could have given him a lot of practical advice. He did, too, but only after he reminded Timothy of the mighty stirrings of eternal life.

Holy Spirit, pour into our hearts the power of Christ. Remove all doubt and double-mindedness. For Jesus' sake. Amen.

The Escape Seekers

Cast all your anxieties on him, for he cares about you. Be sober, be watchful (I Pet. 5:7-8).

Drug addiction is one of the saddest things that has happened to the youth of our land. LSD has emerged as one of the most potent of the hallucinatory drugs. The smallest amount (one ten-thousandth part of a gram) of liquid LSD, usually deposited on a sugar cube, is capable of producing extreme effects. A publication of the New York Medical Society described "a trip" as follows: "All senses appear sharpened and brightened. Vivid panoramic visual hallucinations of fantastic brightness and depth are experienced. Senses blend so that sounds are felt, colors tasted, fixed objects pulsate and breathe. The user is enveloped by a sense of isolation and is often dominated by feelings of paranoia and fear. Confusion, delirium and suicidal inclinations frequently ensue."

Drug addiction feeds on the emptiness of this generation's existence. "Taking a trip" seems the quickest way out of the oppressive drudgery and burdens of life.

To be sure, drugs is not the only way to escape from reality. And, to be sure, not only youth but all age groups belong to the Escape Seekers. We all bungle when it comes to dealing constructively with problems.

Christ invites us all to cast our burdens upon Him, and to be sober. Only in Christ can we face reality and enter upon a challenge. Christ Himself faced the reality of hell for sinners. He arose for them unto newness of life. Christians are under an urgent mandate to bring this resurrection gospel to bear upon their environment.

God of all mercy, we pray for people, young and old, who are deeply troubled by the burdens of life. Draw them to Yourself and bring relief. Amen.

The Word

By faith we understand that the world was created by the word of God (Heb. 11:3).

Your Bible is too small! You confined it to 1400 pages, put it between two covers, tucked it away in a drawer.

But the Bible is the *Word of God*.

God tells us amazing things about the *Word*. God calls His Son the *Word*: "In the beginning was the *Word*, and the *Word* was with God, and the *Word was God*" (John 1:1).

Through the *Word* God made everything: "By faith we understand that the world was created by the *word* of God" (Heb. 11:3). God preserves all things by the *Word*: "By the same word the heavens and earth that now exist have been stored up . . ." (II Pet. 3:7). That *Word* is a power unto salvation: "You have been born anew . . . through the living and abiding word of God" (I Pet. 1:23).

Back of our house is a telephone wire. It is a favorite resting place for the neighborhood sparrows. They chatter and quarrel completely unaware that the wire "contains" *words*. No one can see the *Word* by which God upholds and governs the world. No one can see the *Word* by which He inclines people to turn to Christ. Therefore many deny that *Word*. Their Bible is too small. They rejected the written *Word;* therefore God withheld the power of His *Word* from them. Concerning them Jesus said: ". . . and you do not have his *word* abiding in you, for you do not believe him whom he has sent" (John 5:38).

To us all now comes a renewed invitation to increase our Bible reading. We must see and experience that the Bible is much more than a book: it is the voice of the living God—yes, more, for through the Word we meet Christ our Savior, the Word-become-flesh. Faithful reading of that Word will bring much fruit.

God, take hold of us by Your Word. Strengthen our faith and cause us to grow. May Your precious Word reach many people and bring them to true life. Through Christ. Amen.

Interpretations Belong to God

They said to him, "We have had dreams, and there is no one to interpret them." And Joseph said to them, "Do not interpretations belong to God?" (Gen. 40:8).

Joseph went through baffling experiences: sold by his brothers, framed by a wicked woman, and now suffering in a dungeon in a foreign land. His fellow inmates, the butler and the baker, don't understand their plight either. But in spite of all this, Joseph's faith is fully victorious! It gives Joseph the power to place the things he cannot understand in the hands of God. He confesses, "Interpretations belong to God."

M. L. Schoch tells of the following event which took place in the German concentration camp of Dachau during the winter of 1944. Inmate Rebbe Hirsch reads to his cell-mates from Psalm 23: "The Lord is my shepherd; I shall not want." But in the face of so much devilish inhumanness, that Psalm makes no sense to them. They argue, they discuss, they despair. Then they bow their heads, and Hirsch prays with them. In the bleakness of the camp, the certainty is born that God knows and will deliver from the bitterness of evil. Rebbe Hirsch was transferred to Auschwitz, where he died in a gas chamber. His friends said, "The Lord was with him, and he is with the Lord."

No one can understand why evil is allowed to do its ruinous work in the world. Lives are snuffed out wantonly, children have pain and cry for food, and we don't have the answers to the "why" of it all. Why, Lord, was there no place for the Vietnamese refugees on the face of the earth? Why, Lord, do the tragedies of life strike among us?

All these questions keep us very humble. We see only dimly. But in childlike trust we leave the outcome to God. *He* is in control. He understands. He knows our distress. His own Son, too, died—for our sins. "Interpretations belong to God . . ."

Heavenly Father, take hold of us that we may not slip. Teach us to say amen to whatever we must experience, including the bitter and the dark. Amen.

Awareness

Lord, let me know my end, and what is the measure of my days; let me know how fleeting my life is! (Ps. 39:4).

Patricia Walker, a young, married teacher in western Canada, was informed by the Royal Canadian Mounted Police that her husband had been killed in a car-train accident. Some time after, however, the Mounties returned. There had been a case of mistaken identity: her husband was alive and well. Later Pat wrote, "In spite of the joy, life has not been quite the same since that incident. I have become aware of the fragile hold of life . . ."

We should all realize that this life has an end. That is the concern of Psalm 39. No, the poet is not a pessimist. He wants us to be aware of the frailty of life *so that we can live each moment more fruitfully*. He asks God to show us how fleeting life is. What a difference that will make! Of course, for we will then be dependent on God, we will live on good terms with God, we will cherish the forgiveness of sins, we will dedicate our lives to God, and we will want to know the purpose of life. But above all, we will earnestly seek the redemption which Christ came to bring. And we will treasure the new life of peace.

Could you imagine Pat Walker being upset with her husband the next day because he still had not fixed that dripping faucet? It is the aggregate of small annoyances that undercut the quality of our daily life. Why should we quarrel or feel offended when the Bible tells us that our Savior suffered hell for us? One look in hell and one look in heaven would make us very appreciative of each other. Stop and consider how few our years, how frail our lives. That disarmingly simple bit of wisdom may yet lead us to a lot of happiness.

Lord, teach us who we are, and why we live here on earth. Sometimes, Lord, nothing makes sense to us. Holy Spirit, teach us the secret of living every moment out of the Father's hand. Amen.

Evil's Grip Broken

In spite of all this they still sinned (Ps. 78:32).

Alexander Pope wrote these words:

> Vice is a monster of so frightful mien
>   As to be hated needs but to be seen;
> Yet, seen too oft, familiar with her face,
>   We first endure, then pity, then embrace.

There is much wisdom in these lines. A mysterious kind of blindness causes the sinner not to recognize his sins. Our eyes grow dim to evil. The longer a vice is tolerated, the less painful it becomes to live with it.

Psalm 78 demonstrates how obstinate this blindness is. First the Lord showered His goodness upon the people: He gave them bread from heaven, water from the rock, and deliverance from their enemies. But in spite of all these blessings, they kept sinning with gusto. Then the Lord brought judgment, we read. That led them to repentance, but only for a while. They were soon wandering along the pathways of evil again.

Was there no end in sight? Would they be slaves of evil forever?

And what about us? Must we continue in the grip of vice?

No, we need not!

See the wonderful things God did. He gave His Son as our complete Savior. Note that the work of Christ consists of two chapters. The first one He fulfilled for us on earth: His obedience, His suffering, His death, His resurrection, and His ascension. The second one is His session at the right hand of God; it is the period from His ascension to His return at the end of time. From heaven Christ sent the Holy Spirit to bring dead sinners to life. From heaven He cares for His church on earth. He daily supplies us with His strength! He breaks the power of canceled sins. Evil need not have a hold on us any longer. We can prove Alexander Pope wrong.

Lord Jesus, we thank You for supplying us daily with Your victorious power. Help us to continue in joyous freedom. Amen.

The Sorrow of Riches

He who loves money will not be satisfied with money (Eccl. 5:10).

Sydney Harris reports the following monumental cases of miserliness. Sir Harvey Elwes left a fortune of more than one million dollars, yet he never spent more than $400 a year. James Duke, a founder of a tobacco empire, took pride in living in the cheapest hall bedroom in New York. He was known to begrudge his employees their every paycheck. The seventeenth century Englishman Dick Jarrett left a fortune at his death, but during his life he would sneak scraps of food left by guests on the tavern tables. The recluse Howard Hughes, one of the richest men on earth, worried about petty cash till his dying day.

Money didn't bring happiness to these people, and that seems to be a universal law. Today's verse tells us that he who loves money will in the end not be satisfied with money. He wants more. And when he has more he wants still more. Once committed to Mammon's service, there is no end to the sacrifices he demands.

Christians have traditionally defended the right to accumulate wealth and fortune. Perhaps we were not fully aware of all its harmful implications. With millions starving, we may well wonder whether God meant Christians to use so much money for their own conveniences.

That's one side of the coin. The other is: What do material possessions mean to us, even when we don't count ourselves rich? Does materialism have its little altar in the back room of the house of our heart? Remember, you are truly rich when you own Christ and His cause.

Lord, may our riches be in You. Redeem us from the charm of money and position. Help us to serve those who need our help and understanding. Amen.

The Big Liar

The devil took him to a very high mountain, and showed him all the kingdoms of the world and the glory of them; and he said to him, "All these will I give you, if you will fall down and worship me." Then Jesus said to him, "Begone, Satan! for it is written, 'You shall worship the Lord your God, and him only shall you serve.' " (Matt. 4:8-10).

Satan, chief of the demons, is God's imitator. He suffers from great exaggerations of himself. When he met Jesus on the mountain, he acted as if he created the nations and could do with them as he pleased.

But watch out. Let satan *over-estimate* himself, so long as we don't *under-estimate* him. His power is colossal, and he commands fabulous riches. He was deadly serious in his offer to Jesus—kneel and I will give you the kingdoms of the world. Nero and Hitler are but two of the many who received empires from satan in return for faithful satanic service.

But Jesus rejected satan's proposal. He knew that satan was a liar, that he had nothing to give away, and that his favors would bring nothing but gall and bitterness in the end. Whatever satan offers is sick and beyond redemption.

Jesus met satan head-on. He sent him away in the power of the Father's Word, and then, instead, He offered Himself to His people. He never promised wealth and ease to His followers. He gave Himself as a ransom for their sins. *Don't underestimate Christ!* Once you are right with God, your life has a new foundation. With Christ, God gives you all the things you need (Rom. 8:32).

Believers own all things with Christ. But remember the formula for the use of things: the more you give, the more these blessings will be real to you. In that, too, Christ is the example.

We praise You, Lord Jesus, for defeating satan. Holy Spirit, help us to experience the security of a life of service. Amen.

The Mourners

Blessed are those who mourn, for they shall be comforted (Matt. 5:4).

Alongside its colossal technological achievements, the twentieth century will be remembered for its monumental sorrow. A book on Polish history reveals that one-fifth of that land's population perished during World War II—five million in the ghettoes alone. On a global scale, the war demanded the lives of ten million military men and twelve million civilians. Our own day will be remembered for the massive suffering of Asian and African refugees, and the oppression of millions upon millions under cruel dictatorships. Add to all this the social injustice, the racial discrimination and the pain of the sick and lonely, and we begin to see something of the despair of our times.

But we can only understand a miniscule fraction of the world's woes. Only Christ can truly understand sorrow. He once said, "My soul is very sorrowful to death" (Mark 14:34). In His anguish He pressed out sweat mingled with blood. He tasted the cause of all suffering—the curse of sin.

The thinker Nietzsche once said in a moment of despair: "All I can see is a grey sky with two black ravens flying slowly." Earlier in his life, Nietzsche had answered the question what he thought of Jesus as follows: "Oh, the pale Jew who died the untimely death of a weakling."

Jesus, too, left a word for His people: "Be of good cheer; I have overcome the world!"

Go to your Savior, ponder His work for you, His love for you, and you will be able to go on—even through the darkest night.

Lord Jesus, we commit the suffering and sorrowing people to Your mercy and comfort. Use us to bring them Your comfort. Amen.

Multiplying Mercy

Blessed are the merciful, for they shall obtain mercy (Matt. 5:7).

The religious leaders of Jesus' days were tough taskmasters. They reasoned that in life everybody received what he deserved. When they saw somebody suffer, they simply concluded that he must be a big sinner who was getting his due. Sympathy was short-lived in the atmosphere of such pitiless righteousness.

Jesus presents an altogether different type of righteousness. In this chapter He introduces His new Kingdom. People who take pride in their own goodness find the doors of the Kingdom shut. Only those who know that they have nothing to offer are welcomed. They are the people who despair at the bankruptcy of their sins and accept forgiveness for Christ's sake.

That's why mercy is the order of the day in the Kingdom of Christ. Those *saved* by mercy want nothing better than to *practice* mercy. They extend Christ's compassion to others in distress. Note the amazing sequel. This exercise of mercy boomerangs! The merciful themselves are rewarded with mercy from others, says Christ. This implies that Christian kindness works its own response. Those who receive kingdom mercy become doers of mercy. Mercy multiplies itself. The possibilities are endless. Hatred is so strong today that it tears the human race apart. Every solution seems pitiful in view of mounting distress. Christian mercy is the only answer. Christ calls His followers to be doers of mercy. He Himself will let it echo and reverberate in an ever widening circle of people caught by His infectious mercy.

Phillip Brooks once said, "No possession is truly ours until we have blessed someone else with it."

Lord, You have seen how much fear there is on Your earth. The cruel and the greedy go their way boldly. Give us, Holy Spirit, the courage which only the merciful can experience. Amen.

Plea for Purity

Blessed are the pure in heart, for they shall see God (Matt. 5:8).

Once upon a time, an old Greek myth tells us, there was a king called Augeas who had 3000 cattle and a stable which had not been cleaned for thirty years. It was the strongman Hercules who accepted the king's challenge to clean up the stable. Hercules, however, did not use his muscles for the job. He led the course of two rivers through the stable, and they washed all the filth away.

The moral condition of our continent resembles the Augean stable. A well-known evangelist recently said, "We have become so corrupt that we put Sodom and Gomorrah to shame." True!

Immorality has always been with us. People really lived it up in the Gay Nineties and the Roaring Twenties, but today the sick and unnatural have been added, the morbid and the perverse. In his book *Awakened China*, Felix Green quotes a Red Chinese official: "Western nations with the highest crime rate in the world talk to us about respect for the law; western nations with the highest rate of drunkenness in the world tell us to be sober; western nations with the highest divorce rate preach to us about the sanctity of the home."

That's exactly satan's design. The Western democracies have been endowed with many spiritual riches and cultural treasures. They should be imbued with the spirit of service; they should be bringers of relief, justice and freedom to the struggling nations. But instead they have succumbed to the cancer of moral decay.

No amount of patchwork will help. There is a river, the river of Christ's blood shed for sinners, which can cleanse us from all filth. Our text says that the pure in heart are blessed. Their entire lives are lived before God's face. They shall actually see God.

Holy Spirit, wash us clean in the blood of Christ. Restore the spirit of wholeness to the nations. Clean away the corruption that now mars life. Richly bless the pure in heart. Amen.

Personal Prayer

But when you pray, go into your room and shut the door and pray to your Father who is in secret; and your Father who sees in secret will reward you (Matt. 6:6).

Public prayer is good; personal prayer is better. Jesus tells us to go into a closet and there, in deepest privacy, talk things over with God.

You see, the homes of Jesus' day had one room in them where people stored their supplies and kept their treasures. That room was securely locked. Guests might have the run of the house, but they would not think of peeking into that room. That room represented a man's earthly security. His well-being depended on the contents of the store-room.

And that is exactly why Jesus told the people to pray in that room. Their lives' deepest secrets had to be exposed to God. By withdrawing into that room, they confessed that they depended on God completely for all their needs. God was the only source of security.

That's why we must withdraw with our God in such prayer. We acknowledge that our only hope lies in Him. He bought us at the price of His Son, and now we are His concern. In such deeply personal prayer, we bare our souls before Him. We withhold nothing; we are still before Him. Our relationship with Him is strengthened. The understanding between Him and us is confirmed. We rededicate ourselves and all that we have to Him. We share our problems with Him. We lift up before Him the needs of people in ardent intercessory prayer. In a very deep and personal sense, we dwell with our whole soul upon Him.

From this prayer of the inner room, we emerge as new people—cleansed, refreshed. We return to life, ready to share His riches with others. Let's periodically withdraw from life and seek the face of God.

Teach us, Father, the beauty of the hallowed moments spent with You in secret. Amen.

With Jesus in the Storm

There arose a great storm on the sea, so that the boat was being swamped by the waves; but he was asleep. And he said to them, "Why are you afraid, O men of little faith?" (Matt. 8:24, 26).

An unforgettable experience for the disciples! First the horror of a sudden storm such as they had never witnessed before—the ugly hands of death tearing at their little vessel from all sides. And then the unimaginable relief when Jesus spoke and put death and destruction in their place.

The Lord will do that in your life. But you have to step into the boat with Him first. That is no small matter, for the going will be rough! That little Sea of Galilee will really boil when the winds suddenly swoop down from the mountains around. The disciples felt that Jesus should never have let the storm develop as it had. Imagine, while He slept in the fore-cabin, they almost perished in the tempest. Of course, they should have known better. Jesus may be asleep, but as Mediator between God and man He always watches. And Jesus tells them right out that the real problem is not the storm but the weakness of their faith.

What about *your* faith? Deep down we prefer a calm and secure life. Let Jesus take care of that! If disaster strikes we say, "Now where is Jesus?" He can afford to sleep, you see! Yet, all the while He watches, actually watching mostly *whether our faith is real.*

Are you ready to believe that He is in command always? If you go into the ship with Him, He will change your life completely. Then you will not live for ease and security any longer; your only interest will be that God's will is done in all your affairs. Once we know such obedience, He will take care of the storm and the waves as well.

Lord Jesus, be the captain of my world, my heart, my thoughts. Help me, Holy Spirit to see Christ in every situation. Amen.

You Are a Sheep

When he saw the crowds, he had compassion for them, because they were harassed and helpless, like sheep without a shepherd (Matt. 9:36).

Time and time again the Bible calls us sheep. Why would the Lord apply that humble comparison to us? It surely isn't the picture that we have of ourselves. If we call a person a sheep, he will most likely not react as one.

But the Bible has a better understanding of us than we have of ourselves. Aren't we in fact defenseless as sheep—a most easy prey to devouring animals? We are defenseless amid the forces of sin, even though we often go our merry way as if everything is lovely in the garden. In themselves Christians are helpless in the arena of the world. Against the forces that shape our world, we have very little to offer of our own. Sheep blindly follow each other, but they are completely dependent when it comes to finding grazing ground or avoiding the dangerous abyss. It is often not easy to acknowledge dependence and blindness in this age when Christians, too, have become a success in society. But that's the Lord's description of us—sheep, harassed and helpless.

The Bible, of course, says more. It calls Jesus the shepherd. The shepherd loves the sheep, he protects them, he drives off the predators, he keeps the flock together, he brings the wandering ones back, he leads to new pastures, he avoids the dangerous places. Sometimes he must be hard on the sheep, but it is for their own good. He gently carries the young in his bosom.

Christ is this kind of shepherd to His people.

It all sounds quite out of place in our sophisticated age, doesn't it? But you see, one day that Shepherd gave His life for the sheep. If that means little to you, then you are still quite alone in the wilderness. And this advanced age has really never solved the problem of loneliness, has it?

We must admit that we are helpless as sheep, and we acknowledge You as our Shepherd, dear Savior. Keep us close to You and close to the flock. Amen.

A Straight Course

No one who puts his hand to the plow and looks back is fit for the kingdom of God (Luke 9:62).

In his book *Crusade in Europe*, General Eisenhower tells how difficult it was to stick to the one great goal of the Allied war effort: push through to the heart of Europe. He lists the pressures that tempted him to divert his attention to an attack in the Balkans or a battle in Italy. Every day he had to remind himself again of the purpose of all the war actions: to move toward the heart of Europe.

It is that way in our life.

Jesus tells us that we must live for the Kingdom of God. Do you know what the Kingdom of God is? When Jesus rules in our heart! Then everything we do stems from our heart. So we seek the Kingdom of God when Jesus rules our thoughts, our feelings, our actions, our ideals, our relationships, our work, and our holdings. Our one great aim must ever be to effect the rule of Jesus Christ in every area of life.

But there are evil powers in us which would draw us away from Christ. And around us, too, a host of forces seek to exclude Christ's rule from human concerns. It is not easy to keep that one great Kingdom goal before us always.

In Luke 9 the Lord compares the battle of the Kingdom with the challenge of the plow-man. His goal is to plow evenly and straight. His temptation is to look back; he is uncertain of himself, and he doesn't really dare to march on. The result is a crooked furrow. But he takes hold of himself, directs his eyes toward a fixed point at the end of the field, and proceeds steadily. That's how we must seek to do the Master's kingdom bidding.

Lord Jesus, take possession of our hearts, our lives, our holdings, and our concerns. Lead us in singleness of heart to live a full Christian life. May we bear much fruit. To the praise of Your name. Amen.

Twelve Simple People

The names of the twelve apostles are these . . . (Matt. 10:2).

The Old Testament church was founded on the twelve patriarchs. The New Testament church was founded on the twelve apostles.

The twelve patriarchs were shepherd-kings, royal grandsons of Isaac and Abraham. The twelve apostles were mostly unknown laborers.

But the twelve apostles, though of humble origin, did works for the Lord that were more mighty than the works of the important patriarchs.

This shows what the Master's grace can do in His servants. We probably wouldn't have chosen these men as apostles. Peter talked big, but he was a coward at heart. John and James were of uneven temper: "sons of thunder," Jesus called them once. Thomas was a pessimistic doubter. Matthew had been a tax-collector, and the people thought of him as a traitor. None of them was educated; all of them were unknowns. And the apostle Paul, who was added later, had been a persecutor of the church. A psychological test would have ruled several of them unfit for the ministry.

It appears that Jesus does not choose His ambassadors on the basis of brilliant gifts or noble birth. For you see, the secret of fruitful service does not lie in the greatness of people. At Pentecost, Peter and the eleven preached the gospel and 3000 were baptized. How could the fishermen do it? Because there had been a flame on their heads. The Holy Spirit had taken possession of them. Christ chooses, leads, and gives the Spirit.

Matthew tells us here that Jesus sends out His disciples with one message: "The Kingdom of heaven is at hand." That Kingdom will come through you, too, if you depend on the Spirit. It knows no class distinctions and no unemployment.

Lord, send us too. Equip us with Your Holy Spirit for service, and make us worthy representatives. Amen.

People in Conflict

Now when John heard in prison about the deeds of the Christ, he sent word by his disciples and said to him, "Are you he who is to come, or shall we look for another?" (Matt. 11:2-3).

Some of the readers will recognize themselves in the conflicts of John the Baptist, who was a prisoner of ruthless King Herod in the passage we have just read.

John had done great things for Christ. He had prepared the way for Him. John had high hopes that the Kingdom of God would soon change the face of the earth, now that the Messiah had come. But suddenly it had all ended: John was thrown into prison, and Christ the Messiah seemed in no hurry to establish the Kingdom of righteousness. The weeks went by, nothing happened, and the conflict raged in John's soul. He thought: "Is He the Messiah, or isn't He?"

Then John did something that should be an example of permanent validity to us. He took his distress to Jesus. One day some of his friends were allowed to visit him. He asked them to go to Jesus and find out whether He was the promised Messiah. That's where we must begin. We cannot hope to solve any of our conflicts if we don't have clarity about the Christ.

In His answer to John, Jesus pointed to His *work* and His *person*. He had healed the sick, the blind, the lepers, the deaf, and He had raised up the dead and had preached the gospel. Jesus presents this as proof that He is the Messiah, for the prophet Isaiah had described the Messiah this way centuries before (35:5-6). On that basis, Jesus asks John to accept and trust Him.

Now John has ground under his feet: Jesus was his Savior, Jesus was in command. Even though John could not fully understand Jesus' strategy, he could face life again! He could even face death—the death of a martyr which he would soon die. Jesus can give you that peace. When you find Him, you find yourself, and only then can you come to terms with your world.

Jesus, Savior and Friend, You know the struggles of our heart. Sometimes we feel so hopeless and distraught. Take our hand and lead us on. Amen.

This Divided World

Every kingdom divided against itself is laid waste, and no city or house divided against itself will stand (Matt. 12:25).

In the course of an argument with the Pharisees, Jesus stated the generally accepted truth that a kingdom divided against itself cannot stand. How urgent for today's world to ponder those simple words, for there are so many divisions among us! Wendell Willkie's ideal of One World died with his generation. The 38th parallel in Korea and the ugly Berlin Wall are only symbols of the deeper divisions that fragment mankind.

The estrangement of man and his fellow man is so deep because it is so old. It goes back to Paradise, where our parents Adam and Eve broke with God. From then on, all relationships collapsed. Shame divided Adam and Eve. Hatred drove Cain to put Abel out of his life. How else could it be? Where man does not live for God, he lives for himself. Even his charitable acts are prompted by selfish considerations. Families, once communities of trust, are falling apart everywhere. Labor and management form two hostile camps. In spite of all the beautiful slogans, the advanced nations refuse to face the growing distress of the so-called developing nations. And what more has to be said about corruption, drug addiction, crime, revolution, racial hatred, and wars, before society will realize the nearness of collapse?

The Gospel of Matthew speaks of another Kingdom, a Kingdom that will never fall apart. It is the Kingdom of Christ. Those who accept forgiveness of sins through His sacrifice belong to that Kingdom.

There is something mysterious about the Kingdom of Christ. You can't pinpoint it. It is foremost the rule of Christ in the hearts of His followers. He binds them together into one spiritual body, an "organism" of which He remains the head. His Kingdom is the opposite of division and fragmentation. Our hope for wholeness in this broken world lies in this Kingdom.

Lord, the divisions and alienation all over the place make us so sad; we reach for the heart of our neighbor, but he steps back quickly. Holy Spirit, take away our loneliness and restore the communion of saints. Amen.

He Thought of Me

I am the good shepherd; I know my own, and my own know me (John 10:14).

When George Nixon Brigs was Governor of Massachusetts, three of his friends visited the Holy Land. While there, they climbed Golgotha's slope. From the summit they cut a small stick to be used as a cane. On their return home they presented it to the governor and said: "We wanted you to know that when we stood on Golgotha's mountain, we thought of you." Accepting the gift with all due courtesy, the governor gratefully added: "But I am still more thankful, gentlemen, that there was Another who thought of me there."

Yes, salvation is only possible because Jesus Christ thought of *you*. In John 10 we read that the Savior *knew* His sheep. The verb *to know* has a rich meaning in the Bible. It implies a lasting relationship, a possessing each other in love and faithfulness.

Such "knowing" always demands a *response*. Jesus says here: ". . . and my own know me." Indeed, the sheep hear the Shepherd's voice. They answer His call, and they follow Him.

There must be that moment in your life where you stop in your tracks and ask yourself: What have I done with Christ? What is my relationship to God? What do I live for?

Have you come to that point?

The Good Shepherd left the ninety-and-nine in order to find the lamb that went astray. He will do that for you. Don't avoid that moment; don't avoid *Him!* Only in that encounter can you *know* your Lord. From there you can share your life with Him. He will watch over you. What an overwhelming thing to know: *He thought of me!*

Thank You, Lord Jesus, that we can be Your people. Make us ever again willing to follow You. Thank You, Lord, that You did it all. Amen.

Which Burden?

Come to me, all who labor and are heavy laden, and I will give you rest (Matt. 11:28).

Don't misunderstand this beautiful, well-known text. Jesus is not thinking here of people burdened by sorrow or misery.

What is the case? Well, Jesus visited the cities of Chorazin and Bathsaida. They were Galilean cities in which He had often preached. He had performed many miracles there to confirm the good news. But the response was nil. Why? Because the people thought they weren't so bad. They kept the law and did commendable works besides. They would gladly suffer a bit of inconvenience for the sake of a good return in the hereafter.

And that's why Jesus was angry with them. They didn't realize the terror of their burden of sin and guilt, and therefore they didn't feel the need for the Savior who alone could take over that burden and exchange it for true rest and peace.

That's the heart of the gospel. We cannot meet God's law on our own, no matter how hard we try. Our relationship with Him is completely broken. Our guilt reaches to the sky. Only Christ, the Savior, both God and man, can save us from our sin. He did that by being born for us, by fulfilling the law of love for us, by suffering and dying for us, and by rising from the grave for us.

There have been moments when you groaned under the load of problems. Perhaps some readers, right at this moment, don't know where to turn next. Yes, Jesus is sensitive to the reality of your daily afflictions. But He first puts His finger on a deeper pain to which we may have grown numb. It is the pain of guilt. He will take it over from us if we believe in Him. Guilt is the load of which Matthew 11 speaks. What a relief to relinquish that burden! Christ calls it *rest*. In that rest you can really run!

Thank You, Savior, for taking away our guilt. Show us the Father's face every day. Make us vigorous in Your service. Amen.

When the Devils Danced

Then he [the unclean spirit] says, "I will return to my house . . ." And when he comes he finds it empty, swept, and put in order. Then he goes and brings with him seven other spirits . . . and they enter and dwell there (Matt. 12:44-5).

. . . I saw a Lamb . . . with seven horns and with seven eyes, which are the seven spirits of God sent out into all the earth (Rev. 5:6).

You are a problem-solver. That's good! God is aware of your needs. He fed Elijah under the juniper tree. Jesus healed the sick and gave the 5000 food to eat.

But beware!

Today's passage gives us an example of wrong problem-solving. It tells of a man who had a demon in his life. What a mess he was in! But one day he decided to clean up his life. Out went the demon! Things were going to be different from then on.

But he soon learned that it wasn't all that simple. Demons help each other. The original demon returned for another try, assisted by *seven more demons*. It was ridiculously easy. The man was completely unprepared for such an attack. The house of his life was clean, but quite defenseless. The demons simply moved in and had a devil of a time. The man's life was ruined.

Don't think it cannot happen to you. No matter how clean you live or how cleverly you solve your problems, if you do it in your own strength you will have trouble some day.

The Bible outlines a different course. It tells of Jesus, who sends the Holy Spirit to His followers. In Revelation 5:6 the Holy Spirit is called "seven spirits." The figure "seven" points to the fullness of the Spirit's work. He will fill the house of your life. He gives courage, wisdom and power in every situation. The seven spirits keep the seven evil spirits out. Believers can always go on in the Spirit. You should invite Him in before it is too late.

Lord, how vulnerable we are in the face of the demonic powers of our world! Show us, Holy Spirit, how incredibly naive we are in trying to be a match for those evil spirits. Come, Holy Spirit, make our hearts Your residence, show us how to do good, safeguard us from harm, and lead our thoughts. For Jesus' sake. Amen.

The Paralyzing Power of Unbelief

And he did not do many mighty works there, because of their unbelief (Matt. 13:58).

Jesus came to His hometown of Nazareth where He preached the gospel. But His own rejected Him. Scornfully they asked, "Isn't this the carpenter's son?" And then Matthew reports the dreadful fact that Jesus couldn't do many mighty works there because of their unbelief.

Seldom has the reality of unbelief been pictured more starkly.

Surely we know that the power of God is unlimited. His mighty works of creation demonstrate that daily. And from the Bible we also know that He ultimately governs every event, both good and bad. But the power of God will not be manifested for good among men *unless they believe*. Romans 1:16 states, "For I am not ashamed of the gospel: it is the power of God for salvation *to every one who has faith*." Those who will not believe will not experience the power of God. His power simply cannot work in the poisonous atmosphere of rejection. Ephesians 1:19-20 posits the same condition of faith: ". . . and what is the immeasurable greatness of his power in us *who believe*, according to the working of his great might which he accomplished *in Christ . . .*"

So often we ask why God tolerates evil. It would be far better if we would be more concerned about the presence of massive unbelief in the world. God's power runs in the riverbed of faith. Where faith is absent, God's power cannot flow.

Remember Christ in Nazareth. He appears helpless among His unbelieving countrymen. What a warning for us! The patience and graciousness of gospel preachers may never hide the urgency of the call to faith and repentance. Without God's power, only the power of satan remains.

But the reverse is true too. When we trust and believe, there is no limit to what He can accomplish through us. His power through His children is so great! What riches that we may claim that power every day!

Lord, lead us to repentance and faith. May we not be perplexed in the moment of crisis. May Your gospel reach many people, and may they be saved. Keep Your eye on us. Amen.

Comfortable People with a Comfortable Law

Woe to you, scribes and Pharisees, hypocrites! for you tithe mint and dill and cummin, and have neglected the weightier matters of the law, justice and mercy and faith; these you ought to have done, without neglecting the others (Matt. 23:23).

The people of Jesus' day didn't mind the law of tithing—paying ten percent to the church—because they knew their obligations exactly. Nine percent was not enough; eleven percent was too much. The choice between obedience and disobedience was easily defined. Oh, there might be a problem now and then, but that could be solved. For instance, what about the tenths of such seasoning herbs as mint, dill and cummin, of which only a wee bit was grown in the family vegetable garden? The people thought they didn't have to tithe these, since the law of Moses didn't mention them by name. But the religious leaders decreed that these little extras should also be tithed. And that settled the problem. The people dutifully paid, for, after all, they wanted to be on the safe side.

Remarkably enough, Jesus doesn't scold them for their accuracy. But He attacked the spirit that was underneath all those precise figures. The Pharisees rejected the heart of the law—justice, mercy and faith. The heart of the law made the law much more difficult to fulfill. Once the heart was grasped, it couldn't be reduced to figures on paper. The law requires men to love and to care. The law makes us face our evil nature. Those who know the law properly must surrender to Christ.

Inside every one of us there is a calculating Pharisee. He can only be removed by the grace of Christ. If we confess Him as Savior, He will give us a new heart. Prompted by love, we will do the works of the law gladly.

Lord Jesus, we are really very selfish schemers inside. Show us up for what we are, especially in meeting our obligations. Fill our hearts with love through the forgiveness of sins. Amen.

The Chaplain

Be merciful, even as your Father is merciful (Luke 6:36).

God our Father is great in mercy. He gave of His own love; He gave His Son for us useless sinners. This is what makes His mercy special. The children of the Father do likewise. Having been saved by the Son, they know the secret of giving of their own love, giving of themselves. They are merciful as their Father is merciful.

That is an enormously high ideal.

Is it realistic for us to strive for it?

Consider a few things that go into making us merciful people.

First, we must be merciful to ourselves. How? God accepted us in mercy, and now we have to accept ourselves. God forgave us and remembers our sins no more, so we must live without remorse or regret.

Next, we must learn to put ourselves in the position of other people. We must try to imagine what they are up against. We can actually cultivate bigness of heart.

Finally, we must practice these ideals in daily situations. We must be doers of mercy. That involves making choices. We will face situations where we can comfortably mind our own business, or we can reach out and be a real neighbor to those who carry some burden. There are so many who need your interest, your encouragement, your advice, or your assistance. Be to them a doer of mercy.

St. Martin, who later became a bishop of Tours (A.D. 372), once traveled as a young soldier in the area of Amiens, where he noticed a poor beggar shivering in the cold. He got off his horse, tore his cape or "capella" into two pieces, and draped half around the beggar. He became known as the "capella lender," from which our word *chaplain* has been derived. Our day needs many chaplains.

Dear Lord, we praise Your name for Your wondrous mercy in Christ. Holy Spirit, help us to deny ourselves and to share Your goodness with those who are troubled. Amen.

The Girls Who Missed the Wedding

Then the kingdom of heaven shall be compared to ten maidens who took their lamps and went to meet the bridegroom. Five of them were foolish, and five were wise (Matt. 25:1-2).

Among those who call themselves Christians there are two kinds—those for whom their faith is a motor that drives their life, and those who drag their Christian profession along as an unpleasant burden.

The parable of the wise and foolish maidens pictures both kinds. All ten had been invited to a wedding. They were going to meet the bridegroom toward nighttime. Equipped with lamps, they would form an honor guard of light. But then trouble began. Five of the girls ran out of oil for their lamps. They hurried to town to buy oil, but by the time they returned, the wedding procession had left. So they missed the wedding.

We are all forgetful at times. But we don't forget things easily if they mean a lot to us. The five wise girls had taken extra oil along because their friend's wedding was an outstanding event for them. For the foolish five it was not. Hence they forgot to make proper provisions.

To be a Christian is a unique and wonderful reality. It means that through the forgiveness of sins in Christ, we have actually become children of God. Imagine that! The almighty God who fashioned the universe is our Father! He cares for us and wants to commune with us. That should mean everything to us. We should always be aware of His company, we should seek to please Him, we should worthily represent Him in every situation, and we should eagerly introduce Him to others.

But, oh, the sad reality! We go our own way, and before we know it there are large parts of life where He is absent. Our Christianity has become an unwelcome burden. Hurry, repent, for the Bridegroom can come at any hour!

Lord, awaken us from our spiritual slumber, show us the excitement of a life in God's nearness, help us with eagerness to bring others to the faith, and give us fresh energy to stay in step with You. Holy Spirit, may we never be found unprepared for the great calling we have in Christ. Amen.

Certainty in Chaos

Heaven and earth shall pass away, but my words will not pass away (Luke 21:33).

It is the year of the Lord 410. A bishop of the Christian church in North Africa receives in his study the terrible news that the Goths have invaded Italy and that Alaric's hordes have sacked Rome. The bishop understands that these events mark the end of Roman civilization. That bishop, St. Augustine, then wrote his famous book *De Civitate Dei*—The Kingdom of God. Earthly kingdoms will wane and collapse, but God's civilization will stand the test of the centuries because it is His own eternal cause.

Disasters have ravaged the earth many times since the days of St. Augustine, but the church of Christ has always remained.

We don't know what the future will bring. International relations are poisoned by hatred and despair. Many people have lost their trust in the church of Christ. And we must admit that her shortcomings are many.

All these realities have affected you too. Your church membership is not always as real and lively as it should be. Life without Christ charms you too at times. Wouldn't it be a relief to be freed from the press of the kingdom obligations?

But from the Bible learn this lesson: life apart from Christ will not last. The waves of judgment will wash it all away. But that lesson has a reverse side: God will never forsake you. Who will tell what you are going through these days, or what lies in store for you? Today's text assures you that it is more likely for the globe to disintegrate than for God to forget you for one moment.

God, You rule mankind, and we thank You that we never escape Your attention. Keep us faithful to the end. Amen.

Afraid, Slow, and Blind

*All authority in heaven and on earth has been given to me. Go therefore
and make disciples of all nations . . . and lo, I am with you always . . ."
(Matt. 28:18-20).*

1. To the *frightened* Jesus says today that all power and
authority is His. The whole world exists by His power. If you obey
Christ, your whole life is on a new footing. You then live a *normal*
life. To ignore Him is to live *abnormally*. We often feel awkward in
presenting the good news. Shame on us! It's as if doing the Lord's
bidding makes us odd. That's why God made man in the first place.

2. To the *slow* Jesus also has something to say in today's text.
"Make disciples of all nations." No small task, to be sure. We must
speed up our efforts. We must begin at home. The churches have
to return to the Word of God, lest more members drop out. Such
revived church members will have to learn that they may not leave
their obligations to missionaries and evangelists any longer. They
themselves have to live and preach the new life here and abroad in
whatever capacity of life they find themselves. Millions are
estranged from Christ in suburbs and ghettoes. Two thousand
tribes have not even been contacted for Christ. So, let the slow
repent!

3. And to all who are *blind* Christ says today, "Lo, I am with
you always." We struggle, we witness, we live, *in His company*. He
is always around. Christ wants us to see that. He tells us to open
our eyes and recognize Him. As a child is suddenly not afraid
anymore when it knows its mother is near, so we overcome our fears
and scruples in bringing the gospel because Christ is at hand.

We must stop being so frightened, and blind, and afraid.
Then there will be no stopping the gospel from transforming
millions.

*Dear Lord, help us see the urgency of the great commission. Give us
courage and vision to live and express it, always and everywhere. Amen.*

The Nearness of the Great Judgment

When the Son of man comes in his glory . . . he will sit on his glorious throne. Before him will be gathered all the nations . . . Then the King will say to those at his right hand, "Come . . . for I was hungry and you gave me food . . ." Then he will say to those at his left hand, "Depart . . . for I was hungry and you gave me no food" (Matt. 25:31-2, 34-5, 41-2).

The great judgment is very near. Oh, it may be many years before the judgment actually takes place, but we must nevertheless feel the reality of it today. Remember, Christ Himself will be the Judge. He will conduct the trial in His capacity as Mediator between God and man. It will be the closing act of His great work of salvation. The fullness of the Master's work, the great judgment included, must be real to His followers.

All of humanity will appear before the Judge that day. Those who did His bidding will be publicly vindicated. Those who refused to do His will, will be publicly condemned. The coming judgment must determine how we look at life today. Behind all the suffering for the sake of our faith stands the Judge. Behind all the raging of the powers of unbelief stands the Judge.

All this should lead us to triumphant living, but it should also lead us to sobriety.

It is by grace alone that believers may stand at the Lord's right hand. Yes more, their own works will be exposed at the end of time, works done out of love for Christ today. Believers have been saved for the purpose of service: "I was hungry and you gave me food . . ." That service will be a major item in the trial.

The early Christians perhaps saw this more clearly than we do today. They were very conscious of the Lord's return. Behind persecutions they saw great vistas of victory. Beset by troubles, they nevertheless knew the urgency of good works. That made them dynamic Christians. They made many converts for Christ. They changed the world because their lives were changed.

Lord Jesus, Judge of heaven and earth, fill us with zeal and willingness to do good. May Christianity look better because of our presence. Amen.

The Precious Garment

I will greatly rejoice in the Lord . . . for he has clothed me with the garments of salvation (Is. 61:10).

Clothes have had a strange fascination for people through the ages. After the war, domestic help was hard to get. A lady in New Jersey was only able to get a maid by letting the maid wear her mink coat on her evenings off. Before you dismiss that as a dubious item, remember one thing: almost all people try to express certain ideals in their dress, ideals which they find hard to experience in daily life. The fifties brought the "new look" that wishfully reflected the optimism of a new technological age. The blue jeans and granny dress of the sixties expressed a deeply felt desire to experience simplicity and honesty. The problem has always been to live up to the ideals people express in their dress.

All this has a deeper ground that goes back to our family history. Our first parents, Adam and Eve, were people of great fortune and personal brilliance. Their bankruptcy became our family disaster. They lost their beauty, their standing, and their gifts. What remained was a deep nostalgia for that lost family heritage. So people pretend to be what they no longer are—some with mink and jewels, others with beards and sandals. They try to impress others, be it ever so subtly, but nothing can fill the empty void.

Nothing? Yes, Someone can! A Savior who, we are told, will dress us with very special garments—*the garments of righteousness!* These garments mark us as sons and daughters of the most high God. Our *outer appearance* is then true to our *inner reality.*

Have you accepted those garments? Get them; they are free. Without them you are out in the cold.

Father, our lives have often been untrue. Give us new hearts, Lord Jesus, and help us to show it in a new life. Amen.

Money

For the love of money is the root of all evils (I Tim. 6:10).

The well-known story of Roger Babson's visit to the President of Argentina bears repetition. In their conversation, the President wondered aloud why South America found itself so much poorer than North America. He remarked about South America's natural abundance of trees, copper, iron, silver, gold, its big rivers and large farms. "Why would we still be so poor?" he sighed. Babson knew the answer, but he waited. After a while the President summed it up himself: "South America was settled by men who came for gold; North America was settled by the Pilgrim Fathers and the Puritans who came in search of God."

That assessment strikes us today as a bit glib, I suppose. Apart from its validity as such, the praise implies a painful indictment. The historian Charles Beard observed: "The Bible no longer lies at the heart of our society; it has nothing to do with our civilization." We have chosen the external tangibles—luxurious cars, fashionable homes, frozen crabs, and charcoal-broiled steaks. Today we face the dire consequences. Our traditional style of consumption just can't continue.

Christians should have known. The Bible tells us continually that we must not seek our comfort in material things, but rather in godliness and service to those in need. We must help each other in making responsible use of our dwindling resources. We must discover the true purpose of being God's pilots on spaceship earth.

Lord, open the eyes of the nations that seek after wealth. Open our eyes. Free us from the tyranny of the gods of goods and pleasure. Help us to bless our fellow man. Amen.

Paradise Regained

Finally, brethren, whatever is true . . . honorable . . . just . . . pure . . . lovely . . . gracious . . . if there is any excellence . . . think about these things (Phil. 4:8).

Imagine that there had been no fall into sin in Paradise. What kind of a world would we live in today? Well, there would be no police department, no courts, no hospitals, no welfare services, no army, no old-age homes, no prisons, no drug addiction, no refugee camps, no air pollution, no weed control, no unemployment, no bankruptcies, no oil spills, no bad debts, no energy crisis, no divorces, no accidents. And that would be only a beginning. You just wouldn't recognize a host of things. The front-page news would all be Hosannah-like, the advertising page honestly small, Ann Landers happily retired, and tax return forms the size of a postcard.

Alas, your alarm clock had the ring of a harsh world about it this morning, and your sore back confirmed the reality of a troubled world. And so you got through the day and made the best of it.

Did you? Did you really *make the best of it?* Christians are realists, but they are at the same time *idealists!* Their Savior walked among them and broke the power of evil. He said, "I make all things new." When we follow Him and become extensions of His healing mercy, things become new through us. Wherever we show our face, something of Paradise should be regained.

Paul goes a step further: he challenges us to dwell actively on all the perfections listed at the top of this page. The patient practice of those perfections is Paradise action.

Lord, quicken us to a life of perfection and healing. Holy Spirit, show us the mighty possibilities of Christ's power in us. Amen.

The Rainbow

When I bring clouds over the earth and the bow is seen in the clouds, I will remember my covenant (Gen. 9:14-15).

Try to imagine what Noah and his family faced when they came out of the ark after the great flood. The earth resembled an alien planet covered with silt and slime—a silent landscape of death and destruction under ominous clouds. What an uncertain future that family faced all alone on that hostile globe!

But they were not alone!

As soon as the ark hit solid ground on the heights of Ararat, God came and visited Noah and his family. And God promised them that He would see them through. Then, as a sign of that promise, He set the rainbow around the big clouds so that they could never again pour their wrath on mankind. The rainbow was God's sure pledge of His covenant faithfulness. Never again would the earth be destroyed by the angry waters.

Note a few more things about the rainbow. We read that God said, "When I bring clouds over the earth and the bow is seen . . ." *God* brings the clouds. All events are part of His all-embracing design for earth and mankind. Sometimes that fills us with fear.

But around those clouds is God's rainbow—as a sure pledge that He will protect His children and provide for them. The clouds are necessary, but they will not overwhelm God's people.

One more thing about the rainbow. You must know that a rainbow is formed from ordinary sunlight refracted by the water vapor of the atmosphere into the seven colors of the spectrum. The same happens when light is led through a prism or a piece of crystal. God has always shed light on the pathway of His children. But it is only when heavy clouds surround them that God's light will burst forth in seven splendid colors. The darker those clouds, the more brilliant the colors.

God is faithful; His promises will never fail. All His children will experience His light. But it is in times of trial that they experience the light of the Father's face in all its colorful excellence.

Wonderful God, thank You for the exuberant riches of Your goodness and faithfulness. Give us renewal of faith and trust. Your name be praised forever. Amen.

Truth-fullness

You shall not bear false witness against your neighbor (Ex. 20:16).
I am . . . the truth (John 14:6).

Truth is an amazing thing. It can grow on you.

Israel traveled through the desert. Unless the people could depend on each other's word, life for the fledgling nation would be impossible. So the Lord tells them: "Don't lie."

But *truth* is richer than stating true facts. Before God gave the ten commandments, He told the people of Israel: "I am your God." He meant to say: "We have a covenant together. We are friends, partners. We have a solemn agreement." This gave truth a deep dimension. The people were *truth-full* when they shared life with God from the heart, much like a husband and wife who are *true* to each other in everything.

The New Testament tells us that Christ is the Mediator of the new covenant between God and the redeemed (Heb. 9). He is the bridge between heaven and earth. He bundles up our life and makes God a partner in it. That's why He called Himself *the Truth* in John 14. When we know Christ in us, we don't only *speak* the truth, we *are* truth. We live *true* lives; we are what God intended us to be.

Perhaps you are reading these lines at breakfast time, or after an evening out. Not a very suitable moment to ponder the word *truth*. Still, how important to come to grips with truth, for the very quality of your life depends on it. Truth is more sensitive than a compass needle. You may say things that are accurate, but if you say them in anger or flattery they are not true. Underneath it all is our heart—totally exposed to the eyes of Christ. Truth will grow there when you invite Him in. His presence will add a glow to every touch of affection, and integrity to every moment of fellowship. In Him you become a *true* person.

We thank You, dear Savior, that Your Spirit keeps us connected with You. Help us to bear true witness to our neighbor. Through Your grace, Lord Jesus. Amen.

Thank-fullness

What shall I render to the Lord for all his bounty to me? I will lift up the cup of salvation (Ps. 116:12-13).

Thankfulness—how do you express it?

The possibilities are many.

The jet-set makes it part of the art of gracious living. The telephone operator adds a "thank you" to every sentence as a matter of business routine. And the little poodle wags his tail for a bit of Gravy Train.

Christians may go to Psalm 116 and learn thankfulness from David, the man of God. For David, thankfulness is a combination of things he says and things he feels in his heart. He can't catch it in one simple formula.

Listen how David expresses gratitude.

"I love the Lord."

"I will call on him."

"Gracious is the Lord."

"The Lord has dealt bountifully with me."

"The Lord preserves the simple."

"For thou hast delivered my soul."

If you are really thankful to the Lord, then *say so! Tell* the Lord; *make mention* of all His blessings.

But now David takes us one step further. In today's text he says, "I will lift up the cup of salvation." What a beautiful way of giving thanks! In all his thankfulness, he senses the vibrations of salvation. He is saved! God forgave him and accepted him back. That salvation makes everything else possible. It is the source of all that is good. And so, at stated times, David sings jubilantly of that salvation. He raises a glass: To my God, for salvation!

Open my eyes, O Holy Spirit, and show me the many gifts my heavenly Father entrusts to me every day and night again. Thank You, Lord, for them all. But thank You above all for having adopted me as Your child because of Jesus Christ. May gratitude season the whole substance of my life. Through the Savior. Amen.

A Personal Appeal

I appeal to you therefore . . . (Rom. 12:1).

This month let's study Romans 12.

The letter of Paul to the church of Rome is very beautiful. Believers today ought frequently to take it to hand and to heart.

A beautiful plan underlies this letter. The first eleven chapters explore the agonizing depth of our fall into sin with all its dire consequences. But they also trace the riches of God's grace in the victory of Jesus Christ over death.

Paul is so gripped by the greatness of this gospel that he exclaims at the end of chapter 11:

How great are God's riches!

How deep are His wisdom and knowledge!

For from Him and through Him and to Him are all things.

To Him be the glory forever. Amen.

Having displayed all these treasures in the house of salvation, Paul suddenly turns to us and says: "Now what about you? Will you accept the riches of this amazing gospel for yourselves? I *appeal* to you therefore . . ."

That's what Romans 12 is all about. It tells us how to respond to God's work in Christ. Let's study this chapter verse by verse. Let's follow Paul step by step. Let's do it prayerfully.

We will discover that the foundation of the Christian faith is God's own work. *He* did it all for us through Jesus Christ. But we will also discover that we must *personally* surrender, *personally* take it to heart, and *personally* live this new relationship to our heavenly Father. Only then can we transform God's power into productive Christian living.

God in heaven, bless, we pray, the meditations of this month. Holy Spirit, teach us the secret of Christian living. Help us to serve our Master with joy. Amen.

Visible Christianity

I appeal to you therefore, brethren . . . to present your bodies as a living sacrifice . . . which is your spiritual worship (Rom. 12:1).

Many people think that Christianity is a *spiritual* religion. They are right! It is from God, who is Spirit (John 4:24). Paul here calls it *spiritual service.*

But don't let that give you the idea that *spiritual* Christianity is *invisible* Christianity. Some people feel that way. You would never recognize them as Christians on the job or in their business.

In today's text, Paul tells us that our *spiritual* Christianity consists of offering our *bodies* to God, which means that we must serve Him very practically in daily life.

Some time ago two reporters from a large Toronto daily newspaper decided to test the honesty of the city's auto mechanics. They disconnected one sparkplug wire of a car engine otherwise in perfect shape, and consulted several garages stating that their engine missed. They were charged up to $35.00 for labor and parts, until they came to a mechanic who explained, "You have a loose connection here," whereupon he put the wire back in without cost. When the reporters told him of their previous experiences, he replied, "I couldn't do that; I'm a Christian." His spiritual service had made Christianity visible.

Our Christian example is worth more than many Christian words. But God's *Word* is more than *words*. It is the *power* of God unto salvation. Regular Bible reading brings the Father's power within your reach. You need a re-fill every day. You will then become a practicing Christian, and you will make Christianity visible.

Dear Lord, make our love to You real and practical. Give us the honesty and courage to own up to our Christian profession. Give us wisdom to put our faith to work without feeling smug about ourselves. For Jesus' sake. Amen.

Thermometer and Thermostat

Do not be conformed to the world but be transformed . . . (Rom. 12:2).

A *thermometer* and a *thermostat* look alike, but there is a big difference between them.

A *thermometer* merely registers the temperature, but does not change it.

A *thermostat* not only measures the temperature, it also controls the heating unit so that the temperature will be raised and maintained at the level determined by the thermostat.

Many people are like thermometers. They do what others do. They feel insecure if they are not playing the same game other people play. They don't make a contribution toward the betterment of life because they are too busy keeping up with the Joneses.

And don't think that being a thermometer is an innocent thing. Today's text has good reason for warning us not to conform to the world. For once you conform, the temporary fashion of the world becomes a tyrant which demands more and more sacrifices on the altar of status and prestige. When this tyrant rules your life, you will soon become deaf to the voice of God and blind to His blessings.

Pray that God will use this study of Romans 12 to make you a new person. You need no longer be passively pulled along by the forces around you and in you. You can have the courage and the freedom to be your own person by being God's person, by being what God intended you to be—His friend, His partner, His manager.

Let's explore that a bit further tomorrow.

Holy Spirit, make us sensitive to God's goals and standards for our life. We confess that we are often more concerned about what people think of us than what God thinks of us. Lord, give us more faith. Amen.

To Be Or Not to Be Transformed

Do not be conformed to this world but be transformed by the renewal of your mind, that you may prove what is the will of God, what is good and acceptable and perfect (Rom. 12:2).

Romans 12:2 says that I must be *transformed*.

What happens to me when I am transformed? Well, deep inside of me something happens. God's Holy Spirit reaches into my heart. He breaks the shackles that kept me chained to death. With cords of love He ties me to the heart of God. He does this for the sake of Jesus Christ, who died for my sins. He does this by using the Word of God which I accepted by faith. From now on my old greedy self is no longer in the driver's seat. *Christ* has taken over in me. My new inner self differs from my old inner self in the same way a butterfly differs from a caterpillar.

All this is only talk if I do not demonstrate it in my life. Today's text says that I must now "prove the will of God, what is good and acceptable and perfect." The meaning is clear. I must point out the way of salvation to people around me. I must hear the voice of the distressed, and I must announce the demands of God for society.

And all that will have results.

My personal transformation will transform life around me. A new dependability will mark my relationships, and my daily work will have a quality of thoroughness about it. This will soon enrich the lives of others around me. When many Christians do this together, there will be a transformation on a wider scale and the world will know that God is alive. The glow of hope will bring joy and goodness to many.

Holy God, fill me with new life. Teach me ever from the Bible how to share the new life with others. Use my godliness to bring healing in the land. For Jesus' sake. Amen.

Apostolic Authority

For by the grace given to me I bid every one among you . . . (Rom. 12:3).

Ministers and other church office-bearers have not gained in esteem these last several years. One critic stated, "Far from standing like lonely figures in the ship's prow, the clergy have tended to be found in far greater abundance on the poop deck."

Preachers have become very modest people these days. But none of that is found in the apostle Paul. He speaks here with great authority, "I bid every one among you . . ."

Paul had sound reason for this appeal to authority. He knew he had been commissioned by Jesus Christ. He also knew that the office of apostle was his by grace only. Increasingly, Paul recognized that his strength and conviction came from God only.

That's why Paul never misused his office. The more he became aware of the authority of his office, the harder he worked for Christ.

That is still so today. The appeal to authority is genuine only when it is accompanied by deep concern for the cause of Christ.

The great English preacher Hugh Latimer was once invited to preach in the Royal Chapel at London. On his way to the service a voice in him said, "Latimer, Latimer, be careful what you preach before the king of England." Then another voice spoke softly in his heart, "Latimer, Latimer, be careful what you preach before the King of kings . . ."

Sober observers of society will realize that the future does not look bright. Governments no longer control the course of events. Everywhere people grab what they can, everyone for himself. In the midst of chaos, our God speaks with authority, and His Word is our unwavering standard.

Lord Jesus, we thank You for office-bearers in the church through whom Your Word comes to us with a sovereign claim. Show us, Lord, that we personally are also mandated to be Your representatives! Make us willing and faithful. Amen.

Know Yourself

. . . I bid every one among you not to think of himself more highly than he ought to think, but to think with sober judgment, each according to the measure of faith which God has assigned him (Rom. 12:3).

In Romans 12 Paul says that God is the one who has given us our personal gifts, faith included. God Himself determines the *quantity* and the *quality* of these gifts. The variety is nearly endless. God measures them out carefully to each of His creatures. And He holds us responsible for using them to His honor and the well-being of our fellow man.

This means, therefore, that we must serve God with all our capacities. Christ taught this clearly in the parable of the talents (Matt. 25:14-30).

But at the same time it means that we must not try to do work for which we lack qualifications. "Think with sober judgment [about yourself], each according to the measure of faith which God has assigned to [you]," Paul says.

That sobriety should guide us in daily life. We must recognize our personal limitations. Pity the man who has worked his way into a position for which he is not fully qualified. He labors under fear and tension. He plays games with himself.

Let us remember that God is our Maker. He made no mistakes. He gave each of us a certain number of talents and gifts. If we live in deep dependence upon God, He will provide us with a task in life which is not beyond our ability.

Have you sized yourself up that way?

What a relief, really, what a freedom, to be able to be yourself! You don't have to out-do people around you in order to count; you don't have to impress others in order to make it. You can be yourself—the *self* God designed with special care.

Father, You know me; give me peace with who I am. Wash the poison of jealousy from my system. Help me to respect others for their gifts and to thank You for my own. For Jesus' sake. Amen.

All One Body We

For as in one body we have many members, and all the members do not have the same function, so we, though many, are one body in Christ, and individually members one of another (Rom. 12:4-5).

How does the church come into existence?

Some Christians teach that it involves the following steps: (1) the gospel comes to individual people, (2) some of these people accept the gospel, and (3) they decide to band together and form a church.

But that is not the picture in John 15. There Christ describes the church as a vine of which He is the stem and the believers are the branches. Big branches as well as new twigs owe their existence to the vine. God, the heavenly vinedresser, grafts other branches into the vine. These in turn owe their life to the vine.

The vine with its branches represents the church. There is a deep unity: the vine is there, and, through it, more branches and more fruit.

Romans 12 looks at the church that way. Paul compares the church to a human body. The foot, the hand, the nose, the ear—they all exist because of the body. Christians owe their faith to Christ's saving work which He accomplishes through the church.

This means three things for the believer.

(1) He is very humble because he knows God's goodness. The believer is like a child who one day is suddenly overcome with wonder as to why his adoptive parents showed so much love and concern.

(2) He has a deep sense of security. Once he belongs to God's family, he realizes that the Father and the brothers and the sisters won't let go of him anymore.

(3) He has a deep sense of responsibility. He is both motivated and replenished to do good things for the entire body of believers.

We are so grateful, Lord Jesus, that You have made us part of the body of believers. Help us to serve our brothers and sisters in the faith. Reach out to others, Lord, through us. Amen.

Gifts That Differ

Having gifts that differ according to the grace given to us, let us use them . . . (Rom. 12:6).

In Romans 12 Paul discusses seven important gifts which believers receive from the Lord. But before he does that, he makes an important observation about gifts. He tells us that "gifts differ according to the grace given to us . . ."

How must we understand this?

Well, first we learn that believers have one great gift *in common*—the gift of *grace*. That gift is the salvation they receive because of God's goodness and mercy. The early Christians called that gift of grace *charis*.

Now we read that from that one gift of grace *a variety of other gifts* sprang forth. And those gifts differed a great deal among believers. Their qualities and interests were not all the same. The early Christians called those gifts *charismata*, confessing that these gifts were theirs by the grace of God.

Today we praise God for the wonderful gifts He has entrusted to us. They are something like a pipe organ. The wide range of size and quality of pipes makes a rich harmony of music possible. Thus, every believer is equipped to make his own special contribution toward building the church of Christ. But those who believe must not exercise their gifts because of pride. A believer uses his gifts joyfully, knowing they have come by grace alone.

During the next seven days we will discuss these seven gifts. We will discover that we don't each have these gifts in the same measure. But we will also discover that when there is love in the brotherhood, every one of us will profit from these gifts, either as a giver or a receiver. And in the Kingdom of heaven, a receiver will always become a giver, for gifts may never go unused.

Lord, we are grateful for the grace by which we became children of God. Help us now to use the gifts of grace to bless others around us. And bless us, too, as we benefit from the gifts our brothers and sisters in Christ have received. In Him. Amen.

The Gift of Prophecy

. . . [If our gift is] prophecy, [let it be] in proportion to our faith (Rom. 12:6).

In the next several verses of Romans 12, Paul lists seven gifts God gives His children. The first one he mentions is the gift of *prophecy*.

One recent Bible translation chooses the word *preaching* instead of *prophecy*. This is correct, for that's what prophecy is all about: *telling people about God and His will for man's life*. This can be done from a pulpit, but also from the seat of a bus.

Does that sound unlikely? At a given moment you may be led to share God's love with another. If so, you take the position of prophet. Then be sure it is the Word of God you are sharing; tell only what you know by faith and experience to be true. Paul says: "[let it be] in proportion to our faith."

Sermons must keep pace with the faith and understanding of the listeners. A pastor must not preach over the heads of his people, yet he must challenge them with the richness of God's Word. He must not adorn his pulpit with fancy theories but with the simple Word of God.

Dr. Peter Eldersveld, for many years minister of the *Back to God Hour* radio, once stated, "Put the food down low, so the lambs can reach it. It won't hurt the sheep to stoop a little. Sermons must be as real as a child's world. Such sermons will cut down men to the size of children spiritually, so that they can enter the Kingdom of heaven" (Mark 10:15).

Holy Spirit, make us better prophets. Help us experience the blessings of salvation personally and share them with others. May the gospel preached in the churches today be unmistakably clear, pointing people to sin, repentance, and forgiveness. We pray in the power of the Master. Amen.

The Gift of Service

. . . [If] service, [let it be] in our serving (Rom. 12:7).

The second gift which Paul mentions is *service*. Note that well. Service is a *gift*. It is a privilege to serve. Why? Because that's how we resemble the Master. His whole life was marked by *servanthood*. In Philippians 2:7-8, we read that Christ laid aside the glory of heaven and "taking the form of a servant . . . he humbled himself and became obedient unto death, even death on a cross."

That's why His being a servant was so important. Our eternal life depended on it. His servanthood was the very secret of His victory over hell and damnation for us.

And that's what makes service the secret of our Christian life. In Galatians 2:20 Paul says, "I have been crucified with Christ: it is no longer I who live, but Christ who lives in me."

Service is still the hallmark of Christian living. We resemble the Master most gloriously when we live for others, help them, and care for them.

Some years ago, a writer in the devotional booklet *Today* told about a church gathering where General William Booth of the Salvation Army was scheduled to speak. The general took ill, however, and therefore had a copy of his speech delivered for someone else to read. That speech was probably the shortest ever written. It contained just one word: "others."

The sensitive ear hears the mournful wail of the hopeless around the globe. Believers who are serious about God's will for their lives will earnestly covet the gift of service rather than the pursuit of material gain.

Dear Jesus, compassionate High Priest, make us willing to hear the suffering and understand the needy. Show us clearly by which motives we live. Take the trinkets out of our hands so that we can touch others. May others see Your mercy in us. Amen.

The Gift of Teaching

. . . [he] who teaches, [let him practice that gift] in his teaching (Rom. 12:7).

The third gift which the apostle mentions here is *teaching*. It is a very important part of the church's total ministry in which the members share.

Teaching is important for a number of reasons.

First, because Christianity is a *historical* religion, it is based on *facts* which happened, *events* which took place. Some of these events are the following: God's creation, man's fall into sin, the death and resurrection of Christ, and the work of the Holy Spirit. The church must proclaim these facts. Without teaching, there can be no communication of the faith. Pastors must proclaim these facts in their sermons. Members must be ready to communicate these events to people they get to know. That's why Christ gave the church the gift of teaching.

The second reason why teaching is an important gift is that Christianity is a *way of life*. The Christian faith must be worked out in daily practice, in personal experience and conduct. How is the believer to express his Christian commitment? It takes searching, study, reflection, and reading. That's why Christ gave some believers the gift of teaching. They must guide the church in the Christian walk of life.

Christ Himself shows the way; He was the great Teacher sent from God. His skill with precept and example is a challenge to those possessing the gift of teaching. Often as they teach the Christian way of life, teachers experience a special need of forgiveness. Jesus' own example was always as good as His precepts. Teachers depend on the long-suffering Christ.

Some people plead for more action, fellowship and experiences. That is good, as long as *teaching* the Word occupies the central place.

Holy Spirit, keep us from underestimating the calling of teaching. Lead us into a deeper understanding of the faith. Lord, thank You for the Bible. May we help each other to understand it more fully. Amen.

The Gift of Exhortation

. . . [he] who exhorts, [must show it] in his exhortation (Rom. 12:8).

The fourth gift which Paul mentions is that of *exhortation*. Webster's Dictionary explains that *to exhort* means to urge earnestly by advice, to admonish strongly.

This reflects the meaning of *exhort* in the original language. An exhorter pleads with people because he is concerned about their well-being. An exhorter is something like a sheep dog rounding up a flock of sheep. He is like a mother hen who appears to be upset as she gathers her chicks when danger threatens.

There is something entirely selfless about the activity of exhorting. An exhorter enters into the situation of the people entrusted to his care. He understands their situation. He comforts, he encourages, he helps, he prods, he advises, he guides, he rebukes, and he corrects. But he does all this in love, with disarming kindness.

Exhortation is a vanishing art these days. People want to do their own thing without interference from others. That's because so many don't want to have anything to do with moral rules anymore. They don't want to talk about good or bad; they just want to enjoy themselves and be left alone. They don't see that they are on a collision course. They are blind. But thanks be to Christ, He equipped Christians with the gift of exhortation. The exhorter *sees* very clearly. That's why he is so concerned about people stumbling around in moral darkness. Such exhorters can't help being totally honest, for they want to *save*. Actually, all Christians have this gift to some extent. And they can develop it. When someone today needs a word from you, don't withhold it.

Holy Spirit, help us to express the goodness of our God among men everywhere. Help us to give with Christian cheer in the name of Christ Jesus. For His name's sake. Amen.

The Gift of Generosity

. . . he who contributes, [let him do so] in liberality . . . (Rom. 12:8).

The fifth gift mentioned in Romans 12 is the gift of *giving*. Praise God for the gift of generosity! For it is this gift that enables us to express our *resemblance* to our heavenly Father. Our God is a giving God. He made the world and *gave* it to man. He endowed man with precious gifts of heart and mind. He *gave* His Son. The Son *gave* Himself to save His people from hell. God poured out His Spirit upon the church.

Made in the image of God, gifted contributors imitate His giving. *He* gave to bring glory to God the Father; so must they. *He* gave with the love of His whole heart; so must they. Gift giving is an expression of gratitude for Christ's love; it is a token of God's liberality.

The art of giving can be developed and cultivated. You can learn it by just doing it. Giving always brings joy in its wake. Giving grows on you. It demonstrates that you are not a slave of things.

Interestingly, modern psychology has discovered the benefits of generosity. At a meeting of business executives, Dr. Karl Menninger was asked how to prevent a nervous breakdown. He answered, "Turn the key in your door, walk across the tracks, find someone in need and be of help, and you will probably ward off a nervous breakdown."

Long ago Jesus knew that secret, but He knew that in order to be lasting, the motive behind such an act must be more than self-therapy and more than humanitarianism. It must be an act for God, done for His honor, out of His love.

Holy Spirit, help us to express the goodness of our God among men everywhere. Help us to give with Christian cheer in the name of Christ Jesus. For His name's sake. Amen.

The Gift of Leadership

. . . he who gives aid, [should do it] with zeal . . . (Rom. 12:8 RSV).
. . . he that ruleth, [let him do it] with diligence . . . (Rom. 12:8 KJV).

You will find that the King James Version of the Bible quotes today's text as "he that ruleth, [let him do it] with diligence." When we remember that Jesus said: "He who is greatest among you shall be your servant" (Matt. 23:11), we see that the two translations are really alike. According to Christ, the one who rules is the one who gives aid.

Good leadership is of tremendous value. That's why great leaders are remembered. The English statesman William Pitt possessed amazing leadership gifts. He inspired his ministers with vision and courage and rallied them behind a common cause.

The church, too, has an indispensable need of good leadership. The Bible describes the church as a living body of which Christ is the head (I Cor. 12:12-31). Church leaders must learn from this description. The head never rules the body rigidly, but coordinates each function, integrating every activity into a harmonious whole. So a leader in the church must respect the members and encourage them to express their faith spontaneously.

Such interested and devoted leaders help the church avoid two extremes: that of holding to authority too rigidly and that of abandoning authority completely. Rather than leaving everything to each individual's insight, the gifted leader will help to draw all of the insights into the perfect rule of Christ. With God-given zeal for Christ and His church, the leader prayerfully comes to its aid.

This gift of leadership finds an echo in the hearts of all Christian believers because it makes an appeal to their sense of responsibility. And they are responsible people because they are made in God's image. God established a covenant with them.

Christian authority always produces harmonious growth: those who receive leadership hand it on in the form of mutual aid and concern for each other.

Lord, give to the church leaders who bring out the full potential of the church. Bless those who have the oversight over us. May all our church activities be marked by understanding. For Jesus' sake. Amen.

The Gift of Mercy

. . . he who does acts of mercy, [let him do them] with cheerfulness (Rom. 12:8).

The last gift which Paul mentions in these verses of Romans 12 is *mercy*. Paul is very concerned that the Christians of Rome be merciful for the right reasons. He knows that it is very human to practice mercy for reasons of pride or selfishness. That type of mercy, as we know from our day, accomplishes nothing and is short-lived. It can even be cruel (Prov. 12:10).

In our city one used to be able to dial a telephone number and listen to a message of cheer, encouragement and sympathy—a different one each day. One day calling that number produced nothing but a matter-of-fact announcement: "The number you have dialed is no longer in service." This could almost be called typical of the programed mercy we see today.

Paul's advice is simple, but urgent. Practice mercy with *cheerfulness*. That takes real compassion and sympathy. We can do that only when something has happened to us. We must have seen our own misery from which Christ saved us by His suffering and death. Only when Christ's love compels us are we ready to show mercy to the distressed.

Mercy has three enemies; all three lurk in our hearts. The first one is called *Condition*. He demands that the person to whom we show mercy be cooperative and prove himself worthy of our mercy.

The second one is called *Reservation*. He sees to it that our mercy flows in a sensible trickle. After all, we have many obligations.

The third enemy, named *Result*, cautions us to be sure that our help produces quick solutions. Too bad, but there are just a lot of hopeless cases.

Paul is prepared to defeat these enemies. We will see that tomorrow.

Thank You, Lord Jesus, for saving us in Your mercy when we were totally unworthy of it. Holy Spirit create in us the mind of Christ. May we with grateful hearts share the mercy of the Master. Amen.

Love

Let love be genuine; hate what is evil, hold fast to what is good; love one another with brotherly affection; outdo one another in showing honor (Rom. 12:9-10).

The philosophical Greeks of Paul's day had many theories about *love*. For them love was always *conditional*. They loved those who favored them and who earned their love. Christ came with a totally different concept of love. He sought and saved those who were *unworthy of His love*. He loved those who were unlovable.

Christians should follow the example of their Master. They should love without seeking reward, without setting conditions, and without fear of what will happen if their love is rejected. This is the kind of love the Bible is speaking about in Romans 12, "Let love be genuine."

The practice of such love is no easy assignment. Practicing such love is especially difficult because, as Paul says, it must be expressed in every situation of life: in fighting evil, in showing affection, and even by "outdoing each other in showing honor."

What an impossible assignment! What a mysterious thing love is! I can summon myself to diligence, even to a measure of courage, but can I marshal *love* at will? Can I force myself to produce it? Can I make myself experience love? The key to the answer to this baffling question lies in the word Paul uses to describe love—*genuine*. "Let love be genuine." This points to the origin of love: it comes from God through Christ. He Himself is the source of love. And it becomes ours when we confess Christ as Savior and daily accept His presence in us by the working of the Holy Spirit. Ask Him for it; let Him rule over your heart.

Teilhard de Chardin, though not always a dependable guide, once said, "Someday when we have learned to harness the wind, the waves and the tide, we will harness the power of the love of God. Then, for the second time, man will have discovered fire."

O Savior God, by love we were saved. Help us now to walk in that love. Purify our love, Holy Spirit. Make us strong in hating what is evil. For Jesus' sake. Amen.

The Vigorous Life

Never flag in zeal, be aglow with the Spirit, serve the Lord (Rom. 12:11).

Psychologists and educators often talk about the importance of *motivation*. They know that in order to reach a goal, a person must be excited about it and must feel that it is useful. Many people have little motivation because life seems senseless and is full of frustrations.

But Romans 12:11 calls men to *vital living*. It says, "Never flag in zeal," because there is work to be done. Life makes sense. Christ brings restoration through His victory and He renews our lives. He wants to share all this with the world through people like us. And that's why Paul calls us to serve Him.

Or did you think that it takes heroes of faith to do that—and not a person such as you? Well, then you will be interested to learn that both the Old and New Testaments give examples of famous believers who collapsed under the weight of their hopelessness. The one outstanding example in the Old Testament is Elijah, who wanted to die under the juniper tree (I Kings 19). In the New Testament we have the example of the apostle Paul, who cried, "Wretched man that I am!" (Rom. 7:24). Modern man echoes that despair. Ian Fleming sighed, "I am now ashes; you have no idea how bored one gets with this whole business of living." But that's where the all-important difference comes in. The prophet Elijah surrendered to the Lord. The Lord showed him not to trust the spectacular powers of the world but the "still small voice" of the Spirit. The apostle Paul had to learn not to rely on human knowledge but on Christ's Spirit. Only then could he urge us to "be aglow with the Spirit."

The Spirit knows no favorites. He will gladly make your heart His workshop. That's His specialty. Then you, too, will have new power, and you, too, can have vitality and vigor. "Be aglow with the Spirit!" What motivation to serve!

Lord, we pray for a new measure of power from Your Spirit. Give us complete dedication and obedience to the Master. We have shied away from facing problems that have been nagging us. Help us to be realistic in Christ. Amen.

The Joy of Hope

Rejoice in your hope, be patient in tribulation . . . (Rom. 12:12).

Above all else, the apostle Paul was a practical man. In today's verse he speaks of two things: *hope* and *tribulation*. Paul knew that tribulation knocks hope to pieces. Hopelessness is the most crippling disease that plagues mankind. Whittaker Chambers once put it this way, speaking for many: "I have been to the funeral of all my hopes. I have buried them one by one."

The special thing about the Christian gospel is that it brings hope. Hope is the conviction that whatever happens, Christ is in control. It takes much Bible reading, much prayer, and much practice of godliness to make hope strong. If hope is strong, patience in trial can be learned, for "who shall separate us from the love of Christ?" (Rom. 8:35).

Paul was not unrealistic. He did not engage in religious double-talk. Paul knew that the Christians in Rome faced a dark future which would bring martyrdom to many. But beyond the valley of darkness Paul saw the dawn of victory. That victory was real to Paul because he knew that the death of Good Friday has been overcome by the life of Easter Sunday.

You are invited to live close to the Savior. Then you will experience that Christian hope keeps your life afloat no matter what the future may bring. It allows you inner joy. With it you are a rich person. Paul makes this outright command: "Rejoice in your hope!"

In that hope Christians have done amazing things. As he stood bound at the stake, the English reformer Hugh Lattimer said, "Be of good cheer, Master Ridley. By the grace of God we shall this day light such a candle in England as shall never be put out." And so it was!

Lord Jesus, instill in our hearts a deep awareness of Your victory over the powers of darkness. Without the hope of resurrection we cannot live. Help us to experience its joy. Amen.

The Prayer Vigil

. . . be constant in prayer (Rom. 12:12).

The fourth century church father St. Augustine wrote a book he called his *Confessions*. That book must be understood as a prayer to God. Recounting the crippling power of sin from which by grace God saved him was like lifting his heart to God in thankful confession. It was prayer.

How can we ever find words sufficient to extol the virtues of prayer?

Prayer gives us reassurance, comfort, courage, and direction. It is a power line to heaven through which our strength is replenished. It is the way we experience that God is our Father in Jesus Christ.

The entire twelfth chapter of Romans pictures a dynamic Christianity affecting every facet of our lives. How can we be equal to its challenge? Paul throws the windows to heaven open. He tells us that we can meet the challenge of a Christian life only when we draw Christ into our life by prayer.

Prayer underlies the Christian life. And although we struggle when the finite and infinite meet in prayer, it is not a hesitant God we pray to, but a willing God. Bishop Trench explained it this way: "Prayer is not overcoming God's reluctance; it is laying hold of God's highest willingness." Have you experienced that?

Our fathers used to say, "Ora et Labora"—Pray and Work. So much of our daily work goes wrong because we don't pray fervently; so much of our prayer goes wrong because we don't work.

Holy Spirit, help us to be much more faithful in our prayer life. Draw us back to a close contact with our Savior. Lord Jesus, purify our prayers, because they are so imperfect. We pray for the world of which we are part. Have mercy, Father, on the many who suffer. Amen.

Helpfulness

Contribute to the needs of the saints . . . (Rom. 12:13).

Help the saints! That's the message of today's text. There are two things that the text does not mean. The word *saints* does not refer to people without sin, but to people who are forgiven. And the text does not imply that Christians should care only for fellow Christians; they must help *everyone* in need (Luke 10:30-7).

What does the text mean, then? Well, Romans 12 pictures believers *as members of one body*. And now the members are asked to help each other. That request is simple but embarrassing. For isn't it a shame that the Lord has to remind us to help each other? Christians often worry themselves so blind about their own well-being that they don't see each other's needs. They should feel the pain of their brother's poverty. That's why the Christians of Acts 2 shared things, and sharing gave them "glad and generous hearts, praising God and having favor with all the people" (Acts 2:46-7). But in today's world, the gap between rich and poor Christians is widening.

Then it may be true for us as it was of the early Christians: "And the Lord added to their number day by day those who were being saved" (Acts 2:47). When the body functions properly among its several members, it can begin to meet the needs of the world around it effectively. For then it commands God's blessing.

So then, it is our generosity which strengthens bridges between saints and saints, and builds new ones to sinners. Should you classify yourself among the saints—and you should for Jesus' sake—then remember nevertheless that it was God "who loved you, the sub-man, into a saint," as someone put it.

That process still goes on. Isn't it tremendous to be part of it?

Dear God, we express our thanks for Jesus Christ who brought healing and relief while He was on this earth among us. Use us now, Lord, to display that same compassion so that many who now suffer may know that Christ rules. Amen.

Our Home Our Castle?

. . . practice hospitality (Rom. 12:13).

Paul's request here seems agreeable enough: open your home and entertain people. But it is not quite that simple. Paul wrote in days of stress and strain for the Christian church. People were on the move everywhere because of persecution. Refugees arrived in Rome continually. Paul asked the Christians of Rome to take these people in. They came—poor, upset, and tired. They needed help and understanding. Such hospitality might be risky, inconvenient, and even costly. It involved sharing everything with people who had nowhere to go.

Is such outgoing generosity still our strength today? To be sure, every family needs privacy. But is it Biblical to call our homes our castles as we sometimes do? Christians are still being persecuted; wars and famines rage in many places; children are left uncared for; and everywhere people are on the move, unable to face the perplexities of modern life. Do we have hearts big enough to care about the uprooted people around us?

Hebrews 13 urges us to follow the example of the ancients who emphasized hospitality and because of it sometimes unknowingly welcomed angels into their homes. That is an exciting idea often capitalized on by story writers. Unless we are busy doing good, nothing good happens to us or to the world around us. We leave nothing for God to bless. Christ followed that tradition. Hospitality meant everything to Him, probably because He depended upon it so much Himself. He once said that taking a stranger in is the same as taking *Him* in (Matt. 25:35).

On my desk lies a letter from a pastor to his congregation in Edmonton. He alerts the members to their obligations toward the many people who come to Alberta in hope of benefiting from the oil boom. He urges them to take note of their needs even though some have come to Alberta with not the best of motives. He asks them to open their homes, their church, their hearts to the many newcomers. Yes, in Romans 12 Paul means hospitality to be that real and that practical.

Help us, Lord, to share the riches of our hearts and homes with those who are sad and lonely. For Jesus' sake. Amen.

Don't Hit Back

Bless those who persecute you; bless and do not curse them (Rom. 12:14).

Paul has taught the church of Rome how to live together as Christians. Now, in today's verse, the apostle opens the windows upon the world around them. It was not a pretty world. Christians were hated everywhere; they suffered persecution. And Paul tells these Christians that they must *bless* their enemies.

Persecution takes place when Christians witness to their faith in words and deeds. So today, in one form or another, Christians experience persecution. And our Bible still says: "bless and do not curse." Is Paul asking the impossible here? No, for he immediately opens a second window, a window upon *Christ*. The sermons of Christ form the important background of Paul's words (Matt. 5:10-11, 44; Luke 6:28).

That has a very important background.

Because of our sins, we deserve the curse of God. But Christ bears that curse for those who accept Him as Savior. That's why Christians are *through with cursing*. When they suffer abuse, they look upon Christ who suffered abuse because of them. Jesus prayed for those who crucified Him. Stephen followed that example and prayed for his murderers (Acts 7); so did John Huss, the great Bohemian reformer, who was burned at the stake.

You stand in a great tradition when you forgive those who hurt you. But it is not easy. You can do it only in the power of the Master.

Does all this still seem a bit far-fetched to you? If so, remember that the key idea of today's text is *acceptance*. And acceptance begins deep within your own heart. You must accept yourself; you must come to terms with yourself. And from there you must accept the people with whom you associate daily, at home and at work. Most of your anger is often directed at your own person and those whom you should call "your loved ones." Begin this exercise of love and acceptance there. Only from that platform can you come to terms with your tormentors afar.

Lord, give us grace to forgive whenever we feel wronged. Help us not to be overcome by anger. Instill in us peace and strength so that we can minister to people in need, even though some of them may be very disagreeable to us. Amen.

Multiplying Joy

Rejoice with those who rejoice . . . (Rom. 12:15).

The Christian church has always confessed that joy is an important part of Christian life. When the Westminster Assembly received the first draft of the Westminster Confession, the delegates rejected it because they missed the tone of Christian joy. Only when this was corrected was the famous confession adopted (1649).

Yesterday we read that the Christians of Rome had their share of troubles. But now Paul tells them that they must be joyful nevertheless. And because joy is so scarce in this sad world, Paul advises them to s-t-r-e-t-c-h it. Christians must know each others' joys; they must experience them together. That way joy is doubled and tripled. When scores of Christians do that together, the church will witness a chain reaction of joy. In fact, such joy slips across church fences and touches people everywhere (Matt. 5:46).

The early Christians had the reputation of being joyful people. There was something very winsome about them. Their joy was probably a big factor in their evangelical success.

To share joy is Christ-like. It was worth it to Christ to endure the cross so that He could share the joy of heaven with us. Think of Jesus, think of all that He is, think that you belong to Him—and then "Lift up your heart; lift up your voice; Rejoice!"

Rejoice in glorious hope;
    Jesus, the Judge, shall come,
And take His servants up
    To their eternal home.
We soon shall hear th' archangel's voice,
    The trump of God shall sound, Rejoice!

Holy Spirit, giver of joy, help us to rejoice with others around us. Help us to understand and to accept the joy of our fellow man. For Jesus' sake. Amen.

The Ministry of Comfort

. . . weep with those who weep (Rom. 12:15).

Some people weep at night, but no one knows about it, for they smile in the daytime. Some people don't know how to weep anymore because they are defeated. Sorrow has a firm grip on mankind today.

Paul tells us to weep with the weeping. He does not tell us here how we can do it. But in the letter to the Corinthians, Paul explains that God comforts us so that we may be able to comfort others—not just in any way, but "with the comfort with which we ourselves are comforted by God." Christ is our comfort.

Christian believers are close to one another because they are close to Christ, members of His body. Christ understands sorrow fully. He once said: "My soul is very sorrowful, even unto death" (Mark 14:34). Christ bore the weight of our burdens all alone. As His followers, we share the burdens of our fellows.

When we live close to Christ, we resemble Him in some respects (Eph. 4:13; Gal. 2:20). The more we love Christ, the more we love people. As we express this love, we can begin to understand something of the grief of others. In that Christian love, we can comfort them. We are then able to weep with the weeping.

Toward the end of his life, the well-known preacher F. B. Meyer said: "If I could do my life's work over again, I would spend more time in the ministry of comfort."

Note that he said: "spend more time." Take some *time* for people who need you. It's time well spent. Perhaps that's the essence of the ministry of comfort: have time for each other. Life is short. Lengthen yours by sharing time with sad people.

Dear Lord, give us the strength and the desire to experience something of the sadness of the people we meet. Help us to comfort them with the comfort we have in Christ to sincerely share their burdens. Amen.

The Test of Harmony

Live in harmony with one another; do not be haughty, but associate with the lowly; never be conceited (Rom. 12:16).

Today's message deals with *harmony*.

Harmony combines into one the ideals of peace, agreement, appreciation, and togetherness.

Harmony leads a frail existence in today's broken world. People are callous to each other, interest groups clash in society, and the nations distrust each other. But worst of all, the Christian church itself is fragmented. Thousands of pages have been written about church unity, but little of it has led to real healing.

Today's text puts the finger on the real sore.

There will be no harmony in the church as long as there is no harmony in our hearts. Paul suggests a little test which will indicate whether we are sincere about our search for unity. He asks us: Do you associate with the lowly? Or in today's language: Do you respect the little guy? Do you treat people with sincere kindness? Do you show humble courtesy to those who are less important than you are?

Every little act of conceit adds to the reef on which the ship of home and church breaks to pieces. That's why Paul bluntly states: "Never be conceited."

Christ taught harmony. He told us to be like little children, quite free of envy and spite, open to suggestion, and friendly even to the passer-by. Had Christ carried an air of conceit about Him, He would not have gathered such large crowds when He walked this earth. The Lord of glory humbled Himself to bring harmony among us conceited sinners.

In Christ may we learn to live in harmony so that we may raise one voice of praise to God (Rom. 15:5).

Holy Spirit, guide us in the meek and lowly way our Savior walked. Remind us that each person is the crowning work of God's creation. Unite the redeemed in praise, we pray. To God's glory. Amen.

Evil: Too Big to Handle

Repay no one evil for evil, but take thought for what is noble in the sight of all (Rom. 12:17).

After three young men were expelled from a dance hall in Montreal, they set what they thought would be a harmless little fire in the hallway of that building just to scare the doorman. That little fire turned into an uncontrollable blaze in which some thirty people met their death.

That tragedy illustrates the message of today's text. Don't fight evil with evil. Once you set evil going, you cannot control its disaster course. The history of warfare illustrates this grimly. Evil is just too big for mortals to handle. It devours its own children. Use it as a weapon, and it will turn upon you in growing fury.

Evil cannot simply be pushed aside, for it will push back. Instead, something good must fill its place. The Philippian Christians were advised: "Whatever is true . . . whatever is pure, whatever is lovely . . . if there is any excellence . . . anything worthy of praise, think about these things" (Phil. 4:8).

The gospel is the only guide that teaches us how to cope with evil. God placed the world's evil upon His Son Jesus Christ. Christ paid for the sins of those who accept Him as Savior. That's how evil is dispelled from human lives. There is no other way. Don't nurse a grudge or avenge yourself. Put the injuries which others inflict upon you into the hands of Christ. That's where evil stops.

Christianity is a totally *selfless* religion. It is always directed away from the self and is always oriented toward doing good for others. But the amazing thing is that the more a Christian gives, the richer of heart and mind he becomes.

True happiness is to be what God intended you to be. He made you a giver.

Thank you, Jesus, for rendering good for evil while You were on our earth. Live in our hearts and make us Your imitators. May our meekness and patience be real and true. For Christ't sake. Amen.

The Blessings of Peace

If possible, so far as depends upon you, live peaceably with all (Rom. 12:18).

Paul holds up the peace sign here. "Live peaceably," he says. Paul does not deny that people around us may cause friction. But as far as *we* are concerned, he says, let us keep peace with all people. If we can keep peace without compromising with evil, we must do so. Paul often enjoined believers to live in love, forgiving each other. Peace is a result of forgiveness. Christ taught that peacemakers would be called sons of God (Matt. 5:9).

Here in Romans 12, Paul has two important reasons for requesting us to be peacemakers.

Peace is a mighty concept in the Bible. Peace exists when every obstacle between God and man is removed. You have true peace when you walk and talk with your God. Peace is the very purpose for which God made you. Thus Paul zeroes in at the meaning of life itself: be what God wants you to be!

The second reason Paul urges you to live in peace is an *evangelistic* one. If your life expresses peace, you will draw people who are beset by conflicts and turmoil. Your peace enables them to confide in you and to discuss their problems with you. They will welcome your advice and help. Can you think of a more favorable situation in which to lead someone to the Prince of Peace?

Don't underestimate this peace mission which God gave you. The apostle James surveyed the situation of his day, saw wars everywhere, and wondered in consternation where all the fighting came from. Then, guided by the Spirit, he saw individuals such as you and me, and he stated point-blank: "It is because of the war and lust in your hearts." Peace around us, therefore, depends on peace within us.

Lord Jesus, help us to experience the peace of God which is ours through the blood of the cross. Help us to share it with our fellow man. Holy Spirit, give us the spiritual power to create an atmosphere of peace in which others may be won for Christ. Amen.

God Himself Will Settle It

Beloved, never avenge yourselves, but leave it to the wrath of God; for it is written, "Vengeance is mine, I will repay, says the Lord" (Rom. 12:19).

Have you ever been victimized badly by someone? Then you know how hard it is *not* to be overcome by bitterness. Then you also know how hard it is to forgive.

Some years ago the people of the Italian town of Marzobotto voted on a proposal by the Justice Department whether or not to release from their local prison a German Nazi major who had killed three hundred of their town's people. The outcome was grim for the major: 282 of the 288 people voted *no*.

Who would dare to criticize the people of that town? To forgive is super-human. Forgiveness starts with God. He gave His Son to pay for the foul deeds of people everywhere. Only in the power of God's forgiving love can we understand Paul's request in Romans 12: "Never avenge yourselves."

Does that mean that you must let people walk all over you? No, for God is a God of justice. Today's text tells us to leave the wrong you may have suffered to the *wrath of God*. He will settle injustice in His own time—some of it now, some of it later, and some of it on the judgment day.

There is a holy tension in this verse of Romans 12. On the one hand there is the struggle of self-denial: never avenge yourself. We all know the power of angry indignation when we have been wronged or ill-treated. On the other hand there is something very relaxing about God's command here. When God is your Father, you can afford to take the long view. You can wait; you can hope; you can discuss things with God; you need not be nervous or fret.

Isn't it wonderful to be freed from your own feelings of bitterness?

Father, assure us again that evil will not triumph in the end. Help us not to be overcome by anger. Vindicate those, Lord, who suffer injustice on the earth. For Christ's sake. Amen.

Save Your Enemy

No, "if your enemy is hungry, feed him; if he is thirsty, give him drink; for by so doing you will heap burning coals upon his head" (Rom. 12:20).

Romans 12 is filled with difficult requests, but this tops them all. It is not enough to leave your tormentor alone; it is not enough to leave vengeance to the Lord. No, we must actually shower him with mercy and goodness.

What could be behind a request such as this? Christianity itself. You see, we are totally unworthy of our salvation, and we are also totally unworthy of the many blessings God showers upon us daily. Therefore Christians must bless those who hurt them.

But Paul has another reason. He is always thinking in terms of winning people for Christ. Your sin-hardened tormentor may fear neither God nor man, but your practical Christian love may just find a hole in his armament. Pity the thirsty hangman who is given a drink by his victim. Such Christian generosity is like putting burning coals on someone's head, Paul suggests.

Paul uses forceful language in today's text. He paints an extreme situation: your outright enemy is suddenly at your mercy, and what are you to do? But harder on your nerves, perhaps, is the person whom you could not call your enemy but who is still obnoxious to you, who gets under your skin day after day in the office. Paul tells us not to be obnoxious in return, for you will then sink to his level and will suffer damage to your soul. It all amounts to one question: What is victory? Is it that you get even with a disagreeable person at work? No, victory is that you take your disagreeable feelings to your Father in heaven.

Lord, fill our hearts with love and forbearance toward those who seek our harm. And may this light from above shine in their darkness. Holy Spirit, grant us the grace to follow Christ. Amen.

The Grand Finale

Do not be overcome by evil, but overcome evil with good (Rom. 12:21).

The last verse of Romans 12 is short and sober, but it is the capstone of the Christian faith.

Consider the record. God created man and the world for Himself. Man was to devote his life on earth to his heavenly Father. All that was ruined. How? By evil. Evil is that ugly force of satan by which he set man up against God in heaven. Evil spoiled the very purpose for which man was made.

But God has the last word. His Son Jesus Christ triumphed over satan. He broke the power of evil. At the return of Christ, evil will be completely expelled from the earth and heaven and earth will be united into one glorious new creation. By fighting evil today, we may have a foretaste of that great future.

Romans 12 is echoed in Revelation 22, the very last chapter of the Bible. In verse 11 of that chapter, the good and righteous are encouraged to persevere in their goodness. Romans 12 is one big challenge to live the goodness of Christ every day from morning to night. It takes a lot of faith to recognize in the ringing of the alarm clock the trumpet call of Christ to holy action for Him. Sometimes we feel tired and discouraged. Then we long for the end. Revelation 22 teaches us to pray for the speedy return of Christ. And Christ responds by saying, "Surely I am coming soon." Until then we ask our Father for strength to do good, the good that overcomes evil. Don't lose heart; your goodness will produce a whole lot of restoration in God's world before Christ's return.

Holy triune God, accept our praise for the triumph of our Savior over the forces of satan. Restore us to a life of joyful service. Bless, Lord, the meditations of this month. Grant us this day a foretaste of the great sabbath to come. We pray for the speedy return of our Lord. Amen.

Prayer for a Blessing

"I will not let you go, unless you bless me" (Gen. 32:26).

This month let's talk about prayer.

Do you have a good prayer life? Do you have problems with your prayers? Do you believe that God hears your prayers? Do you wonder sometimes whether asking God for things will annoy Him? Do you have the feeling that prayer seems to be a one-way street—you talk but no one hears? Do you think that prayer "changes things"? And does it make you feel better? After each "amen," you face the same problems in life again. Perhaps your prayers have become mechanical, not truly alive, not truly born of faith. And if you believe little, you ask little, and if you ask little, you expect little, and if you expect little, you pray little. A vicious circle is the result. In the meantime our lives become cluttered, and that frustrates our prayers still further.

The life of Jacob illustrates this for us (Genesis 28-33). Surely he was a believer, but he made mistakes, schemed, and floundered. Finally his life became so complicated that he was stuck on all sides. Did prayer help in that situation? Well, one night Jacob met God and they wrestled together. In the end, Jacob broke down before God. That was the most wholesome experience Jacob ever had. And it immediately bore fruit. One strong prayer welled up from Jacob's heart: "I will not let you go, unless you bless me." God answered that prayer: "And there he blessed Jacob" (vs. 29).

There are no two people alike, and our circumstances differ from Jacob's. But we may firmly believe that God is deeply concerned about every detail in our life, so we bring everything to God in prayer. We must first break down before Him and hand Him the reins of our life, for only then can we pray that most fundamental prayer, "O God, bless us." Standing on that blessing we can ask Him to provide in the affairs of the day.

O God in heaven, You seem to be so far away at times. Renew in us the certainty that You are near to us in Christ, our Savior. Forgive us our sins of doubt. Bless, Lord, our prayers. Assure us again that You will truly hear our prayers. Give us a deep desire to commune with You truly through the power of the Holy Spirit. For Jesus' sake. Amen.

Prayer for Unworthy People

"O Lord God, destroy not thy people and thy heritage, whom thou hast redeemed through thy greatness" (Deut. 9:26).

Today's text gives a remarkable insight into Moses' spiritual caliber. He prayed for forty days and forty nights.

What urgent matter prompted this prayer marathon?

Sin!

The people had rejected God. Only a few years before, God had liberated them from Egypt. But they forgot quickly and followed false gods. Then the Lord told Moses that He had given up on the people.

Moses immediately recognized the dreadful consequences. There was only one course open to him. Moses secluded himself with God for forty days. Moses prayed. He begged God to have mercy on His rebellious people. We call this kind of prayer *intercessory prayer*, because he prayed for his people and prayed for the salvation of millions of people after him.

God heard Moses' prayer. He accepted the people back in His grace, and many years later Christ was born from those people. His coming was the fruit of Moses' prayers.

Christ's ministry, too, was marked by much prayer. Like Moses, He once spent forty days and forty nights with God in the wilderness (Matt. 4). His very life was *intercession* for His people. He died for their rebellion against God. But He died triumphantly, paying fully for the sins of all who believe in Him. And those who are saved through Christ become imitators of Christ. They carefully observe the needs of the world and of people around them. They bring those needs to their God in prayer. Intercession is for them a very important task. The cause of God among men, you might say, exists because of these prayers.

Today the Lord invites you to be an intercessor. Have you noticed the many people around you who need your prayers? God has placed them on your way. Don't let them down. Lift them up in prayer to your Father in heaven.

Father, how wonderful that our prayers are so important and that they do so much. Holy Spirit, give us the desire and the words to pray. Lord, help us to understand the many needs around us. Keep interceding for us, Lord Jesus. Amen.

Prayer for a Special Favor

"O Lord of hosts . . . remember me . . . give to thy maidservant a son, then I will give him to the Lord all the days of his life" (I Sam. 1:11).

It is quite biblical to pray for things. The Lord Jesus taught us: "Give us this day our daily bread." The Lord knows that we have legitimate needs and desires. He made us that way. A cow is content to chew the cud. Let our ambitions surpass that contentment.

But the Bible adds a recipe in the use of God's gifts. He wants to be our partner in the enjoyment of His blessings to us.

Hannah begged God for a child, but she immediately dedicated her son to the Lord. When still a young child Hannah took the little Samuel to the temple to be God's servant there. God blessed that noble deed. Samuel's ministry to the nation was a great contribution to the coming of the Messiah, Jesus Christ. Thus, in the end, Hannah's humble request for the joy of motherhood became a wonderful thing of salvation.

The Lord invites you today to share your every concern with Him in prayer. Nothing is too small or too big for His full attention. Feel free to bring your fondest wishes to the Lord. Full personhood means that we have worthy desires. The Lord created us that way. But we must always ask ourselves: What is the motive for this wish? Will it help me serve the Lord better? Will it make me a better person? Only such prayers will bring happiness and blessings. How wonderful it is to realize that the Lord purifies our prayers before He sends them on to the Holy God! That's why we pray for Jesus' sake.

Holy Spirit, help us to pray for the right things. Our motives, Lord, are sometimes a mystery to us. Shape our desires; help us to surrender fully to the demands of Christ's Kingdom. For Jesus' sake. Amen.

Prayer for Vision

"O Lord, I pray thee, open his eyes that he may see" (II Kings 6:17).

Helen Keller, the famous blind author, once said, "Sometimes I am glad that I am blind, for I see much better than the people who travel through this enchanted world as if it were a barren waste."

The Bible tells us that many people are so blind that they see nothing of God in life. In II Corinthians 4:4 the apostle Paul gives the reason: "The god of this world [satan] has blinded the minds of the unbelievers, to keep them from seeing the light of the gospel."

There once was a prophet in Israel—Elisha—who lived in the little town of Dothan during the troubled days following the defeat of wicked king Ahab. One dark night, a Syrian army surrounded Dothan in order to take Elisha a prisoner. When his servant saw the troops the next morning, he nearly died of fear. But Elisha sat there calmly in his rocking chair, fully relaxed. His secret? Spiritual X-ray vision. Around the enemy army he recognized God's heavenly host, an army of angels complete with chariots of fire. Then Elisha prayed for his servant, "Lord, open his eyes that he may see." God heard the prayer and the servant saw and his fears were gone.

Perhaps you, dear reader, see nothing but anxieties and obstacles around you. Perhaps this very moment there is a gnawing fear in your heart. Do problems loom large in your life? Are there no solutions, you think? Have you suffered too many disappointments? Pray that the Holy Spirit will open your eyes so that you may see the mercies of your God all around you. And remember also that you need the help of fellow believers in reassuring you that God hears prayers.

Lord, show us Your great works in Christ and Your mighty hand unfailingly around us. Father in heaven, help believers in distress and danger. For Jesus' sake. Amen.

A Prayer of an Underprivileged Boy

"Oh that thou wouldst bless me and enlarge my border, and that thy hand might be with me, and that thou wouldst keep me from harm so that it might not hurt me!" (I Chron. 4:10).

Jabez, who uttered the prayer above this meditation, was an unfortunate youngster. His birth had been very difficult. His mother had expressed her pain and fear in the name of the boy. *Jabez* means *sorrowful*. Psychologists today would probably say that the mother projected her fear and despair upon the boy.

All this might have left Jabez a discouraged boy with an enormous inferiority complex. If he had become a misfit, he could have blamed his unhappy childhood and the lack of love in his up-bringing. But Jabez did no such thing. He recognized his disadvantages, but he didn't fret about them. Instead he took his burdens to the Lord in prayer. He asked the Lord for help and protection in the difficulties he faced. The answer came with amazing simplicity: "And God granted what he asked."

It should be mentioned in passing that Jabez was of the tribe of Judah, from which Jesus Christ was also born. Though Jabez may not have realized it fully, his prayer for well-being was connected with the Messianic vision in the tribe of Judah.

Broken homes, unemployment and corruption have victimized many youngsters today. Who of us has been able to avoid misfortune and setbacks? Those wounds heal very slowly; the scars hurt. What a danger that we surrender to self-pity and anger! Then the result is worse than the cause. Take a good hard look at yourself. Have you faced your problems in the awareness that Christ gave Himself for you though He was without sin? Take, then, your plight to the Lord, and make a new, clean start in His power!

Lord, hear us now as we pray for healing in our hurt and for power in our problems. Father, it is so hard to accept, so difficult to forgive. Give us peace in our hearts. Take away our sins. May we see new opportunities and fresh goals. Open our eyes to see the needs of others. Use us to bring Your kindness to those around us. Amen.

Prayer for a Whole Life

"Grant to Solomon my son that with a whole heart he may keep thy commandments, thy testimonies, and thy statutes, performing all . . ." (I Chron. 29:19).

The great missionary Hudson Taylor once said, "Preaching is not enough. Our lives must be a visible sacrifice. We tell men that worldly pursuits are vain; our lives must prove it. If we cannot put men right by approaching them with a message, we often can do so by love."

David prayed basically the same thing for his son Solomon, who was about to succeed him as king of Israel. David prayed that his son would not only *know* the commands of God but also *perform* them. His whole life would then be a demonstration of godliness, and the nation would follow in his footsteps.

Solomon spoke many godly words. They were even published. But alas, his deeds became increasingly evil. And the people imitated his deeds, not his words.

We must pray the prayer of David more fervently for ourselves and our children. Let us pray much that the Lord will make us responsible Christians in word and deed. We must pray for a life that is *whole*, for then our witness is also *whole*. It is not enough to witness in words only: our life must bear out our words. And it is not enough to witness with a good life only. Even unbelievers do that (Luke 6:32-4). Our spoken testimony must be unmistakably plain: only in Christ is there salvation!

As life goes on, we will be drawn again and again into that bad dilemma: shall our witness for Christ be mostly *word* or mostly *deed*? In Christ, word and deed are one. He is the Word become flesh. His person and life *embodied the message* of God's salvation. He did what He said. The more we consider that in faith, the more wonderful life becomes. We will become more and more doers of the Word. Make that your prayer, and you will never go wrong!

Holy Spirit, restore my life to wholeness. Help me to practice what I preach. Help me to show in my life what I believe in my heart. May many see the Christ in me. In His glorious name. Amen.

Prayer for Power and Light

"Oh that we may see some good! Lift up the light of thy countenance upon us, O Lord!" (Ps. 4:6).

David, the writer of Psalm 4, was worried. Everything had gone wrong in the land. Despair hung heavy as fog. The people were tired. They were afraid. They cried to God for relief, "Oh that we might see some good!"

Ten years ago we thought we lived in very difficult times. Since then the energy crisis, inflation, threatening recessions, unemployment, terrorism, and famine and poverty in Africa, Asia and South America have come, and no solution is in sight for the problems in the Near East. Mass depression has taken hold of mankind's soul. "Oh who will show us any good?"

David, the young king, knew that God had sent him to lead the people to light. But what could one man do in the face of so much despair? Note what David did. He prayed for his people. "Lift up the light of thy countenance upon us, O Lord." In the Hebrew language that expression could be used for a mother who brings her face close to her little child's, dispelling his fear.

We must pray for such a world, for its pain is ours. Prayer is not everything, but it is a great deal. Human efforts in building a better world have failed. Big budgets, ambitious programs, and skillful diplomacy could not prevent collapse everywhere. The world just cannot go on without God's help. Let us all pray for God's relief. He blessed the nation when David prayed for blessing. He will bless the nations today when there is repentance and obedience.

In response to the question why prayer is necessary for Christians, a confession of the church gives this answer: "Because it is the chief part of thankfulness which God requires of us, and because God will give His grace and Holy Spirit only to those who with hearty sighing unceasingly beg them of Him and thank Him for them." Note that the Holy Spirit works *in answer to our prayers*. And the Holy Spirit can change hearts!

Father, show the world the light of salvation. Have mercy on the human race. Lord, we are surrounded by so many impossible situations. Send us Your solace. Amen.

A Prayer of Joyful Amazement

What is man that thou art mindful of him? (Ps. 8:4).

In Eugene O'Neill's play *The Great God Brown*, the central figure, Brown, lies dead in the street. A policeman bends over his body and asks the bystanders, "Well, what's his name?" Someone replies, "Man." The policeman, with notebook and pencil, demands, "How do you spell that?"

How do you spell *man*? Do you spell it *customer*, or *competitor*, or *colleague*, or *classmate*, or *one-of-the-masses*?

The Bible says that God spells man *My child*! He made man that way. He opened His heart to man. He gave man a name. He gave man a task and everything he needed for that task. And He was a father to man. Imagine . . . *My child*!

When man turned his back on God, wandering off as a lonely stranger, God didn't give up on man. He came to man in Jesus Christ. Christ died for man's sin. He gave man His Spirit, who will open his eyes to see that God spelled man *My child*.

The writer of Psalm 8 saw it and accepted it. His heart was flooded with joy. He sang out in praise and prayer: "What is man that thou art mindful of him?"

Two questions are very important in your life: How do you feel about *yourself*? How do you feel about the *people* around you? Jesus Christ died for you so that you may have life! In Him you can come to terms with yourself and have peace in your heart. That makes you a person of dignity! If you have discovered that for yourself, you can also think highly of people on your way. You will recognize them as very precious, you will care about them, and you will be ready to share God's love with them. Do it!

Dear God, how wonderful it is to be saved in the grace of Christ and to know the Holy Spirit in us. Thank You, Lord, for having made us children of God. Forbid, dear God, that we should ever lose the sense of wonder for so great a salvation. In Jesus' name. Amen.

Prayer in the Face of Death

Even though I walk through the valley of the shadow of death, I fear no evil; for thou art with me; thy rod and thy staff, they comfort me (Ps. 23:4).

The Chinese people, in one province, used to set one small room in their house aside in which they placed two caskets as a constant reminder of the brevity and frailty of life. Praise worthy as this token of sobriety might be it was not without grimness.

Psalm 23 presents a more uplifting vision of life and death. True, the writer acknowledged that death is a frightening reality. He saw it as a dark valley! But the amazing thing is that he was not afraid of death. He tells us that for him death had lost its evil. For him death was a door that leads to a friendly God.

Christ has come as the fulfillment of Psalm 23. He died for believers and took away their sins. When they die, they are ushered into God's presence. Death for them is no longer the doom of judgment, but rather a glorious homecoming.

Are you afraid to die? Perhaps you have pushed that question out of your mind. But there are the reminders. A young man you knew, killed in an accident. A mother who couldn't be missed, taken by cancer. And you yourself, are you still as energetic and alert as you used to be? Does time seem to fly faster than ever? We have no abiding city here, says God's Word.

Will you have peace when you die? There is only one way to get it. Go to Jesus Christ and confess your sins. Leave your guilt at His cross. Only then can you face your God without fear and terror in the moment of your death.

Praise God for such boundless salvation!

Lord, please take our sins and guilt away. Be our shepherd now and when we go through the valley of death. Fill us with the presence of the Holy Spirit. Give us courage to share such tidings of life with people who need us. May we live this new life to the full. In the name of Christ our Lord we pray. Amen.

Prayer for Self-discovery

I acknowledged my sin to thee, and I did not hide my iniquity . . . Then thou didst forgive the guilt of my sin (Ps. 32:5).

A newspaper picture showed a man toting a big picketing sign in front of a stadium in New Zealand. "Don't let Billy Graham scare you," it read. The sign-bearer was undoubtedly a man of concern. He really felt that convincing people of sin is a harmful thing. Many knowledgeable people feel that way. During my ministry I have often met people who were told by their psychiatrist that they should stop worrying about sin.

Strange that experts can be so blind on this score! The Bible wants happy and peaceful people. It points out the way clearly: get rid of your sins! How? By taking them to Christ. Christ paid for the believer's sins. In Him there is complete forgiveness. And that is the basis for deep happiness.

David had fallen into all kinds of sins. It really didn't bother him at all. A modern psychiatrist would have sized him up as a well-adjusted person. But when the Lord led David to confession and forgiveness, he looked back upon the past and then realized that he had not been happy at all. In fact, he tells us that his body had "wasted away." Forgiveness became the gate to a life of happiness and peace. It not only made him a new man inside, it also gave him health and vigor.

Notice that for David, forgiveness and healing became ingredients in his prayers. David delighted in his peace with God. He kept thanking God for taking that awful guilt away, and he continued praising his Father for so much grace. That made his prayers very rich.

We may pray such prayers. We found the address for guaranteed healing; afterwards we kept reminiscing with the great Physician.

Lord, take away our sins. Fill us with assurance and acceptance. May new vigorous health be ours. Help us to esteem ourselves highly for Jesus' sake. Thank You, Savior, for giving Yourself to us. Amen.

Prayer in Loneliness

I say to God, my rock: "Why hast thou forgotten me?" As a hart longs for flowing streams, so longs my soul for thee, O God (Ps. 42:9, 1).

Loneliness is a cruel enemy. It is a tyrant that keeps people prisoner. There is a concentration camp in Siberia, I'm told, which is so isolated that the gates are left open. Prisoners can walk out, but escape would lead to certain death in the immense tundra.

The writer of Psalm 42 was an exile in the land beyond the northern borders of his country in the mountainous region of Hermon. Some years ago I visited that area. At Banias our guide pointed out the source of the Jordan River—a rush of tumbling water from a crack in the steep mountain side. We read Psalm 42 together: "Deep calls to deep at the thunder of thy cataracts; all thy waves and thy billows have gone over me" (vs. 7).

But the loneliness of the psalmist had a deeper cause. He missed the intimate presence of his God. His heart went out to the temple in Jerusalem. There blood was sprinkled before God's face, and because of this blood believers shared in the forgiveness of sins. That brought them close to their God and close to each other. Oh, how he longed for that closeness!

Do you feel isolated and forsaken? Don't you have anyone who can understand you and share with you? Do you wish you had interesting friends and nice people in your life? The writer of Psalm 42 cried to *God*. That was the right beginning. He sought forgiveness of sins. He felt the closeness of God. And God gave him brothers and sisters. He became part of a community. Have you taken that first step?

Holy Spirit, bring us close to our heavenly Father and to other Christians. Help us share our love with the many lonely people around us. Bring every wanderer home, we pray. Reach the forgotten ones, Lord, for Jesus' sake. Amen.

Prayer for Security

. . . cleanse me from my sin! . . . rebuild the walls of Jerusalem (Ps. 51:2, 18).

Imagine that you were standing on the moon looking at the earth. Under proper conditions and with the right equipment you could see just one manmade object on earth—the Great Wall of China. Its size is enormous: 1900 miles, fifteen feet thick, with some 25,000 massive stone towers strung along the entire distance. The wall was built by emperor Chin Shih Ti some 200 years before Christ in order to shield China from the attacks of the Huns and Tartars on the north. Every third man in China was ordered by the emperor to work on the Great Wall. Twisting through the most barren and mountainous parts of China, it took more than a million lives. It brought near ruin to a once prosperous nation. But the tragedy was that it never brought safety. It has been said that the cost of the Great Wall in life and treasure was so great that the Chinese never got over it—but the Huns and Tartars did.

Thus the wall stands today as a grim monument to man's failure to find security. The Word of God knows a better way. "Cleanse me from my sin," David prayed. In the way of confession and forgiveness, God came into his life. Only then could he pray for security: "Rebuild the walls of Jerusalem."

We will probably never quite realize how deep the urge to search for earthly security is. We may experience real concern for God's Kingdom, yet the touch of money plays a large role in our feelings of security. The fear of failure is very real among us.

God invites us now to share our insecurity with Him. Let's tell Him our failures and weaknesses; let's think of Him as very real and concrete. God, who bought us at a great price, will also look after us. The walls of Jerusalem are very strong.

We must admit, dear Lord, that we try to build our own walls of security. Lead us to repentance and faith. Give us the safety which only the care of our heavenly Father can provide. We pray in the forgiveness of sin, through Jesus Christ. Amen.

Prayer for Wisdom

Behold, thou desirest truth in the inward being; therefore teach me wisdom in my secret heart (Ps. 51:6).

The great English mathematician and philosopher Isaac Newton, whose theories became the foundation for modern science, once said of himself, "My life seems to have been only like a little boy playing on the seashore and diverting myself now and then by finding a smoother pebble or a prettier shell while the great ocean of truth lay all undiscovered before me."

That seems unimaginable. How could a man of such learning, who worked so tirelessly for the well-being of mankind, think so little of himself? Did he suffer from an inferiority complex? No, on the contrary, he was a wise man. He realized that life is short, that there is so much to do. Yet, even in his industrious life, many opportunities were wasted. Newton tried to understand what life is really all about.

There is an ocean at our feet, but we dig a shallow hole in the beach and play in a puddle. What is it that makes life worthwhile? What do we live for? What makes us really happy? How can we have fulfillment? The girl in the office with you, the man at the other desk—how do they cope with the futility of the daily humdrum of living?

Today's Bible verse is a cry to God for *wisdom*. Lord, tell me why am I here, show me what to live for, tell me how to go about it.

Wisdom is to know who we are, why we are here, and how to manage our affairs toward one goal.

And that, dear reader, begins in *your heart*. The text at the top of this page says that we must have *truth* in the inward being. Truth is that we know God as Father and covenant partner. Do you know that deep within? If so, then pray every day again for wisdom and God will answer your prayer.

Teach me wisdom, Lord, in the secrecy of my heart. Holy Spirit, show me, tell me, point the way. Help me to discern foolishness, trivialities, and stupidities. For Christ's sake. Amen.

Prayer for Courage

In thee, O Lord, do I take refuge . . . For thou, O Lord, art my hope, my trust, O Lord, from my youth. Upon thee I have leaned from my birth (Ps. 71:1, 5-6).

There is a version of the domino theory that holds not for nations but for people. One of our children's teachers put it humorously: "The dog is afraid of the lion, the cat is afraid of the dog, the mouse is afraid of the cat, my wife is afraid of the mouse, and I am afraid of my wife."

The chain reaction of fear in daily life is not that funny. Someone said, "The students are afraid of the teacher, who is afraid of the principal, who is afraid of the superintendent, who is afraid of the board, which is afraid of the parents, who are afraid of the students, who are afraid of . . ."

Probably true. Fear plays a much bigger role in human relationships than we realize.

The poet of Psalm 71 honestly admits his fear. He has become old and feels helpless and threatened. But he takes his fear to the right address. He calls upon God and cries for relief. Prayer helps: God hears him. Courage grips his heart, and his lips sing the praise of God. The end of this psalm is a hymn of rejoicing.

We tend to think that our fears are caused by people and situations. And that, of course, is true. It is unimaginable what some people go through. And it seems that for some people, there is no end to suffering: they get one thing after the other. But always remember that *fear has a deeper root*. That root lies buried deep within ourselves. We forsook God and made common cause with satan. We are as children in a dark night who lost their father. But the Father we forsook sent His Son, and the Son searched for the wayward and brought them home! What a reunion!

Have you met the Son?

Let Him bring you back to the Father.

Then you also will experience inner peace and courage to live life to the full.

Heavenly Father, accept us, too, as we follow the poet's example and come with all our fear. Fill our hearts with courage. Give us the honesty to face life's problems. And, Lord, after we have received strength from You, fill our hearts with praise. Amen.

Prayer for Joy

I will also praise thee with the harp for thy faithfulness, O my God; I will sing praises to thee with the lyre, O Holy One of Israel. My lips will shout for joy (Ps. 71:22-3).

At one point in the graduation exercises at the Naval Academy in Annapolis, the commanding officer announces solemnly, "You are now commissioned officers in the United States Navy." That signals the end of all solemnity. Loud hurrahs burst forth, caps and programs sail through the auditorium, and everywhere there is yelling and hugging.

I have witnessed something of that joy in believers who confessed their faith and were received into the fellowship of Christ and His people. But I also know of Christians who seem heavy-hearted, who don't experience a sense of great liberation, and who even frown on the exuberance of those who have tasted the new wine of salvation.

To be sure, the expression of joy should not be contrived. It should come from the heart, really and sincerely. But that doesn't mean that we shouldn't express it openly. Joy must be shared.

That's why the poet of Psalm 71 prayed fervently for joy and promised that he would make his joy known in shouting and praise.

Do you long for that kind of exuberant joy? Good, because it is a necessary ingredient of salvation. You can't do without joy. Follow the example of Psalm 71 and ask the Lord to give you the experience of joy. Think deeply about the work Christ did for you. Imagine that! You have been adopted by God, the almighty creator God! You own the world with Him. Give that reality a big place in your life. Express it, share it, and the awareness of salvation will grow deeper and stronger.

One little footnote should be added. Psalm 71 tells that joy was expressed with the help of two musical instruments—the lyre and the harp. That means, among other things, that it is a great idea to use effective tools in expressing our happiness in the Lord.

We praise the name of God and His Son, our Lord Christ! Holy Spirit, fill us with joy and thankfulness. Give us, Lord, courage to make it known. And let others be touched by our joy. Amen.

Prayer for Better Management
in God's Creation

The heavens are thine, the earth also is thine; the world and all that is in it, thou hast founded them. Blessed are the people . . . who walk, O Lord, in the light of thy countenance (Ps. 89:11, 15).

During the first world war, the Turks held some Arab territory in the area where once the Garden of Eden was located. They exacted a tax for every tree on each man's property. The Arabs responded by cutting down every tree, except the very fruitful ones. As a result the undergrowth died, humidity altered, the climate became drier, top soil blew away, and life became a nightmare for many.

We can easily blame people far away for mismanagement of God's creation. But all too numerous are the examples on the American continent of polluting the air, contaminating the water, and squandering irreplaceable resources.

How is it that we are so thoughtless about the well-being of God's creation? It is because we are often thoughtless about the precepts of God for daily life. We think we own our lives and our little holdings. How mistaken! God owns it all and He made us stewards, custodians. We are not here to accumulate wealth, but to serve God and our neighbor with our substance.

The prayer above today's meditation spells out two fundamentals for responsible living.

First, we must confess that the earth and its fullness belong to the Lord. There is no such thing as absolute human ownership. God owns all things. We are His stewards, His custodians. We must manage things for Him to His praise and for the well-being of our fellow human beings.

Secondly, we must "walk in the light of God's countenance." This means that we share His company in what we think, feel or do. He is on the scene when we make a mess of things and when we seek our own advantage without regard for the needs of people around us. It also means that we manage the available resources with an eye to the happiness of the generation after us.

"Blessed are those people . . ."

Heavenly Father, liberate us from our greed and insecurity. Replenish the earth, Lord, and help us to care for Your creation wisely and lovingly. Use us in bringing relief to the hungry and dignity to the dispossessed. Amen.

Prayer for God's Closeness

O Lord thou hast searched me and known me! . . . thou discernest my thoughts from afar. Even before a word is on my tongue, lo, O Lord, thou knowest it altogether (Ps. 139:1, 2, 4).

Prayer is a strange thing. Suppose God didn't exist. Then prayer would be senseless. But if God does exist, prayer appears to be senseless too, for God knows everything anyway. "Before a word is on my tongue, lo, O Lord, thou knowest it altogether." You can even go a step further. God not only knows everything, He also determines everything. "The counsel of the Lord stands forever" (Ps. 33:11). So why pray, if the Lord goes His way anyway?

The answer lies in Psalm 139.

Note a few things.

Psalm 139 is one long prayer. Prayer is a form of intimate speech—in this case, between two friends. God is the Big Friend, David the little friend. They talk together happily.

But, sad to say, the friendship had its unhappy moments. David wasn't always a good friend. Thoughtlessly he wandered away from God. But God didn't respond in kind. He ran after David. He found him and explained to him his foolishness. Then David repented and the two friends made up.

Out of that joyful reunion, David's prayer of joy was born. There was so much he had to tell God. Of course, God knew beforehand what David would say, but He listened carefully anyway because He loved David and delighted in everything David told Him. And God acted upon what David said (Ps. 65:2).

Did you realize that God is that eager for your prayers? In Psalm 116:2 we read that God "inclined his ear" to believers. When someone is ill, we put our ear over his mouth to hear every whispered word. God listens that intently to our words. It's almost embarrassing, isn't it?

If you have wandered away from God, you had better make up with Him quickly and then tell Him everything.

O God, how wonderful that You hear our prayers and that prayer changes things. Forgive us our silence. Help us not to leave unsaid what should be said. In Jesus' name. Amen.

Prayer for Average Means

"Two things I ask of thee . . . give me neither poverty nor riches (Prov. 30:7, 8).

This morning the 8 o'clock news mentioned the passing of Bertha Adams. She was a familiar figure in Palm Beach, Florida, where she made her living by begging. A week before her death, a judge declared her incompetent and committed her to a rest home, where she died weighing a scant 60 pounds. When authorities checked her belongings, they found nearly a million dollars in cash. Bertha had no will and apparently no relatives. No one knows how she acquired her fortune.

Money is one of the strangest things this earth has ever known. It can make gentle souls vicious, honest people cheats, and wise people fools. Though the Bible warns us that the love of money is the root of all evil (I Tim. 6:10), even Christians, at times, are hard after the dollar. Money makes money, and it is a bewitching experience to be part of the process.

But the godly man Agur who wrote Proverbs 30 went to the Lord and prayed earnestly that he might be *neither rich nor poor*. He wanted to be free. He wanted nothing to clutter up his beautiful relationship with God.

Praying such a prayer is not easy. You can only pray it when you have settled for a certain kind of life—a life in which not you but God is central. You realize that God has a program for the world. You willingly offer your services, and you trust that God will provide for your needs. You then learn to see that both riches and poverty could become obstacles to a life of meaningful service. Neither the proud nor the bitter can serve with joy. Therefore let that prayer be yours: "Give me neither poverty nor riches."

Lord, we don't want to lean on things for our security, but You know the beguiling power of riches. Help us to see that clearly. Give us unwavering trust in Your provisions for our lives. You know that we need the means to make ends meet. Look after us always, heavenly Father, and give us joy in service. Amen.

Prayer for Health

Heal me, O Lord . . . (Jer. 17:14).

The Hebrew prophets were deeply spiritual people. They cared about the salvation of Israel and of the whole world. But note that salvation for them was not only something for the soul, but for man's entire life. Salvation put a man straight with God, and that had everything to do with his daily life, his work, his food, his health, and his happiness.

One day, when the prophet Jeremiah was ill, he prayed that the Lord would heal him.

We learn two things from this simple prayer. "Heal me, Lord . . ."

First, we must recognize that all healing is from the Lord, even when God usually works through means. The best doctor can only help when God blesses his efforts. Without God, the best medicines would not bring relief. So we pray for healing with a believing heart.

Secondly, this prayer also implies that health is a precious treasure which we must guard carefully. Do we? Is our diet balanced? Do we eat too much, or too little, or too fast? Do we work too hard and sleep too little? Don't we exercise even modestly? Do we worry unduly? Do we harm our health with drugs, nicotine and alcohol? Do we leave broken relationships unmended? Do we shy away from having complete peace with God and the people around us? That, too, can hurt our health.

It has been estimated that some 37 million people will occupy a bed in one of the 72,000 hospitals in the U.S. It has also been estimated that half of them would not have to be there if they would take care of their health properly.

Everywhere people toil away at building financial security. But many never reach retirement age, and many who do can't enjoy retirement years because they have spent their health in making provisions for retirement.

Christianity is the religion of wholeness. Health is a gift to cherish and to guard.

We promise, Lord, that we will take care of ourselves better and live more responsibly in Your presence. Motivate us every day to do that, because our good intentions are not matched by our endurance. Give much grace to the sick and the suffering. Amen.

Prayer for Relief

"Behold, O Lord, for I am in distress, my soul is in tumult, my heart is wrung within me, because I have been very rebellious" (Lam. 1:20).

The winter of 1944-45 was one of grim suffering for the Netherlands, occupied by Nazi armies. Thousands died of hunger and cold. But a Christian minister in Rotterdam, one of the hardest hit cities, made a startling statement from the pulpit one Sunday. He said, "More people are dying of fear than of hunger."

It has always been that way. Fear lurks continually in some dark corner of our soul. Even very prosperous people are often inwardly frightened. "Millionaires seldom smile," said Andrew Carnegie, himself a wealthy man.

Experts have written books about fear and how to overcome it. They tell us that there is no reason to be afraid—if only we face dangers and threats squarely.

Well, God also wrote a book in which He tells us a lot about fear. In His book, the Bible, He says that there is real reason to be afraid. We will face judgment, says God, because we have sinned. That's the root of all fear. But God also tells us that Jesus Christ took our place in God's fearsome judgment. He took our place in hell. Thus Christ empties our fears if we accept Him as Savior.

The prophet Jeremiah suffered bitterly at the hands of his enemies. He took his fear to God. He didn't hide his feelings; he emptied his heart before God. But he did more. We read that he confessed his sins. He said, "I have been rebellious."

You need not be ashamed of your fears. Tell God your problems. He knows what life is like. He is a God of great compassion and is very sensitive to the pain of people. But go a step further. Scrutinize your ways, inspect your heart, let God's Word shine in every dark corner. Own up to your sins and confess your rebellion. Then God will forgive you, your eyes will be opened, and you will recognize His protection all around you.

Father in heaven, help us to face our fears, lead us to confession, grant us forgiveness in Christ, and make us strong in the power of the Holy Spirit. Amen.

Prayer of a Frustrated Prophet

"I pray thee, Lord, is not this what I said when I was yet in my country? That is why I made haste to flee to Tarshish; for I knew that thou art a gracious God and merciful . . . Therefore now, O Lord, take my life from me, I beseech thee, for it is better for me to die than to live" (Jon. 4:2-3).

Christianity doesn't always suit us. We have our preferences and they don't always harmonize with God's plans for us. We take roads which lead away from God's destiny for us. So God has to frustrate our imaginations and put roadblocks on our pathway.

All this can be painful.

Today's passage tells us about a prophet called Jonah who ran away because he disagreed with God. God had told him to go to Syria and preach in the capital city of Nineveh. Jonah wasn't interested in a big revival in that city, partly because he didn't like the people there and partly because he was out of touch with God. Jonah was a thoroughly disgruntled man, and there was no peace for him. That's why he was not ready for the task God gave him. His life had come to a standstill. He wasn't even on speaking terms with God. Amazingly, however, God kept coming back to Jonah. God even argued with him. This finally led Jonah to the point of pouring out his heart before God. He withheld nothing—not even his misgivings. He accused God of being too merciful. His cry was far from a model prayer, but the Bible records it, nevertheless, as a prayer.

Why, you wonder, would the story of Jonah be in the Bible? Undoubtedly to show us that God has the final say in our affairs. Jonah wound up doing what God told him to do. But as an appendix, the book of Jonah also shows us that we can go to God with our problems before we have solved them, including our frustrations and misgivings.

Lord, sometimes we feel downcast and we would like to run away from it all. But Lord, we confess that we have nowhere to go but to You. Continue to hold us in Your grace. Amen.

Prayer for Rescue

Lord, save me (Matt. 14:30).

The disciple Peter was a courageous man. When leaders in both church and state hated Jesus, it became extremely risky to be counted in Jesus' company, but Peter stuck with the Lord.

In Matthew 14 we read of another example of Peter's courage. The disciples were in a ship on the Sea of Galilee. That night a severe storm arose. Jesus was not with them at the time, having gone off to the hills for prayer. Toward dawn, Jesus came walking on the waves to join them. As soon as the startled disciples recognized Him, Peter stepped overboard and walked on the waves to meet the Master.

Could you match that courage and faith?

But, you see, this event was not recorded in the Bible in order to show us Peter's courage and faith, but rather his *fear!* At a certain moment Peter took his eyes away from Jesus. Then, suddenly he saw only the angry waves, and he panicked and sank away in the water. Frightened to death, he cried to Jesus, "Lord, save me!"

Have you ever cried to the Lord for help? Then you have learned that such a moment of total dependence became your moment of triumph. For then you surrendered to the Lord. In a deep Christian sense, courage is to acknowledge our utter *weakness* and to accept *rescue from Christ.*

Do you have the courage to face the bankruptcy of your sinfulness? And have you gone to Christ for forgiveness? Yes, that takes courage, because it implies that you will shun sinful situations. It means that you will withdraw from dubious company. But go ahead, do it. Christ will come to your aid. He stands behind you in every problem. Tell Him about the things that upset you; He understands.

Yes, some problems are very real and frightening. But in the end we must admit that fear did its worst in us when we took our eyes away from Jesus Christ. He reassures His followers today that He will be with them forever.

Lord, sometimes we feel downcast and we would like to run away from it all. But Lord, we confess that we have nowhere to go but to You. Continue to hold us in Your grace. Amen.

The Prayer of Christ's Deepest Suffering

"My God, my God, why hast thou forsaken me?" (Matt. 27:46).

See how much Christ suffers on the cross.
Judas has sold Him.
Peter has denied Him.
His followers have fled.
The bystanders mock Him.
The soldiers, indifferently, throw their dice.
High overhead the sun burns down on His naked body.
But His suffering goes deeper than that.
Consider His last prayer: "My God, my God, why hast thou forsaken me?"

That's when Christ suffered our hell, for hell is to be forsaken by God. Christ is forsaken. He bears hell for us. Those who accept Him as Savior will never be forsaken of God.

Perhaps you are very lonely. To feel forsaken is a bitter experience. But when you go to Jesus, your loneliness will lose its sting. He will bring you back to God. God will accept you. Christ's suffering on the cross guarantees that.

Today we read this prayer of Christ again. How brief it is—only one line. But who can fathom its depth? Standing at a distance, we can only confess that the Savior did it all for us. Humbly we accept that gift. In the way of that confession and acceptance, we can face the future. There is nothing in our distress that Christ has not experienced before. He knows it all. So to Him we go with all our needs. Praise God for such salvation and such assurance!

"My God, my God, why hast thou accepted me . . . ?"

Lord Jesus, remember us in moments of distress and loneliness. Bring us back to the Father. Speak to us from the Bible. Fill our hearts with trust. Help us to accept our fellow man. Strengthen the ties of love among us. Bless the worldwide community of believers. Amen.

Prayer for Help

But he was in the stern, asleep on the cushion; and they woke him and said to him, "Teacher, do you not care if we perish?" (Mark 4:38).

In this passage Mark tells us that Jesus and His disciples were caught in a sudden storm while crossing the Sea of Galilee in their little fishing vessel. Scared out of their wits, the disciples quickly woke up Jesus, who was asleep in the ship. They forgot normal courtesy: "Teacher, do you not care if we perish?"

There are a number of things we must note in this desperate one-sentence prayer.

First, look at the exact wording. It says that Jesus was asleep on *the* cushion, not *a* cushion. The evangelist Mark puts it that way because he means to indicate the special place of the helmsman of the ship. But in this case the helmsman is asleep. Quite a test for the disciples. I am sure I would have failed that test. We generally can take quite a bit *if we see the sense of it*. But sometimes we go through baffling experiences that make no sense; the great Captain no longer seems in command.

Second, note that this prayer comes from hearts full of doubt and despair. Jesus asks His disciples, "Have you no faith?" But it was at the same time a very honest prayer. The disciples took their distress to the right address—Jesus Christ. Jesus readily responded to their prayer and stilled the storm.

He is an amazing Savior! Open your eyes to it, and you will discover more riches in Him each time you face situations in Him. We may be weak, we may panic, but when we take it to Him He will never send us away empty. He will do that today for you. He remains the Lord of waves and storms—including the storms and waves in your heart. He will still them too! Have you already offered Him the captain's chair in your heart?

Lord Jesus, Captain of our life and of all circumstances, fill our hearts with new trust and confidence. Hear us, O Lord, when we cry for help. Amen.

Prayer for a Little Boy

And Jesus asked his father, "How long has he had this?" And he said, "From childhood. And it has often cast him into the fire and into the water, to destroy him; but if you can do anything, have pity on us and help us" (Mark 9:21-2).

Today's chapter tells us of a father who prayed to Jesus for his little boy. And no wonder, the boy was terribly ill. But note that the father prayed at the same time for himself. He realized that he needed the Savior as much as his suffering son.

The great love of that father for his son was matched by his great faith in Christ. He believed that Christ could and would help them. This exhausted father surrendered to Christ. And the great Physician healed them both.

To raise a family is no small matter. We need help. We need help to beautify every moment and help in correcting what is wrong. Christ will give that help. If only we trust in Him. If only we pray much for one another.

Our families suffer their share of the world's woes and ills. People turn to experts for relief. But the best experts cannot help us if we as parents have not taught our children how to love and trust.

The petition of this father and the answer of Christ teach us a dramatic lesson about the power of intercessory prayer. This you must discover as you pray for your children and others in your life. We are a solution-oriented generation. We reach for means and devise our techniques. But intercessory prayer must come first, for all life and all healing is from our Lord.

Lord, help us to understand our children. Remove the barriers that keep us from leading them to Christ. Give us love and affection for one another. Help us to be a blessing to everyone with whom we have contact. For Jesus' sake. Amen.

Prayer for the Spread of the Gospel

*"Lord, now lettest thou thy servant depart in peace, according to thy word;
for mine eyes have seen thy salvation which thou hast prepared in the
presence of all peoples, a light for revelation to the Gentiles, and for glory
to thy people Israel" (Luke 2:29-32).*

Soon after Jesus was born, His parents took Him to the temple
"to present him to the Lord" (vs. 22).

They were welcomed there by a wonderful old man called
Simeon, who broke forth in a prayer of praise when he recognized
the Christ-child. In that prayer he summed up the entire mission of
Christ by saying that it provided *light for the Gentiles.*

That sounds acceptable enough, but we must realize that *we
must bring that Light.*

The early Christian church probably saw this more clearly than
we do. They were excited about their salvation. Because it gave
them a new, joyful life, they talked to many people about it. Thus
the gospel spread quickly. It once happened that a pagan
philosopher walking by the sea fell into conversation with an old
man of gentle face and manners. That conversation led the
philosopher, Justin, to Christ, and he became a famous defender of
the faith. In the course of time, he died as a martyr so that he
became known in church history as Justin Martyr. That was
evangelism in the early church, and that is evangelism at its best.

Notice another thing about Simeon's prayer: it's a prayer of
praise, a prayer of thanksgiving. Simeon doesn't say here in so
many words that we must spread the gospel. He simply thanks God
for the Light to the Gentiles. Say no more, Simeon; we get the
point. How can we hide Light and Glory in us from those who
don't own the Lord and therefore own nothing?

Evangelism is a matter of course.

First you set your eyes on Christ: Hallelujah, what a Savior!

Then you set your eyes on people lost in sin: sheep without a
shepherd . . .

From that vision a message is born.

*Holy Spirit, fill our hearts with the excitement of faith. Give us a deep
desire to share the Good News of salvation. Bring many to Christ through
our testimony. For Jesus' sake. Amen.*

Prayer for Better Prayers

"Lord, teach us to pray" (Luke 11:1).

Don't feel bad if you find praying difficult. But do follow the example of the disciples. They went to Jesus and asked, "Lord, teach us to pray."

Jesus gladly complied with their request. In response He taught them the *Lord's Prayer*. Study it carefully. It contains some basic principles which you may apply to your own prayers.

First, in prayer recognize God's greatness. You pray to God who made heaven and earth.

Second, in prayer praise your God. His name must be honored and adored.

Third, in prayer pledge new obedience to your God and ask Him for strength to do His will as revealed in the Bible.

Fourth, in prayer ask God to provide all your daily needs. There is no concern too big or too small for His attention.

Fifth, in prayer seek forgiveness of sins. And remember, you cannot really pray if you don't forgive others.

Sixth, in prayer ask God to make you part of the army of Christ in its never-ending fight against temptation and evil.

Seventh, in prayer let the quality of thanksgiving and reverence never be absent. You owe everything to God in Christ.

Every prayer is a momentous event. On the one hand, a prayer is so simple—a child talking with his Father.

Never lose that childlike quality in your prayers. From the heart share your concerns with the One who always hears and understands. You come as you are.

On the other hand, prayers are rich and deep because God is so immense in His greatness. The more you know about Him, the richer your prayers will be. There is more to learn about prayer because there is more to learn about God from the Bible.

The disciples sat at Jesus' feet and learned about prayer. He still invites students to come and learn their lessons. Daily. From the Bible.

Lord, teach us, too, how to pray. Give us more faith. Cleanse our prayers, Lord Jesus, so that they reach God's heart. Amen.

Prayer for Resilience

"I do not pray that thou shouldst take them out of the world, but that thou shouldst keep them from the evil one. As thou didst send me into the world, so I have sent them into the world" (John 17:15, 18).

Have a heart for three-year-old Henry out in Texas. His blood does not have the ability to fight off germs. So from babyhood on, Henry has been kept in a room-sized plastic bubble, fully shielded from the world's contamination. Researchers hope that they can soon supply Henry's blood with the missing ingredient that will enable him to build up resistance against infection. What a day that will be when Henry can step out of his antiseptic environment!

Something similar holds for our Christian life. We cannot keep ourselves isolated from the nasty world. Sin is all around us. Sin is among us. Sin is in our heart. What we need is inner resistance against evil. We can have that in Christ when we accept Him as Savior and love Him as Lord. Sin then no longer has dominion over us. Jesus prayed for us before He ascended to heaven. He asked God not to keep us from the world, but to make us strong in the fight against sin. How we need that!

We have a mission in this world. There is nothing antiseptic about that mission. We are sent into a broken world, and sin has created distressful situations everywhere. As Christ touched the lepers, so we reach out to the hopeless. We share their plight, we seek to relieve their needs, and we share with them the healing power of Christ.

What a difficult task! How easy for me to write this on paper, how hard for all of us to perform it!

But the Savior keeps His eyes on us. And He prays for us as we go.

Parents know that kind of praying. There comes a time when their children leave the home. All that the parents can do then is pray. They pray, "Father, give my boy, my girl, the inner strength of Christ's Spirit."

We pray for courage, Lord, to go out and to be involved with people and their problems. Help us to understand their needs and to share with them the restoration in Christ. Amen.

Prayer from Scripture

And when they heard it, they lifted their voices together to God and said . . . "Why did the Gentiles rage, and the peoples imagine vain things?" (Acts 4:24-5; Ps. 2:1).

What shall we pray about?

We have, of course, our personal needs. And there are many needs around us about which we can pray. Yet, at times our prayers grow stale. We repeat the same phrases. Slowly prayer loses its vigor.

Today's passage opens up a storehouse of source material for our prayer life—*the Bible itself!*

Consider the situation. Peter and John had healed a cripple and preached to a large crowd. The religious authorities were upset and had the two apostles arrested and jailed. The next morning, however, they were set free and quickly returned to their fellow believers who had been waiting anxiously. Now, what else could those believers do than thank God for the deliverance of their leaders? But the amazing thing is that they prayed *in the words of Psalm 2*. The very special occasion demanded a very special prayer, and so they took it directly from Scripture.

Your prayer life, too, could be enriched if you made the Bible part of your prayers. Study the Bible, and you will find that Bible reading inspires prayer and that prayer drives you back to the Bible. And that, when you come to think of it, is not so strange. In the Bible, God speaks to us; in our prayers, we speak to God. We actually can only speak when we first hear. The Bible and prayer are the two components of a dialogue between heaven and earth, between the Father and His children.

How I love thy word, O Lord!
Daily joy its truths afford;
In its constant light I go
Wise to conquer every foe.

Thy commandments in my heart
Truest wisdom can impart;
To my eyes thy precepts show,
Wisdom more than sages know. Amen.

A Prayer That Goes Unheard

Then the kings of the earth . . . hid in the caves and among the rocks of the mountains, calling to the mountains and rocks, "Fall on us and hide us from the face of him who is seated on the throne, and from the wrath of the Lamb" (Rev. 6:15-16).

This, too, is church history. It happened in the Roman Colosseum during the reign of Emperor Marcus Aurelius who persecuted the church of Christ. A large crowd had gathered to see a Numidian lion burst from his cage and maul a small group of Christians condemned to martyrdom. Suddenly the door under the arena was opened and a keeper led out . . . a lamb! The crowd roared approvingly. What a clever way of ridiculing those Christians with their weird teachings about the Lamb of God!

Today believers still suffer for their faith. Perhaps not in this form, but mockery and hatred come in many disguises. Powerful leaders ridicule Christians and the Christian religion with benign smiles.

But let no one be deceived. In the last book of the Bible we read that the day of reckoning is coming. Many of history's important people will be there. All those who opposed the cause of Christ will be there. All those who ignored Him will be there. They will be overcome with fear. Desperately they will search for a way out. Frantically they will look around. They will pray to mountains, "Fall on us and hide us from the wrath of the Lamb." But the mountains will remain starkly unmoved. They cannot hear these prayers. There is no escape. The Lamb will judge. The day of grace is past.

But we, today, live in the day of grace. We can pray a far better prayer, a prayer of confession and forgiveness, a prayer of thanksgiving, a prayer for guidance. Such prayers reach the heart of God. The end of those prayers will be a happy reunion with Christ in the day of judgment.

O Lamb of God, we come with thanksgiving for the wondrous salvation in Christ. Lord, may we never harden our hearts, but accept our Savior now. Amen.

A Prayer for the Return of Christ

The Spirit and the Bride say, "Come." And let him who hears say, "Come." He who testifies to these things says, "Surely, I am coming soon." Amen. Come, Lord Jesus! (Rev. 22:17, 20).

World history—what a baffling thing!

Who can record all the sorrow, all the injustice, all the chaos, all the senseless suffering?

Can evil go unavenged?

Will futility have the final say?

Are we victims of the cruel whims of chance?

No, Christian believers can *never* accept that!

They cry to Christ to come quickly. Their cry is like that of children who call for their parents in a sudden moment of distress.

This prayer of the church is found in the last book of the Bible, the last chapter. It is a very urgent plea, almost an order which demands instant response. "Come, come, come, Lord Jesus." And the Lord does answer immediately, "Surely, I am coming soon" (vs. 20).

That deep longing for Christ's return must be a quality of *our* faith too. Christ watches the world. He keeps track of every event. The day of reckoning is coming. One day evil will be purged away from this globe. Christ will return with all the saved, and heaven will envelop the earth, and the whole creation will stand aglow with the presence of the Lord.

Amid all the tears, amid the injustice of our age, we make that last prayer in the Bible our own. We pray it with God's children of all ages and all places. Evil will not go unredressed. Suffering has not been in vain.

Let this one prayer echo through your soul and become the very quality of your life, "Come, Lord Jesus . . ."

We pray with believers everywhere: Come quickly, Lord Jesus! And until You come, uphold the church, make her faithful, and let there be much endurance. Lord, we cannot wait to see the earth full of the glory of God. Amen.

God Meant It for Good

As for you, you meant evil against me; but God meant it for good, to bring it about that many people should be kept alive, as they are today (Gen. 50:20).

This month we will examine the fascinating events which occurred when the people of Israel, under the leadership of Moses, threw off the tyranny of cruel Egypt and marched through the trackless wilderness toward the promised land.

It is important that we see some background events, and also note the ultimate purpose of this epic desert journey.

Genesis 50 describes a meeting of the sons of Jacob as they faced an embarrassing situation. Years before, they had sold their younger brother Joseph as a slave to Egypt, not caring what would become of him. Joseph, however, rose to the position of prime minister of Egypt, and when he learned that his father and brothers in Palestine were starving, he invited them to Egypt and offered them a good living. Joseph's gesture was noble, but his explanation was far nobler. He told his brothers that the whole situation was God's own design to provide relief for Jacob's hungry family. "What you meant for evil, God meant for good."

Actually God's design was even richer than Joseph could imagine at that time. The arrival of Jacob's family in Egypt was only the first link of a much bigger chain of divine action. The family of Jacob was destined to become the people of Israel who would travel through the desert to Palestine, and from whom would be born the Savior of the world, Jesus Christ. That was the deepest meaning of Joseph's prophecy: God meant it for good.

In the meditations of this month, we will follow the nation on its desert journey. We will be struck by two things. God controls all events. Yet He uses the efforts of His people and demands their full obedience.

This is the central principle of the Christian faith. Every believer is saved by grace and called to a life of service.

Dear Lord, we pray for a blessing upon the meditations of this month. Help us not to be too busy these summer months to have our daily devotions. Thank You for salvation by grace and for the challenge of a life of fruitbearing. Amen.

The Courageous Midwives

But the midwives feared God, and did not do as the king of Egypt commanded them, but let the male children live (Ex. 1:17).

Many years after Joseph and his brothers had died, a king ruled in Egypt who became alarmed about the size to which the people of Israel had grown. "They will soon be bigger than we are," he told his servants. "We must get rid of these foreigners among us."

So he commanded the midwives in Israel to kill all the male children that were born. Satan's hatred lay back of that cruel scheme. Satan knew that God intended to use the people of Israel in making salvation available to all nations, and therefore he decided to destroy them, using Pharaoh as his willing, though unwitting tool.

But Pharaoh's plan failed. The midwives of Israel kept the babies alive. Back of that courageous love we recognize the hand of God, for the midwives feared God, we read. Though they probably didn't understand the great purpose which God had with Israel, they nevertheless did their duty. Thus the midwives made a contribution to the coming of Christ.

And that's still how the cause of God is served. The battle between Christ and satan goes on to this day. Christ is winning the victory today, and He uses the faithfulness of His followers to accomplish this. That's why we honor the memory of the midwives. We are proud that we may stand with them in the great tradition of being co-workers with Christ.

When you are busy with your daily task again, think back a moment to these midwives and what God did through them. It may well serve as a strong reminder to you that you should work with care and responsibility, even at the cost of personal ease and comfort. God will crown your days with His blessing.

Almighty God, we express our thanks for the courage of the midwives in Egypt. Arouse Christians everywhere to stand strong in the battle against evil. May the Kingdom of Christ come with all its healing power through such obedience. In Jesus' name. Amen.

The Bungling Beginner

He looked this way and that, and seeing no one he killed the Egyptian and hid him in the sand (Ex. 2:12).

The outstanding leader of Israel during its wanderings in the desert was Moses, who was probably the greatest figure of the Old Testament (Deut. 34:10).

But notice the humble beginning of his career. When still a young man, he happened to witness a quarrel between an Egyptian and an Israelite. In a burst of patriotism he killed the Egyptian and quickly buried him in the sand.

The result was that both Egyptians and Israelites disowned Moses, and he had to take refuge in the wilderness of Midian.

That was a very sobering experience for this young Hebrew, who up to that time had moved in high court circles as the adopted son of Pharaoh's daughter.

Did Moses deserve the high honor of being the leader of God's people? Moses knew better. Did he deserve the credit, ultimately, for a job well done? No, all praise should go to God. Moses might serve and work hard, but he accomplished what he did by the grace of God.

In the end two things stand out in God's dealings with His children. He does not select workers for His cause on the basis of their shining qualifications. He recruited a lot of misfits and failures for His army. To be His co-workers is a thing of grace. It is an undeserved honor for even the best among us. And that's not where His grace ends. Once we have been inducted into His forces, God continues to provide and to supply. In the end there remains nothing but humble praise to God. He Himself gained the victory through His people. So let us take heart: our every effort in His service will be used in His overall plans.

Lord, You know the extremes in us. Sometimes we feel defeated and unworthy. Sometimes we feel proud because of a little success. Teach us to depend on Your grace. Make us hard workers for Your cause. For Christ's sake. Amen.

God Hardened Pharaoh's Heart

But I will harden Pharaoh's heart, and though I multiply my signs and wonders in the land of Egypt, Pharaoh will not listen to you (Ex. 7:3-4).

Moses and his brother Aaron presented Pharaoh with the same request over and over again: "The Lord says, Let my people go."

It was hardly surprising that Pharaoh refused. Israel was a source of cheap labor on which the economy had become dependent.

Amazingly enough, however, the Bible tells us that the ultimate cause of Pharaoh's stubbornness lay with God Himself. God hardened Pharaoh's heart. And the Holy Spirit wants us to be very certain about that fact. This part of the Bible mentions no less than twenty times that God hardened Pharaoh's heart.

We will never be able to understand all the implications of this act of God. This much is sure, however. All the evil schemes of satan are ultimately taken up into God's overall strategy. The Exodus from Egypt is God's own work, and He is totally sovereign in His work. His enemies will acknowledge that (Ex. 14:4). It is good for us to accept that sovereignty of God without hesitation, for how could we face life in this age without it? Evil has gone rampant in the world. There is so much suffering in the world. It is all so totally beyond our understanding. The greatest minds have busied themselves trying to understand sin and pain, but they were unable to lift the veil that shrouds evil in mystery. Our only hope is that God knows, that He is in control, that He will bring about ultimate victory. This gives us new courage. The New Testament refers to God's dealings with Pharaoh and makes the same point: God is mighty and will save those who confess Him as Father. He will redress all evil. That God is your God!

Almighty God, we stand in awe of Your holiness and sovereign power. Help us to accept Your rule for our lives. When we suffer or when we feel victimized in this world of darkness, give us a clear vision of the greatness of our God. Amen.

The Great Passover

. . . and touch the lintel and the two doorposts with the blood which is in the basin . . . and when he sees the blood . . . the Lord will pass over the door, and will not allow the destroyer to enter your houses to slay you (Ex. 12:22-3).

God's people were ready to leave their great prison. One by one the Lord had broken the shackles that kept them bound in slavery. But one strong shackle remained to be cut—*the shackle of their own sinfulness*. They didn't deserve to be set free, for they were unworthy of God's grace and kindness. They had often forsaken God and had trusted the gods of Egypt. They had as much to fear from the Angel of Wrath as the Egyptians did.

Because of this, their only hope lay in God's act of mercy. He told them to kill a lamb, the Passover lamb, and put some of its blood on their doorposts. That blood was a symbol of God's forgiveness. Because of that forgiveness, the Angel of Wrath bypassed the homes of the Israelites. And being forgiven, there was nothing that could stop them from leaving Egypt and marching toward the promised land.

Many years later, Christ Jesus made the actual payment for the sins that had been placed on all those lambs. He was the Lamb of God that took away the sin of the world (John 1:29).

Have your sins been forgiven? Jesus will not send you away if you seek Him (John 6:37). He offers you, too, wonderful liberation from satan's hold on you. That will then be your great exodus. Nothing needs to delay your freedom march. Granted, there is still a big desert to face, but believers walk through it in the company of God.

We are often absorbed in making provisions for the future. We toil away at our jobs, we fret about the education of the children, and we manage our funds with care. True, good management of our resources is next to godliness, but the foundation of our well-being, now and forever, is our peace with God, which we can accept free of charge through Christ Jesus. The forgiveness of sins should be our first concern through life. Once we have that, God will provide in all other needs.

We bless the name of Christ who shed His blood for sinners. Lord, bid many come and be set free from the slavery of sin. Help us to use our freedom to serve our God with gladness. Amen.

Judgment of Death

At midnight the Lord smote all the first-born in the land of Egypt (Ex. 12:29).

The night was dark in Egypt. Silently the Angel of the Lord entered home after home and swiftly did God's bidding. A great cry was heard in Egypt. Nearly every home mourned the death of the oldest son. God's final judgment had come to a nation which had enslaved His people. Nothing could stop this punishment because there was no blood on their doorposts.

In Eastern countries, the oldest son was a symbol of hope for the future. In the oldest son, one generation reached out for a new and better day. God took that hope away from a people that hated Him and His children.

God has never changed. Throughout history He has judged people who persecuted His followers. That is still true today. Woe to the nation that hurts the church of God. Its future will be sealed in gloom and despair.

Remember, persecution can take subtle form. When a society blocks the free exercise of the Christian faith in education, welfare, politics, and industrial relations, the judgments of God will surely follow.

Exodus 12 does not only speak of judgments, it also points to mercy and forgiveness through the blood of the Passover Lamb. Today Jesus Christ, the great Lamb of God, offers forgiveness to the nations. When people live for Him and make room for His cause on earth, the future becomes bright with hope.

We must remind each other, once in a while, of our importance. Our presence here on earth is a big factor in the survival of the nations. If it weren't for the Church, the communion of believers, this globe would not be in existence today. And a whole lot of things in society would have disintegrated if it weren't for that Christian presence. Now, more than ever, your intercessory prayers and Christian service are needed.

Lord Jesus, we confess that we have often thought little of the holiness of God. Holy Spirit, help us to walk in His commandments. Heavenly Father, may the nations realize how grim the future is without God. Amen.

The Great Test

When Pharaoh drew near, the people of Israel lifted up their eyes, and behold, the Egyptians were marching after them; and they were in great fear (Ex. 14:10).

This final test was undoubtedly the most difficult one of all. Israel had suffered more than words can express. At last the great exodus had taken place, and the borders of Egypt were behind them. The years of cruel oppression were now a memory. Ahead lay the promised land, described by the Lord as "a land flowing with milk and honey." And then, suddenly, joy turned into a nightmare. Before them was the Red Sea and all around them the angry army of Pharaoh in hot pursuit. "And they were in great fear." Lord, Your people have suffered enough! This is just too much!

We are able to take a lot by the grace of God. But there is a limit, we say, especially when painful problems have been solved and then the same problems start all over again. Or when we are healed from a long illness, and then, suddenly, more surgery is needed. That's when we collapse in despair.

This chapter sheds some light on why God sometimes leads us into that second valley. God wanted to demonstrate to Israel that they could prevail in the battle between God and satan only *in the power of the Lord*. The deepest secret of Christian living, ultimately, is *total dependence upon God!*

All that makes so much sense: God made the universe, He made us, He gave His Son to redeem us, He sent the Holy Spirit to lead. How shall He then not freely give us *all things* with Christ and the Holy Spirit? Yet the lesson to trust Him alone and not ourselves is so hard to learn! Therefore He teaches us painful lessons. But even amid those tough tests, He comes to our rescue. He did that to Israel. While they cried in despair, He parted the waves of the Red Sea and led His people to freedom.

Great God, we pray for grace to look away from our weakness and see the protecting hand of our heavenly Father. Help us, Lord, to trust even in the darkest hour. Remember all those who suffer distress. Amen.

The Song of Miriam

Then Miriam, the prophetess, the sister of Aaron, took a timbrel in her hand; and all the women went out after her with timbrels and dancing. And Miriam sang to them: "Sing to the Lord, for he has triumphed gloriously" (Ex. 15:20-1).

Exodus 15 describes a very joyful moment in Israel's desert journey. They sang. They celebrated. They danced.

Of course.

The Lord had delivered His people from their enemy. The waters of the Red Sea, instead of swallowing up the people, had respectfully invited them to pass through safely. Now they were free, they could live, and they could thank their God. How could they express their praise? By singing and dancing. Imagine Miriam, Moses' sister, going on 90 by then, leading the people in that great celebration.

Ah, the art of celebration! Many believers never quite master it. Church services have become quite formal. We hesitate to express our feelings of exuberance and elation. We warn against excesses, sometimes to justify our inhibitions.

Hasn't the Lord done great things for us? Hasn't He triumphed gloriously? Pray, then, that the Lord may give more ageing Miriams to lead us in the art of praise and celebration. For in the way of praise and celebration we learn to communicate with each other and the Lord. And that equips us to share the joy of redemption with those now far from the Kingdom.

Deeper, of course, than the outward expression of joy is the source of joy itself—the heart of the believer which Christ has claimed as His throne. The condition of that heart determines the integrity of our celebration. It is quite pathetic when mouths sing exuberantly while the hearts know only anguish. But it is also a shame when believers have experienced great relief but lack the personal freedom to make it known and praise God for it. They should go to school at Miriam's. They need lessons.

Praise be to our God for ever and ever. Thank You, dear Lord, for salvation, for relief, for joy, and for a challenge. Amen.
(Let all say, Amen, Amen.)

The Bitterness of Marah

And the people murmured against Moses, saying, "What shall we drink?"
(Ex. 15:24).

How quickly we forget.

The Lord surrounds us with goodness. He provides every day. His Son, Jesus Christ, paid for our sins. He promised to bless us forever. But in spite of all that, a minor irritation or setback can upset us and make us bitter.

Less than a week after Israel had walked safely through the Red Sea, the people suddenly exploded in anger against Moses and the Lord. Why? Because they had run out of water, or rather, the water near their camp proved to be bitter, unfit for human consumption.

This sad episode was not just an incidental thing. The writings of Moses describe nearly a dozen other occasions of the people "murmuring" against Moses and the Lord. It was an evil that lodged deeply in their hearts. The problem at Marah was not so much that the *water* was bitter, but that their *hearts* were.

The Lord's response to the nation's bitterness was twofold. He enabled Moses to cure the water by putting a piece of wood into it. He also provided a cure for their hearts. The Lord said, "Hearken to the voice of the Lord your God . . . for I am the Lord your healer."

Don't underestimate the lesson which the sad episode at Marah contains for us. It is all so deeply human. We prepare ourselves for the big battles of life. We pass the big tests with honor and respect. But how often we find ourselves unprepared for *the little irritations of life.* They easily bring out the worst in us. What a sobering experience to realize suddenly that so much anger lurked deep within our bosom. What damage our explosion of anger did to our marriage, family, and Christian community. What a great blessing, then, to hear God's invitation to come to Christ, who will wash us clean every day again. No one else can take the bitterness away from us. No one else can heal the scars. O come, let us adore Him!

Lord, we know our moments of bitterness and frustration. We are so impatient and so easily upset. Come, Savior, forgive us; come, Physician, heal us; come, King, and rule our lives. Amen.

The Sweetness of Elim

Then they came to Elim, where there were twelve springs of water and seventy palm trees; and they encamped there by the water (Ex. 15:27).

Someone said to me, "Hardships can be good for us, because they bring us closer to God." That is true. The Lord can bless our setbacks in such a way that we learn anew to depend upon Him.

But it is equally true that God can bless periods of peace and rest. Such periods may set the stage for growth and development, if we use them as a gift of God. The memories of those good times may continue to inspire our lives for years to come.

Today's Scripture verse tells about *Elim*, a place of rest and beauty. The people needed Elim. Try to imagine the problems of a nation traveling in the desert, carrying belongings, caring for the children, preparing meals, and tending the animals. And all that under primitive conditions! How they needed that rest at Elim! It was great just to laze under the palm trees, just to have plenty of water to do the laundry, and just to play with the children.

Today the name *Elim* still has a sweet ring. Institutions of mercy have chosen it as a name. We all need our Elims. Treasure those precious moments of rest and relaxation. They clean the air, they sharpen our vision of God, they deepen understanding and peace within us, and they give us new vigor to serve God (Mark 6:31).

You should ponder this some more and discuss it with people around you. For, you see, it takes some thought and prayer for us to discover the secret of this kind of enjoyment. That secret has never been spelled out in travel brochures; it is not necessarily part of expensive vacation trips. The ingredients of an Elim experience are reflection, rest, quietness, fellowship, meditation, contentment, inner peace, goodwill, sobriety, and exuberance. Christ knew that secret when He took some time off and withdrew in the wilderness.

Lord, we thank You for the moments of rest and tranquility. We praise our Savior for having brought peace by His sacrifice for our sins. Bless, dear Lord, all that is lovely and harmonious in this great creation. Amen.

The Miracle of Manna

Then the Lord said to Moses, "Behold, I will rain bread from heaven for you." Now the house of Israel called its name manna; it was like coriander seed, white, and the taste of it was like wafers made with honey (Ex. 16:4, 31).

Worry is bad for us because it warps our vision. Today's Scripture passage tells us about this. Israel was on its way to the promised land. They traveled with a purpose, for their national existence would lead to the salvation of the world. They had to trust, therefore, that God would give them food and drink during the journey through the wilderness.

Slowly a tragic change took place. The people forgot that they were marching for the salvation of the world. Their horizons shrunk to that small, dreary part of the desert which was their daily lot. And that's when they began to worry. What shall we eat tomorrow in this forsaken wilderness? Fear soon grew into anger, and the familiar murmuring began again. "Why didn't you leave us with the fleshpots in Egypt?" they complained to Moses.

Again God was gracious. He announced that bread would rain from heaven and that there would be enough for everybody. The people called that wonderbread "manna." Later Jesus compared Himself with that manna (John 6:31, 49, 58). He is the bread from heaven that brings the people back to God. He represents them before the triune God. He provides in all their problems. And from day to day He assures them that when they seek the Kingdom of God, He will add all things to them (Matt. 6:33).

Chances are that you worry about your income and your bills. Chances are also that you make little progress in solving your problems. It makes you tired and nervous. It robs you of a lot of joy. Worry dims your vision, and you begin to miss out on a lot of wonderful things. You will probably also grow blind to the tasks which the Lord meant you to do in His Kingdom. No one, of course, can predict the future. But you can check the record of your heavenly Father: He has never broken His word! He will back you up too!

Savior, be our hidden manna too. Restore us to grace and fill us with power. Help us to recognize our daily food as a token of our Father's love. Amen.

Prayer Slays the Enemy

Whenever Moses held up his hand, Israel prevailed; and whenever he lowered his hand, Amalek prevailed (Ex. 17:11).

The battle of faith never ends. Israel kept running into enemies. This time it was Amalek, a warlike desert tribe which attacked with fury and swiftness. Unknowingly, Amalek had become a tool in satan's hand, for the prince of evil hated the purpose for which the nation was marching toward the promised land.

Two things stood out in that battle. God fought *for* His people, but He also fought *through* His people. The victory was all *His* work, but He *used* His people to attain it.

Moses dramatically symbolized that.

He sat on the hill overlooking the battle below. As he watched, he prayed, with his hands lifted toward heaven. When his arms got tired, the battle went against Israel. But with the help of Aaron and Hur, his hands remained high and the battle was won. God did it all, but He used the prayers and sacrifices of His people.

Don't underestimate your calling. God's cause doesn't flourish automatically. His Kingdom on earth grows through the prayers and works of His people.

Today strong forces are arrayed against the cause of God. As a result, confusion and distress are widespread. Christians are now urgently summoned to action, action supported by prayer, because God remains in charge.

Notice one other thing in this chapter, Exodus 17. As Israel travels on through the desert, God leads them to greater maturity. Sure, He takes care of them one hundred percent; they would not survive one second without that care. But God mobilizes the people to play an ever greater part in the drama of preparing salvation for the world. That responsibility is an honor and a great joy, but it also brings along struggle and sacrifice. A large segment of humanity is in great need today, and God asks much involvement on your part to serve in this benighted world. Have you heard His summons?

Take hold of us, almighty Father. Make us strong against satan's rage. May church and Kingdom grow through our dedication. Deepen in us a sense of dependence on our God. For Jesus' sake. Amen.

A Piece of Good Advice

So Moses gave heed to the voice of his father-in-law and did all that he had said. Moses chose able men out of all Israel, and made them heads over the people . . . And they judged the people at all times (Ex. 18:24-6).

The Chinese reportedly have a proverb that goes something like this: give a boy a fish, and he will eat one day; teach him how to fish, and he will eat always.

Moses received similar advice from an unlikely source—his father-in-law, Jethro. Jethro, you may remember, lived in the land of Midian, a corner of the wilderness of Sinai through which the Israelites happened to pass at that time. So Jethro stopped by for a visit. It didn't take him long to notice that Moses was far too busy. From morning to evening, Moses conducted court sessions settling the people's conflicts. But there were always more people waiting. So Jethro suggested that Moses select helpers—wise people who could do much of that work for him. And Moses was humble enough to accept that advice. It probably saved him from a nervous breakdown. Thus Jethro, a humble, desert shepherd-priest, made a fine contribution toward the well-being of Israel and thus, indirectly, toward the coming of Christ.

Later the disciples of Jesus stumbled upon the same wisdom and appointed deacons to assist them (Acts 6:1-6). It probably was a big factor in the church's spectacular growth as described in the book of Acts.

Many ministers today would do well to delegate more work to their parishioners. There is a variety of tasks and a variety of gifts. There are jobs for which church-members are better suited than church-ministers. We must all see again that the church's total ministry depends on teamwork. There really are no individual workers in God's Kingdom. All of us, as members of one family, *cooperate* and *share* in one comprehensive calling.

Lord, we confess that we are one body of believers, and that we are responsible for each other. Help us to assist and be assisted in Christian wisdom and modesty. For Jesus' sake. Amen.

The Great Law

"I am the Lord your God, who brought you out of the land of Egypt, out of the house of bondage" (Ex. 20:2).

The film *The Ten Commandments* is a colossal and spectacular portrayal of the events around the giving of God's law. It is also a colossal and spectacular misunderstanding of the ten commandments. The reason is simple. The film completely ignores the *introduction* to the law, the verse above this meditation. These film makers never understood that God announced Himself as *covenant God*, that is, as Father of His children. He had adopted them by His love and grace. They were His. And because they were His, He now taught them how to live as His children. "I am the Lord your God who freed you from the slavery of sin . . ."

Having failed to recognize God as Father, the film makers could only picture Him as an unpredictable and even cruel deity.

Those who love God, however, discover a beautiful secret about His Law. God *supplies* first, and only then does He *demand*.

That's why Christians treasure the ten commandments today. Christ's own life fulfilled those commandments. He obeyed them for us. He paid for the sins we commit against them. The Bible tells us that Christ lives in the hearts of believers. If, therefore, we obey the law of God, it may be said that Christ does it through us (Gal. 2:20).

Receiving the ten commandments at Mount Horeb was an outstanding event in Israel's desert journey. God intended that law to be a challenge toward a life of service, a way in which to walk with joy, a vehicle to help them go places, and an armor to safeguard them against satan's attack. The people didn't always see it that way. They soon found the law a burden and a straightjacket. But *you* don't, do you, dear reader? You know that in Christ, the law is God's special gift to us. What an honor! What a treasure!

Father, we are sorry that we often see the ten commandments as a hindrance to our freedom. We admit, Lord, that we have often brought misery to ourselves and others by breaking Your law. Give us more faith and love Holy Spirit, so that we may do God's will with joy. In Christ's strength. Amen.

The Covenant through Blood

And Moses took the blood and threw it upon the people, and said, "Behold the blood of the covenant which the Lord has made with you in accordance with all these words." . . . and they saw the God of Israel . . . they beheld God (Ex. 24:8, 10-11).

It is striking how often God interrupted Israel's journey through the wilderness.

He did that mostly to renew the *covenant* with His people.

A covenant is a solemn agreement, an understanding, a league, a mutual promise.

In the covenant, God came very close to His people. We read here twice that Moses and the 70 elders *saw* God.

The covenant was renewed, we are told here, by blood sprinkled upon the people. Blood symbolized that God had forgiven the people's sin. Sin was the great barrier between God and His people.

New Testament Christians share in the same covenant joy. God made a covenant with them in Jesus Christ (Heb. 13:20). Christ's blood removed the believer's sins so that he can see God again. God is the believer's life partner.

This is one of the reasons why we must interrupt our daily routine with moments of meditation and worship. It strengthens our covenant relationship with God. It is also the reason why God Himself sometimes interrupts our life. We become involved in so many things that we forget the covenant. Then all God's traffic lights go red, and we stand still and begin to ask ourselves what life's travels are all about in the first place. Maybe your setbacks are God's way of leading you to covenant renewal. He is an all-wise and loving God. Maybe He has a more fruitful covenant life in mind for you. Your present sufferings are part of God's training program with you.

When it comes down to it, the only real life is covenant life. All other life is illusion.

Dear God, forgive us for having so easily forgotten the covenant for which Christ gave His life. Come very close to us, heavenly Father. Help us to sense the loneliness of moments spent without our God. Amen.

Willingness of Heart

The Lord said to Moses, "Speak to the people of Israel, that they take for me an offering; from every man whose heart makes him willing you shall receive the offering for me" (Ex. 25:1-2).

God asked the people of Israel to build Him a tabernacle. The tabernacle was a beautiful tent which functioned as a dwelling place for God among the people. It was a symbol of His covenant love. What a wedding ring is to a married couple, the tabernacle was to God and His people.

The construction of the tabernacle was a high point in Israel's travelings. God invited the whole nation to share in the building program. A love offering was taken up. No directions were given about how much each individual was to give. The only norm for this giving was the willingness of the people's hearts. It worked out just fine that way. When all the gifts were collected, there turned out to be too much (Ex. 36:6-7).

That simple norm of *willingness of heart* is still a great factor in Christian conduct. In Christ we love our God, and that love relationship spans our entire existence. That makes life worthwhile and beautiful. So we must invest in that relationship. In "willingness of heart," we must give unstintingly of ourselves, of our prayers, of our concern, of our energy, and of our means.

You had perhaps not realized that life is so covenant-oriented. Take, for instance, an average family. A family is a covenant community. Parents nurture their children to maturity. A mark of maturity would be that children don't have to be forced to carry out the garbage; they would pitch in with the family chores because they grew up in that kind of an atmosphere, an atmosphere of care and togetherness. That's the covenant spirit. Now apply that to God's covenant with you as it spans your whole life. You will see His faithful care over you, and you, in return, will want to share your life with Him. You will want to be part of His program on earth, for you have discovered the joy of a willing covenantal heart.

Holy Spirit, change our hearts. Fill us with the love of Christ. Give us a new outlook on life. Help us every day to give ourselves in God's service, as Christ gave Himself for us. Amen.

The Golden Calf

And he received the gold at their hand, and fashioned it with a graving tool, and made a molten calf; and they said, "These are your gods, O Israel, who brought you up out of the land of Egypt!" (Ex. 32:4).

Luther is supposed to have said that satan is the ape of God. It is indeed true that satan imitates God. And the worship of false gods is often modeled after the worship of the true God. The tragic episode of the golden calf demonstrates that.

Notice how many similarities there are between this idol worship and the service of the one true God.

While Moses was absent, Aaron, the high priest, quickly gave in to the demands of the people for a visible god and became the *priest* of the golden calf.

The people duplicated their generous giving for the tabernacle by bringing gold in abundance, from which the image of the golden calf was cast.

The joy of godly celebration was imitated in a rowdy party of eating, drinking and dancing around the calf.

And to top it off, the people then credited that dumb idol with having brought them out of Egypt!

All this is hard to imagine. God had been so good to the people! He had so clearly manifested His power to them! How could they turn to idols so quickly, so easily?

But . . . would *we* have done any better? Don't idols have their fascination for us? How subtle the role of idols is! We may confess that God is the Giver of all good, yet money means so much to us as a basis for security. We thank God for accepting us in Christ, but in our hearts we often crave for the approval and praise of people. Unbeknown to ourselves, we lean on idol gods.

The sad episode of the golden calf, and Aaron's pathetic part in it, demonstrate human frailty—our frailty. We thank Christ for not only bringing us to God but also for keeping us in God's fold. People such as us need a shepherd who never takes His eyes off the sheep.

Help us, dear God, to recognize the idols that keep us captive. Lord Jesus, set us free and lead us to serve God in singleness of heart. Amen.

The Anger of Moses

And as soon as he came near the camp and saw the calf and the dancing, Moses' anger burned hot, and he threw the tables out of his hands and broke them at the foot of the mountain. And he took the calf which they had made, and burnt it with fire (Ex. 32:19-20).

Hold your breath.
Moses comes down the mountain.
He has met personally with God.
He radiates God's holiness.
He carries the stone tablets of the law which God had dictated to him.
He rounds the mountain bend.
And then, below, he sees the people.
They are singing and dancing.
Around and around they go, around the calf, a silent idol.
Moses' hands tremble.

He lifts up the stone tablets and dashes them to pieces against the mountain of God. As an angel of wrath, he descends upon the people. Superhuman power possesses him. He lifts the golden calf off its footing. He burns it. He grinds it to powder. He throws the ashes into the drinking water. Now he makes the people drink it.

How can Moses, the meekest man on earth (Num. 12:3), blaze with such anger? He could do this because he had just seen something of the holiness of God and had understood something of the price paid for man's salvation. Only people of such spiritual stature possess the quality of righteous indignation "as one of the sinews of their soul" (Thomas Fuller).

A deeply disillusioned world must pray fervently for leaders of such sterling integrity.

Lord, people everywhere have become cynical about the moral quality of their leaders. We pray that justice and mercy may again become the pillars of life. Give us all that quality of holiness so that Your name may be honored. In the mercy of Christ we pray. Amen.

Cheating God

You shall not offer anything that has a blemish, for it will not be acceptable for you (Lev. 22:20).

From Sunday School we remember the story of the farmer who reluctantly agreed to fatten a "church calf." One day a calf was found dead in the pasture and he sadly announced, "The church calf has died."

That streak of cheapness runs in everybody's soul and is of long standing. Moses reminds the nation here not to sacrifice animals with a blemish.

This reflects badly on the people. Verse 18 tells us that Moses was talking about a *freewill offering*. Imagine the situation. Someone receives many blessings, and thankfulness wells up in his heart. He promises God a gift. But when it comes to the actual giving, he selects a sick animal.

Absurd, you say.

Certainly, but that's how contradictory we often are ourselves. Not so, you think? How about a little inspection of your religious inventory?

First we note this problem that bothered you; you asked God to help you, but now you keep worrying about it. Is that honoring His faithfulness?

Next we see this fine confession: God must be glorified in all of life. But, what's that—are you too embarrassed to witness for Him?

Didn't you say that you were an unworthy sinner saved by grace? Why, then, did you find it so hard to forgive the one who wronged you?

And if you believe that Christ is a complete Savior, shouldn't you forgive yourself and stop punishing yourself for that one big mistake you made?

Enough said, don't you think, about our sickly-looking sacrificial animals? Consistency, in the Christian life too, is a jewel. It's part of the ongoing battle of true piety.

Holy Spirit, show us who we really are. Burn away our cheapness. Take possession, Lord Jesus, of our heart. Help us to take God seriously. Help us to trust His every word. Amen.

All-Inclusive Responsibility

And when you reap the harvest of your land, you shall not reap your field to its very border, nor shall you gather the gleanings after your harvest; you shall leave them for the poor and for the stranger (Lev. 23:22).

... but in the seventh year there shall be a sabbath of solemn rest for the land ... you shall not sow your field (Lev. 25:4).

While still traveling in the desert, Moses instructed Israel to use their future homeland responsibly. He said, in effect, "When you work the land, keep an eye on *God*, on *the land*, and on your *neighbor*."

What an unimaginable, marvelous provision!

Just let these three things sink in.

(1) Keep your eyes on God. Yes, God is the owner of everything. We own nothing without Him. We are stewards, custodians, caretakers. God must be honored in all that we do and have. Our family, our home, our job, all the mines, the factories, the fields, the financial reserves, the oceans—they all belong to Him.

(2) Keep an eye on the land. The land is there to supply people with daily food. Be kind to the land. Don't ruin it, for you must eat from it. It must be worked carefully. Replenish it. Let nature experience the mercy of its keepers.

(3) Keep an eye on your neighbor. In Israel the vagabond and traveler could usually find some leftover corn in the field. And the family of the poor fellow who went bankrupt did not have to lose hope: every 50 years property was restored to the original owner.

That's how God intended the nations to develop the globe. We should have lived modestly with some time on our hands to do wonderful things. Instead we became hurried materialists facing a world of problems.

Some years ago a number of evangelical leaders met in Chicago and concluded correctly, "Before God and a billion hungry neighbors we must rethink our values regarding our present standard of living and promote more just acquisition and distribution of the world's resources."

Lord, help us to be merciful to this bountiful creation. Use us to feed the hungry and to show concern toward our fellow man. Make us owners by the grace of God. Amen.

Our Poor Brother

And if your brother becomes poor, and cannot maintain himself with you, you shall maintain him (Lev. 25:35).
. . . they would have us remember the poor, which very thing I was eager to do (Gal. 2:10).

Another word about the poor.

There is the popular misunderstanding among us that Western industrialized nations give hefty amounts in aid to poor nations. Our aid is not all that spectacular. The United States allocated about .27% of its Gross National Product in foreign aid in 1978 (.60% in 1960). Sweden gave 1.01% of its G.N.P. Canada fell slightly below the latter figure. The rather low U.S. figure was one of the reasons that led Mr. John Gilligan to resign as head of the U.S. Agency for International Development. Before he left, he stated, "Last year the people of the U.S. lost more money at the gambling tables in Nevada than we have in our development program. We spend more money on dog food than we do on the 600 million people in this world who are malnourished."

The situation of world hunger is further aggravated by the shrill contrasts in riches among the nations. The average per capita income in Jordan is $261; in nearby Kuwait it is $9,600. The average an Egyptian has to live on is $230 per year; his neighbor in the Arab Emirates on $31,300. The Western nations live in luxury compared to many nations in Africa and Asia. Global advertising has shown the Third World how the First World lives.

Legislators, we are told, trim foreign aid programs because of the voters' wishes. Individuals count! *You* count! That's why, in today's text, God addresses His individual people to solve a national problem. When your brother becomes poor, maintain him . . .

Lord, this is a very greedy world, and so many suffer without hope. Father, bless the generosity of Your people to create a mood of responsibility and helpfulness among the citizens of privileged nations. For Jesus' sake. Amen.

God's Law and God's Person

. . . if your soul abhors my ordinances, so that you will not do all my commandments, but break my covenant, I will do this to you. I will appoint over you sudden terror . . . (Lev. 26:15-16).

The writer Dostoevski, who stood in the Christian tradition, once said, "If God does not exist, everything is permissible."

The thinker Sartre, who stood in the atheistic tradition, turned that around and made it his creed: "Everything is permissible; therefore God does not exist."

Our obedience to the Lord ultimately depends on what we think of Him. If God is real to us, His commandments will be dear to us. We don't do His will because we *have* to, but because we *want* to. We obey God because we love God. We stand strong in temptation when we sense the nearness of God.

All that, and more, is the concern of today's Scripture passage. God visits His people in the desert and is very honest with them. "Reject My commandments," God says, "and you break your covenant relationship with Me; that is, you reject Me as a person." And what is there left to live for when God is no longer present? Today's text states it clearly: "I will appoint over you sudden terror." Their sin was its own punishment. They wanted God to be absent, and the absence of God unavoidably brings along fear. That's what makes hell hell: God is not there. He withdrew His love.

For years mankind has torn down God's standards of decency and devotion. Terror now stalks the globe. There are so many who are afraid to live and afraid to die. Yet there is not a great return to God. People are blind to the cause of their fear. They seek some diversion in the pursuit of pleasure, the possession of material things.

Today's text calls us to obedience, but it also implies an urgent task: bring the gospel to the people.

Holy Spirit, live in our hearts and keep us ever close to the Father. Help us to delight in God's law. May it be to us the way of life. In Christ's name we pray. Amen.

The Invisible Hand of God

. . . the sound of a driven leaf shall put them to flight . . . and they shall fall when none pursues. They shall stumble over one another, as if to escape a sword, though none pursues (Lev. 26:36-7).

Victor Hugo once wrote, "Napoleon has not fallen because of a superior enemy, but because he embarrassed God."

There is probably a lot of truth in that statement. History cannot be understood apart from God's interference. God's invisible hand is always at work, blessing or breaking down, as He pleases.

Moses pointed that out to Israel. He said in effect, "You may seem strong and rich, but if you forsake God, you are very weak. The sound of a wind will scare you silly."

To that reality the history of mankind bears witness. Empires rose and fell. Why? Because God withheld His blessing. Fortunes were amassed, but somehow never brought the owners happiness, because God disturbed them.

The invisible hand of God is a very real factor that shapes our lives, overriding all other factors. We plan, we toil, we scheme, we calculate, and we smile when we think we have arrived. But if we have not served God and depended on Him, He is likely to pull the rug out from under our satisfaction.

It is very human to want happiness and peace. All sorts of manuals have been written about how to feel good. Most of these books suggest that we tap the reservoirs of power hidden deeply within us. They advise us to be positive, with a touch of aggression. But the wisdom peddlers cannot teach us one basic thing: *how to face ourselves and our Maker.* Thus they never bring lasting peace because they don't have the right diagnosis. The end is terrible disillusionment—hands that clutch some gold, but hearts that are empty and cold. Those who have a wrong estimate of God have a wrong estimate of everything else. "Therefore they shall fall when none pursues."

Holy Spirit, lead us to complete surrender to Jesus Christ. Lord, we confess that unless You bless us, all our toil is in vain. Amen.

Conflict among Great People

Miriam and Aaron spoke against Moses . . . and they said, "Has the Lord indeed spoken only through Moses?" And the anger of the Lord was kindled against them (Num. 12:1-2, 9).

The trio—Moses, Miriam and Aaron, members of one family—was used mightily by the Lord as leaders in Israel as long as they agreed and worked in harmony. When Miriam and Aaron became jealous of Moses one day, leadership fell apart. And Israel's journey was delayed seven days.

What caused Miriam and Aaron to oppose Moses? Basically, they lost the vision of the nation's calling: the coming of the Messiah, Christ.

When that vision of hope grew dim, everyday problems became demons. It upset Miriam and Aaron that their brother Moses appeared to be more important than they were. They began to watch his ways. Soon everything he did offended them. One day it reached the boiling point, and they gave him a good piece of their mind.

That's how satan works. He did so already in Paradise. Imagine Adam and Eve owning the whole world. What more could they want? But satan suggested that they need not take a back seat to God. That did it. They questioned God and lost their whole world in the process.

What makes the events in today's chapter so gripping is that they happened to people of whom we would never have expected it. Miriam and Aaron were intelligent people of goodwill. Why would they get so upset about Moses, their own brother, the most gentle leader Israel would ever have?

These questions imply a compelling lesson for us all. Satan sows the seeds of conflict and anger in our hearts at moments when we feel nobly disposed toward our fellow man. He will find us easy prey when we think we have a way with people. Let's never take good relationships for granted. Let's examine our motives in personal honesty. Conflicts among Christian believers are tragic. They can set the cause of the Lord back for years.

Lord, take pride and jealousy away from our hearts and help us to esteem our fellow men and to respect those who give leadership in church and state. For Jesus' sake. Amen.

The Pessimistic Spies

"And there we saw the Nephilim . . . and we seemed to ourselves like grasshoppers, and so we seemed to them" (Num. 13:33).

Watch out for the discourager!

He subtly undercuts noble motives, he makes a good cause look silly, and he ridicules people who sacrifice for the common good.

At the battle of Saratoga (1777), a man was arrested and court-martialed because he spoke disheartening words to the soldiers in the critical hour.

Ten of the twelve spies sent out by Moses to scout the promised land spread gloomy tidings about the colossal power of the native people. The people of Israel, when they heard that report, rebelled against Moses and threatened to return to Egypt.

The real tragedy was that the spies were blind to the power of God and the task He had given them. They forgot the miracles God had done. They didn't care anymore about the salvation that would come through them as a nation. That's why they were weak and angry.

If we don't see the greatness of God and if we don't do His bidding, our strength melts away and the forces of evil threaten to overcome us.

There is something poignant about the attitude of the spies for our day. Mankind faces terrible problems. The very bigness of those problems tends to immobilize us. We say, "It's no use; our efforts will never be more than a drop in the bucket." The voice of the hopeless will easily be drowned out by the silence of the discourager. Israel faced a great challenge when it stood before the gates of the promised land. The discouragers almost succeeded in shutting that gate effectively. Kingdom people again face a challenge in the world, a challenge awesome in size but also awesome in urgency.

Thank God that His cause does not depend on our personal courage. Let us keep our eye on God, who will not forsake us. He calls us to great things for Him in His power.

Lord, we are grateful that the Bible tells us of people who were weak in themselves, but strong in God. Holy Spirit, open our eyes to the mighty deeds of our God. Make us faithful to the end. Amen.

The People Murmured

And all the people of Israel murmured against Moses and Aaron; the whole congregation said to them, "Would that we had died in the land of Egypt!" (Num. 14:2).

God's people in the desert knew moments of happiness, but far more numerous were the moments of anger and sadness. Every time again we read that the people "murmured" against Moses and the Lord. Yesterday's meditation showed us a reason: the people took their eyes away from the Lord. Today's text shows the inevitable result: everything seemed gloomy and threatening. In their blindness the people turned against God and His servants from whom they had received nothing but good.

According to a recent issue of *Time* magazine, *science* has begun to nose around in that shifty terrain of the happiness phenomenon. It is trying to analyze happiness and to determine what makes people happy. The results have been disappointing so far. No one seems to have quite succeeded in telling us what happiness really is, let alone providing a formula for it. Prof. Jonathan Freedman of Yale University found that employment, living conditions, sexual satisfaction, religion, and degree of wealth have little to do with happiness. He concluded his study vaguely, with this statement: "Happiness is in the head, not the wallet." In ancient times Seneca had discovered that already. He said, "Unblest is he who thinks himself unblest." And the gentle wisdom of Abe Lincoln had confirmed it: "Most folks are about as happy as they make up their minds to be."

Being a Christian doesn't automatically bring happiness. There are, alas, many unhappy Christians. Yet, deep within their hearts, Christ-believers know a beautiful secret, a quiet trust in Christ as their Lord and Savior. Nurse the flame of that loyalty and commitment; let it set your life aglow. That's what makes happiness grow. Happiness has to be cultivated.

Dear Savior, if our happiness has shriveled because of much distraction, then give Your peace, Your joy, Your newness. Lord, there are many people in my life who struggle with problems. Help me to encourage them and to add to their happiness. Help me to share my joy. Amen.

Bogged Down in the Morass of Sin

While Israel dwelt in Shittim the people began to play the harlot with the daughters of Moab (Num. 25:1).

How hard it is to sustain enthusiasm for a vision and a challenge! Israel found it that way. Today's chapter describes a period of relapse in which the people slowed their pace. They began to hanker for the pleasures of the world. These verses tell us that they committed immorality with the people of Moab. That sin became an obstruction to their destination and, in a deeper sense, to the birth of the Messiah.

Satan finds immorality a very effective barrier to the progress of God's cause. Later, in Palestine, the sin of lust continued to hurt the service of God. And the Apostle John warned the New Testament church against those evils (Rev. 2:19-29).

Today, immorality has reached epidemic dimensions. Scores of movies, filthy and utterly perverse, draw big audiences around the world. Venereal diseases have become as common as influenza. Over a million abortions are being performed annually in the U.S. Other Western nations follow closely in proportion to population. Moral evil is not only committed freely, it is increasingly being defended openly. When standards disappear, we live in a moral jungle. The quality of life disintegrates visibly around us. When there are no standards of right and wrong, of guilt and innocence, Christianity will spread much more slowly because there is nothing to appeal to in people.

We renew our prayers for God's mercy on the human race. He will not suffer the progress of His Kingdom to be obstructed forever. There is hope for the world when Christians rededicate themselves to their God. That call comes to us all.

Holy God, make us strong against temptation. Free mankind from the slavery of lust. Give us the Spirit's liberating power. Open the eyes of people everywhere so that they may recognize moral decay. Amen.

Women's Action

Then drew near the daughters of Zelophehad . . . And they stood before Moses . . . saying, ". . . Give to us a possession among our father's brethren." And the Lord said to Moses, "The daughters of Zelophehad are right; you shall give them possession of an inheritance among their father's brethren" (Num. 27:1-2, 4, 7).

Several of today's issues were already present, in one form or another, in the Old Testament. Take, for instance, the role of women, on which today's verses throw some light. We read here of five sisters whose father had passed away in the desert. Since there were no male survivors in the family, they would not have a possession in the new country. Those women decided on a bold course of action. They went to Moses and asked for their own inheritance in the future land.

Now, that may not seem a very spectacular thing from our modern point of view, but there is more to it than meets the eye, even more than the five sisters may have realized. You see, Old Testament believers hoped for the coming of the Messiah. That's why the possession of a piece of land meant so much to them. On that land their children would one day welcome the Christ of God. That land was a pledge that God's promise would come true.

The daughters of Zelophehad made an *honorable* request—honorable because they insisted on sharing, ultimately, in the task which God had in store for the nation Israel. In their action they reflected something of the dignity of Adam and Eve in Paradise. That's why the Lord told Moses to grant their request.

That principle has never changed. There is a clamor for rights by people which is prompted by greed. But not all of it is. People cannot live in honor and serve with dignity unless certain basic rights are secure. The Zelophehad sisters were worthy spokesmen for their sisters of the centuries.

Lord, we are thankful for the boldness of these five sisters. Help us to be equally determined to seek opportunities to serve. Thank You, Lord, for the great contribution many godly women have made toward the cause of God on earth. Amen.

Love

And you shall love the Lord your God with all your heart, and with all your soul, and with all your might (Deut. 6:5).
. . . but you shall love your neighbor as yourself: I am the Lord (Lev. 19:18).

We sometimes tend to think of the Old Testament as containing mostly *law*, and the New Testament mostly *love*. But that's a false notion. The soul of all the laws in Deuteronomy and Leviticus is *love*! God's people were never to keep those laws from a spirit of fear or even duty. God saw His people in Egypt, poor ignorant slaves, and He called them *His people* and made a covenant with them. They did not deserve His love; He gave it freely. He adopted them as His own children for His own sake. Now, as His covenant people, they might return that love to their God. That's why He gave them His commandments. In keeping them they were able to express their love to God and one another in a concrete and practical way.

Reading of Israel's travels through the deserts, we must conclude that the people found the love practice very hard. Reading our own life, we must admit that we find the love practice equally hard. There is a certain risk in loving. We shy away from it. But in the way of much prayer, we must learn that love has its own great rewards. The Christian writer C. S. Lewis once stated, "There is no safe investment. To love at all is to be vulnerable. Love anything, and your heart will certainly be wrung and possibly broken. If you want to make sure of keeping it intact, you must give your heart to no one, not even to an animal. Wrap it carefully round with hobbies and little luxuries. But in that casket—safe, dark, motionless, airless—it will change. It will not be broken; it will become unbreakable, impenetrable, irredeemable. The alternative to tragedy, or at least to the risk of tragedy, is damnation. The only place outside heaven where you can be perfectly safe from all dangers and perturbations of love is hell."

Holy Spirit, create in us more and more the mind of Christ that we may love from the power of His love. Help us to understand situations, problems and challenges where our love is needed. For Christ's sake. Amen.

Writing a Song

Now therefore write this song, and teach it to the people of Israel; put it in their mouths, that this song may be a witness for me . . . this song shall confront them as a witness (for it will live unforgotten in the mouths of their descendants). . . So Moses wrote this song the same day, and taught it to the people of Israel (Deut. 31:19, 21, 22).

Here we read of singing again. In Exodus 15 we witnessed the singing of the people under the direction of Miriam, Moses' sister. This time God commissions Moses, just before his death, to write another song. God tells Moses to teach the children of Israel that song. They must sing it over and over again. They, in turn, will teach their children, and so this song will be part of the spiritual treasure of the generations.

Never underestimate the power of a song. Good singing has comforted and encouraged believers throughout the centuries. Christian songs have been powerful tools in the spread of the gospel. Such singing is a gift of God.

Israel spent many uncomfortable years in the wilderness. One wonders what they did for recreation. Was there time for games? Did the Israelites play much with their children? These references to songs indicate that the people knew the art and joy of *singing*. It gave them new courage. It's amazing how singing will restore hope and trust. Moses' song recounts the faithfulness of God and His glorious acts of salvation. Singing the songs of God opened their eyes to the greatness of their God. Singing is one of the most effective educational tools ever devised.

We thank God that there is fresh interest in new Christian songs today. We need that. Anti-Christian forces reach many hearts with haunting lyrics. The Red Chinese regime, we are told, is very concerned about the songs their people sing.

Let's make room for song writers who have caught the vision of our conquering Christ and the blessings of a victorious life of faith. And let us rediscover the joy of singing the praises of our God. Such singing will be a boost to Christian living.

Praise be to our God for the gift of singing. Holy Spirit, help us express our joy and our love in hymns old and new. Inspire composers and poets to lead us in singing from Your Word. Amen.

The Greatest Prophet

*And there has not arisen a prophet since in Israel like Moses, whom the
Lord knew face to face (Deut. 34:10).*

The end of the desert journey was in sight.

God invited Moses to climb Mount Nebo and see the promised
land. That was a joyful experience for Moses, but at the same time
a painful one. It was his own disobedience that closed the door of
the land to him (Num. 20:10-13). So when today's Bible verse calls
him the greatest prophet of the Old Testament, that does not mean
that he was a perfect man. No, Moses was great because his hope
was so completely in the redemption of his God. That's why we feel
close to Moses. He was a man like us. And that's why we don't
hesitate to view Moses as an example here. His weaknesses did not
hinder him in working for God with unflagging zeal. His one
passion was to *serve*. He gave himself totally in God's cause. We
like to stress *gifts* for certain tasks. Not bad. But Moses did it all by
force of sheer hard work. And that goes a long way.

Several centuries later, God invited Moses to climb another
mountain, the Mount of Glorification (Matt. 17:3). There the
greatest prophet of the Old Testament met the Great Prophet of the
New Testament, Jesus Christ. Moses shared great glory with
Christ. That was possible because Christ was not only fully God
but also fully man. He took the sins of His followers upon Himself
and paid for them. That's why we feel so close to Christ. Our
Savior fully conquered our death and opened for us the door to the
promised land, a life of serving God in gladness of heart.

We conclude the August meditations with our eye focused upon
Jesus, our great Savior. He led us out of the land of slavery and sin,
He guided us from the day that we believed in Him, and He will
provide for us in the future. Let us follow without fear. He will not
fail us. To Him be all the praise and adoration.

Hallelujah!

*Triune God, we humbly and joyfully give thanks for all the wonders of
salvation and for Your triumph of grace over the forces of darkness. Help
us, dear God, to walk faithfully in the ways of service. In Christ's name.
Amen.*

Hope for the Home

. . . for the son treats the father with contempt, the daughter rises up against her mother, the daughter-in-law against her mother-in-law; a man's enemies are the men of his own house. But as for me, I will look to the Lord, I will wait for the God of my salvation; my God will hear me (Mic. 7:6-7).

The vacation season is over and most families have returned to the normal routine of the day. A suitable season, it would seem, to reflect on wholesome family living. For some who read the meditations of this month, there will be regret for mistakes which cannot be undone. But we will see from the Bible that Christ's saving power is strong enough to bring healing to your life and to the complexities of family dynamics.

In the chapter we just read, Micah tells us of a period that resembles ours. There is a lot of violence and family life fares badly. The home is battered by conflict and torn by strife, Micah reports.

Keen observers of our day have sketched similar grim situations and made dire predictions. A report to the White House Conference on Children called the future of the family itself into question. To this, Paul Popenoe, founder of the American Institute of Family Relations, responded by saying that no society has ever survived after its families have deteriorated.

Note carefully, the prophet Micah does not share such hopelessness. He knows a way out. Look to the Lord, says Micah. Wait for the God of your salvation; your God will hear you.

Christianity is the religion of hope—hope that comes from God, "the God of my salvation." The meditations of this month are devoted to a discussion of that hope for the family.

Dear Lord, we are so grateful for the salvation through Christ that also came to our families and our marriages. Protect our homes against enemies from within and without. Help us, Holy Spirit, to express Christian love and concern for each other. For Jesus' sake. Amen.

A Bible in Every Home

He answered, "Have you not read that he who made them from the begin-ning made them male and female . . . ? What therefore God has joined together, let not man put asunder" (Matt. 19:4, 6).

Satan knows how greatly a nation benefits from healthy family life.

Naturally, he tries very hard to destroy a nation's homes.

One of his cleverest—and unnoticed—attacks has been: keep people from reading the Bible. This has been a successful strategy. Few people take time to listen to God talk to them through Bible reading.

The results have fully measured up to satan's expectations. There is great confusion in the land about the nature and purpose of marriage and family. The most outrageous theories about marriage and family are being spun out before a gullible public. The weirdest advice is being given to a new generation, advice that suits the easiest-going consciences. What they all have in common is that a fixed standard of right and wrong is totally lacking.

In Matthew 19 the people present Jesus with difficult marriage problems. And Jesus immediately responds, "Have you not read . . . ?"

Ah, yes, if only they had read the Scriptures, they would have known how God designed the institution of marriage. If only we would read and know the will of God for our homes! Do you read the Bible? There is no other light that can show us the way. The Bible clearly spells out the message of salvation in Jesus Christ. But that same Bible also presents God's blueprint for marriage and family.

Read that Bible thoughtfully, and the Holy Spirit will lead you, too, in joyful and responsible home life.

Lord, let there be a genuine return to the Bible. Help us all to understand Your will for our lives. Lord, open many homes to Your Word. We face so many problems. Lead us to light by Your Word and Spirit. Amen.

As It Was from the Beginning

Then the Lord God said, "It is not good that the man should be alone; I will make him a helper fit for him." And the rib which the Lord God had taken from the man he made into a woman and brought her to the man. Therefore a man leaves his father and his mother and cleaves to his wife, and they become one flesh (Gen. 2:18, 22, 24).

In the beginning God created man, called Adam. Man was perfect and lived in a perfect place. And yet there was something—no, *someone*—lacking. God noticed it right away. He spoke, "It is not good that Man should be alone; I will make him a helper fit for him."

Then God created Woman.

Man and Woman were very much *alike*. Woman was made from Man's substance. They were both fully human, children of God, made in the likeness of God, destined to represent their God on His earth.

Though called to headship, the man must not dominate or exploit the woman. They are one flesh, one spirit, made for mutual enrichment and service.

But Man and Woman were also very much *different* from each other—the one was *man*, the other was *woman*. And God gave them to each other in marriage. They were to possess each other in marriage. They were to complement each other. They were to share life together. They were to serve each other. They were to be faithful to each other. Their physical and spiritual unity was to be crowned with the birth of children.

In Matthew 19:4-5 the Lord Jesus points back to that original situation of Adam and Eve in Paradise. He implies that through His payment for our sins, we can find the way to God, and thereby to God's will for marriage. Christ's redemption is very rich and broad. It is so big that it can make marriage and home life beautiful.

Heavenly Father, we are so grateful for the institution of marriage. Holy Spirit, lead husbands and wives who have lost the vision of the marriage challenge to understanding and service. May all of life thus be blessed. Amen.

Who's in Charge Here?

Wives, be subject to your husbands, as to the Lord. For the husband is the head of the wife as Christ is the head of the church, his body, and is himself its Savior (Eph. 5:22-3).

Family life will be happy when it is conducted according to God's design for the home. And God has arranged the home so that the husband and father is in charge. In spite of what Women's Lib may say, a family flourishes only when a husband and wife know their God-given relation to each other. God's Word spells that out clearly, and it is in harmony with the qualities God entrusted to man and woman at the time of creation. Knowing how He made man and knowing the purpose for which He made man, God stipulated that "the husband is the head of the wife, as Christ is the head of the church."

This authority of the father has been widely misunderstood and misrepresented. Television often pictures the father as a buffoon who exerts his authority in a stubborn, clumsy way and in the end must surrender. This is a far cry from the kind of authority God had in mind. God intended family authority to create a setting for beautiful love relationships, mutual harmony, and understanding. There is nothing egoistic about this authority. It comes much closer to service and sacrifice. Christ Himself is the great example. He leads His church into a blessed, productive life.

The husband and father is responsible for setting the stage on which his wife and children can grow and flourish in the way of peace, blessedness, and imagination. There is a subtle but very real difference between the gentleness of moral authority and the abrasiveness of authoritarianism.

Would you trade the exercise of such authority for a situation where a husband is his wife's (best?) friend and a pal to his children?

Dear Lord, restore Your Word to homes in the land everywhere and bring husbands and fathers to a renewed awareness of their responsibility and task. We confess that all authority comes from You. Use us to the benefit of all whom we may meet today. For Jesus' sake. Amen.

No Exit

The heart of her husband trusts in her . . . She does him good . . . all the days of her life (Prov. 31:11-12).

Marriage has no exit.

At least, it shouldn't have.

Many people secretly fashion an emergency escape.

When they feel their marriage isn't working out, they slip away through that door.

The result is terrible insecurity. Every quarrel is a potential threat to the marriage itself. Every argument may send one of the partners scrambling for the emergency exit.

The Bible tells us that the basis of marriage is trust and faithfulness. Marriage is a lifelong union of love. Husband and wife may not even allow the thought of breaking up that union to enter their minds, for without that trust, love cannot flourish and life cannot develop.

A home built on such firm understanding and trust will provide the security needed for the growth and development of the children. The members of such a family can afford to have shortcomings, and their mistakes don't cause panic, for the abiding safety of the home will soothe the pain, solve the problems, bring solutions, correct wrongdoing, and lead to healing and relief.

How wonderful when a husband can testify with our text today, "His heart *trusts* in her." Notice: *his heart*. It is the foundation of his life. And of the wife it is said, "She does him good all the days of her life." It's a lasting institution. She is surrounded by abiding goodness.

Is your situation far removed from this ideal? Then remember again that Christ's grace was mostly applied to broken situations, and that healing works gradually.

Merciful God, we lay before You the sorrow which unfaithfulness has brought to so many homes. Holy Spirit, lead people to repentance and restoration. Give solace to innocent victims. Preserve our love, for we are frail. Amen.

Marriage Motives

Husbands, love your wives, as Christ loved the church and gave himself up for her . . . and let the wife see that she respects her husband (Eph. 5:25, 33).

Attitudes and motives play a big role in marriage. Many marriage partners are out to *get* more than to *give*. They entered marriage for their own satisfaction. They put on a show of love which was not real love. They may flatter each other with attention and compliments, but basically only for one reason: to have a more responsive partner. Soon the thrill wears off, and they begin to realize how flimsy the basis of their marriage really is.

Paul tells the Ephesian Christians to love each other after Christ's example. He came into this world to *give*—not to *get*. He loved those who were unlovable. He died for unworthy sinners who had no intention of following Him. By His Spirit He overwhelmed dead, stubborn people like us. He gave them life. Thus they became more and more like Him. Believers can now love each other without looking for the reward it brings. A husband, says Paul, can now love his wife just for her own sake. And the wife respects her husband for what he is and returns his love.

All this has a remarkable dimension. While the marriage partners are out to give and to serve, they receive blessed rewards, without laying claim to them. And the opposite is true too: those who married in order to *get* will have nothing in the end.

Note also that blessings keep multiplying in such selfless marriages. Children, for instance, great imitators that they are, will also learn the art of *giving* rather than *getting*. They will learn to care about their fellow man, and they will love the coming of the Kingdom. What a joy!

Lord, teach husbands and wives and all of us the meaning of Christian love. Holy Spirit, help us to be as aggressive as Jesus Christ in seeking those who need us. For Jesus' sake. Amen.

The Home's Twin Foundation

By wisdom a house is built, and by understanding it is established (Prov. 24:3).

The Christian home and family are built on the double foundation of *wisdom* and *understanding*, says today's text.

You can't define wisdom and understanding very easily, for they have to do with living, dynamic relationships between people in ever changing situations.

To be wise and understanding means that you can look at things from a distance. It means that you don't take yourself overly seriously. It means that you can enter sympathetically into someone else's situation. It means that you cultivate the habit of investing in the happiness of your fellow family members. It means that you have discovered the joy of showing concern and kindness in the small things of daily life. Wisdom and understanding make you strong enough to endure patiently whatever little inconveniences and injustices you may have to put up with.

There is one condition that must be met before wisdom and understanding can have full sway in your home. You must come to terms with *yourself*. Do you know how? You must accept yourself and have peace with who you are. At the same time you must be liberated from your egotistical *self*. Those two things can happen in you through Christ.

Christ came to suffer and die for your sins, sins which made you a prisoner of your old selfish nature. And that, in turn, restores you to healthy self-esteem and personal dignity. You have become a *free person*, free in Christ. Without that freedom you cannot exercise the wisdom and understanding of which today's text speaks. In childlike dependence, expect it all from Christ. That's where Paul got his confidence: "But we preach Christ crucified . . . the power of God and the wisdom of God . . . Christ Jesus, whom God made our wisdom" (I Cor. 1:23-30).

Holy Spirit, connect us ever more fully with Christ, the Source of all wisdom and understanding. Help us to care for people in our lives who are dear to us, and all the people with whom we associate. Amen.

"Mixed Marriage"

Now an Israelite woman's son, whose father was an Egyptian, went out among the people of Israel; and the Israelite woman's son and a man of Israel quarreled in the camp, and the Israelite woman's son blasphemed the Name, and cursed (Lev. 24:10-11).

A youth counselor once warned young Christians not to marry outside their faith. He said, "Some mixed marriages work, but don't let that fool you. Suppose you wanted to fly across the Atlantic and asked the ticket agent, 'Is it a safe trip?' and he answered, 'O yes, every once in a while a plane gets through.' I doubt whether you would take the trip."

Marriage is a very intimate relationship. If one partner is committed to Christ and the other is not, togetherness at a deep level is impossible. Tensions and frustrations are the result.

And what about the children of such a home? Usually they become the victims of the tensions between father and mother. Today's text gives us an example. It tells of a boy whose mother was an Israelite woman and the father an Egyptian. "He went out among the people of Israel," we read. That's the Bible's gentle way of saying that he wandered around aimlessly and was up to no good. It didn't take too long before he got into a fight. In the heat of the argument he blasphemed the name of God and cursed. Apparently he was a very angry, "mixed-up kid." He was the *result* of much unhappiness, and he became the *cause* of more unhappiness.

Two things remain to be said here. The Lord will sustain all those who cry to Him in their distress. He will help those who can't cope with the problems of a "mixed marriage." But you, young people, who have not made the choice of a life's partner, make sure you date, court and marry someone who shares your commitment to Christ.

Lord, You know the problems of Your children. Please give counsel and wisdom to those who are in distress. Guide young people to seek a partner in the Lord. Amen.

Family Affection

You shall be happy, and it shall be well with you. Your children will be like olive shoots around your table (Ps. 128:2, 3).

An unknown poet wrote:

> We flatter those we scarcely know,
>   We please the fleeting guest.
> And deal full many a thoughtless blow
>   To those we love the best.

May that not be true of your family. But we know our weaknesses. Our homes should and could be havens of happiness, but we don't always succeed in making them that. We all admit that good family life is very important, yet so much of our soul's concentration is directed toward our work and personal concerns. As time goes on, there are moments when we wonder whether our family is still revolving around the hub of love. Someone said, "If you bungle the job of raising your children, it really doesn't matter what else you do well."

Many people have become pessimistic about the future of family life. A century ago Engels wrote, "The family will not have to be abolished; it will be allowed to wither away." Engels' somber prediction has not fully come true, but there is no doubt that our generation has not been successful in building happy homes.

Psalm 128, as a Messianic psalm, looks forward to the coming of Christ, who not only redeems family members but also family relationships. His love to us is not only a source of strength, it is also our assignment.

Patience, observance, thoughtfulness, and affection are virtues we can all claim from our Savior Jesus Christ. In His grace and power we can practice them. They are their own rich harvest: a marriage and home where affection is freely expressed and received, and where children thrive.

In the Master's power *you* can do that! You will experience what André Marois said: "Marriage is a long conversation that always seems too short."

Lord, we pray, come into our hearts and home, with Your love. May we understand the needs of our children. Amen.

Redemption Through the Family

*The Lord God said to the serpent . . . "I will put enmity between you and
the woman, and between your seed and her seed; he shall bruise your head,
and you shall bruise his heel." [Adam] called his wife's name Eve, because
she was the mother of all living (Gen. 3:14-15, 20).*

Sin is the great family destroyer. Adam and Eve were ashamed
of each other when they broke their tie with God. Cain killed his
brother Abel.

But, praise God, His grace was more than a match for man's
sin. God came with a mighty promise to Adam and Eve. Eve would
become the *mother* of the promised seed, the generations from
which Christ the Savior would be born in due time. God used
marriage and family to bring healing and restoration to the earth.

Adam understood. From that time on he called his wife *Eve*
which means "Mother of all living." The hope of salvation lay in
Eve's *motherhood*.

The Christian family still plays a large role in God's program
of redemption. The church of God has grown in number and
strength through the faithful nurture her young members received
in Christian homes. Standards and ideals of Christian conduct were
instilled in the hearts of new generations *through the home*. Such
Christian upbringing led the children to see that Christ wants to be
served everywhere in life. And the real desire for evangelism has
always come through the concern for the lost, a concern which the
children saw *in the lives of their parents*.

Ours is an age in which the search for *meaning* is very
prominent—and rightly so. Let us remember, then, that a big share
of meaning in life lies in our homes, in our families, in our
marriages. The well-being of church and society depends to a large
extent on the well-being of the home. So, come to life as soon as
you walk over the threshold of your home.

*Lord, help us to see how great a role our family life plays in the salvation of
people and the coming of Your Kingdom on earth. Help us as parents and
children to make the best of these golden years. Amen.*

Family Nurture

Fathers, do not provoke your children to anger, but bring them up in the discipline [nurture] and instruction of the Lord (Eph. 6:4).

The home influence is an enormous factor in the upbringing of your children. You have the task as parents to show your children that they belong to Christ and must serve Him.

The sentence above this meditation speaks of discipline or nurture.

Nurture is a beautiful word. It portrays many things. Nurture implies firmness, but not with undue force. Nurture shows by patient example, not imposing one's ways or convictions. Nurture is instruction with sensitivity toward the children's needs and feelings.

Nurture implies discipline and admonition, but always permeated with love and understanding. Nurture directs the child to commit his heart to Christ as Savior and Lord.

Nurture opens the windows of family life to the big world around us. The parents show by example, word and attitude how to serve Christ in church, state and society.

Nurture sets the stage for a lively exchange of thought and opinion. The children can express far-out ideas without embarrassment. And parents lay out the Christian direction amid all the spiritual forces that compete for their children's loyalty.

Nurture makes the home a daily retreat, a place to confide in one another, to have heart-to-heart talks, and to renew strength and courage.

All of these, of course, are not virtues confined to the home. In the way of dependence on Christ, you can become the kind of person who is a blessing to the people on his pathway.

Heavenly Father, help us as parents to bring up our children in the nurture of the Lord. We often fail, but give us wisdom, strength and patience every day again. And cause us to be good neighbors to people around us. Amen.

Prepare Your Children for a Calling

For this child I prayed; and the Lord has granted me my petition which I made to him. Therefore I have lent him to the Lord; as long as he lives, he is lent to the Lord (I Sam. 1:27-8).

Hannah was a woman of great determination. She wanted a child very badly. She prayed and prayed, and God gave her a son whom she named Samuel.

But Hannah was not only determined to *get* from God, but also to *give* to Him.

Hannah brought up her little son for God's service. One day, when he was still a young boy, she took him to the temple, where Samuel remained as God's servant.

Hannah knew only one motive in her determination to receive and to give. She was a woman who longed for the coming of the Messiah, the promised Redeemer of the world. And Hannah's son became involved in the Messiah's coming. Samuel's illustrious career as a prophet hastened the coming of Christ. The godly upbringing Hannah gave her son was the foundation of Samuel's great career.

Now, there is one thing you must remember about Hannah: she had a lot of family and marriage problems. This woman knew of sleepless nights and bitter tears. How could she manage to do all these wonderful things for the Lord? She kept her eye on that one great goal: the coming of the Messiah. That goal beautified and hallowed every family chore.

Consider your personal and family life. Perhaps you face some very difficult situations. You may have convinced yourself that you are disqualified from doing something significant for the Lord and His people. Nonsense! Keep your eye on the cause of God and the coming of His Kingdom. Such a sense of calling will beautify your family relations and dissolve tensions and fears.

Lord, there are great things to be accomplished for You through Your people. Help us in equipping them for it. Holy Spirit, give us the endurance to do it. Amen.

Do You Take Time for Your Children?

And he [the father of the demon-possessed boy] said . . . "Have pity on us and help us" (Mark 9:21-2).

Mark 9 tells us about a father whose little boy had been terribly ill from his early childhood. Note how close the father was to the boy. He asked Jesus, "Have pity on *us*, and help *us*."

This closeness was undoubtedly a result of the boy's pitiable condition. Even so, is there any reason why we should not be close to our children?

The only way you can build this closeness is to spend time with your children. But it all depends on *how* you spend time with them. A busy father who works hard at his business and in the community may spend an occasional evening in front of the television set with his children, but he is not really spending time with them.

The family would have been far better served if the father had given ten minutes of *undivided attention* to his teenager, or if he had listened attentively to his little boy or girl for only a little while. Your children don't demand many hours of your time. What they need is your zeroing in completely on what they want to share with you, with a mind clear of other concerns. And then remember what they said, mull it over, and pray about it.

The father in today's text had that kind of a relationship with his little son. We read that he *brought him to Jesus*. To lead children to Jesus is not an easy assignment. By God's grace you can do it if you have regularly invested something of yourself in your children. Trust and respect are bridges across which you can invite your children to the Savior.

Heavenly Father, help us to point each other to Christ, the Source of power, purpose and meaning. May our hope not be in our own goodness, lest our fall be very great. Amen.

Raising Children by Grace Alone

The Lord was with Joseph, and he became a successful man (Gen. 39:2).

The Bible never dwells very long on the goodness of people. Tracing the interesting history of Joseph in Egypt, we cannot help but be impressed with his firm stand against evil and his courageous attitude in personal tragedies. Nevertheless, the Biblical account never offers a word of praise for Joseph's "goodness."

The reason will be clear if we note what the Bible says instead. We read, "The Lord was with Joseph." The same sentence is repeated in verses 21 and 23.

That one little phrase, repeated three times, is of immense importance for us personally and for our homes.

Now, would that we learned that lesson! We have a tendency to *program* our children to be "good" and to avoid the "bad." Our children soon realize that it is to their advantage to be "good," and that "badness" doesn't pay. Our children also learn quickly that the community will accept or reject them depending on how "good" or "bad" they are. And since children yearn for approval, they will mostly fall in line.

But notice how dangerously close we have come to hypocrisy and works-righteousness, for our goodness was motivated by the urge to please others. Let's quickly see the main events of salvation again. Our sin created a bottomless abyss between God and us. Christ bridged that abyss and connected us with God's power. To be "good" is to accept as real that God will be with us *as He was with Joseph*. Let us consider tomorrow what happens when we let God have His way in us.

Heavenly Father, help us to point each other to You as the Source of power, purpose and meaning. For Jesus' sake. Amen.

Strong by Grace Alone

*But he refused and said to his master's wife . . . "How then can I do this
great wickedness, and sin against God?" (Gen. 39:8-9).*

Parents often worry whether their children, once they leave the
home, will continue in the Lord's ways and will stand strong in
temptations.

They hope that their children will measure up to Joseph, the
young Hebrew boy sold as a slave to Egypt. Faced with un-
believable temptation, Joseph came through victoriously under
very difficult circumstances.

What was the secret of his power? Not his goodness, as we saw
yesterday. No, Joseph stood firm because *he knew his God was
near.* Through loneliness and suffering, the presence of God had
become precious to Joseph. The *will* of God meant so much to
Joseph because *God Himself* meant so much to him. When this
sudden temptation came, Joseph immediately called his heavenly
Father to the scene: *"How can I sin against God?"*

It is not enough for parents and the church to call youth back
to a respect for standards of good conduct. Parents and children
must meet Christ and, through the Holy Spirit, walk intimately
with God. Obedience and fruitbearing are a result of God's own
doing through us.

The apostle Paul was very concerned that the church of
Galatia persevere in the faith, so he shared a precious personal
secret with them: "I have been crucified with Christ; it is no longer
I who live, but Christ who lives in me" (Gal. 2:20). Our children
will stand strong when they have learned that secret from us: let
Christ do it through us.

*Dear God, help each one of us to know You personally and to be filled with
Your presence. Restore us to a blameless life and the great calling of Your
Kingdom. Through Christ's power. Amen.*

Bad Advice for the Lovelorn

But Amnon had a friend, whose name was Jonadab, the son of Shimeah, David's brother; and Jonadab was a very crafty man (II Sam. 13:3).

Amnon, the son of King David, is in love. That should be a wonderful thing, but it isn't in Amnon's case—first of all, because he is in love with his half-sister Tamar, and secondly, because Amnon's love is very impure.

Into this situation steps his friend Jonadab, worldly-wise beyond his years and very unprincipled. Jonadab relishes his role as counselor to an anguished friend. His advice leads to quick and easy fulfillment of Amnon's unholy desires.

Now, as you read this, think for a moment. Who are your friends? What are their principles? What are they to you? What are you to them? Our associations with people have far more consequences for us than we think. Consider the results of Jonadab's advice. Tamar leaves the house "a desolate woman," and Amnon himself is murdered by Tamar's brother Absalom, who, in turn, falls victim to further family intrigue.

Some questions are unavoidable.

Wasn't there anyone in David's household to whom Amnon could have turned for help? Did no one notice his distress and confusion? Why weren't any provisions made to guide Amnon and Tamar once the damage had been done? Were they all strangers to each other in the palace family? What had become of standards for godly living? Was there no longing in David's family for the coming of the Messiah Redeemer?

But then, perhaps we should honestly face some of these questions in our own homes. Are the lines of communication open? Is there opportunity for good advice to be given and heeded?

Lord, open our eyes to each other's needs at home. Make us people who understand and care. For the sake of Christ's Kingdom. Amen.

Family Unity

When the boys grew up, Esau was a skilful hunter, a man of the field, while Jacob was a quiet man, dwelling in tents. Isaac loved Esau . . . but Rebekah loved Jacob (Gen. 25:27-8).

Terrible damage is being done to the modern family. We can coin all sorts of fancy phrases to describe the tragedy and its causes, but it all comes down to this: we have become so selfish and cold-hearted that we simply cannot stand being together anymore. Counselors tell us that marriage partners often don't even bother defending themselves. They just want to leave and be free.

One religious broadcast recently told of a sociologist who advised young people that they should enter marriage expecting that they will have been married three times before life is over. The grim fact was that this sociologist saw such a trend as a reasonable development. "After all," he remarked, "it is impossible to expect two people to be properly suited to one another over a whole life span; people change and develop too much to expect them to be able to continue to live under one roof for a whole lifetime."

Many fall for this sort of "scientific" reasoning. The fact of the matter is that a nation cannot survive without healthy family life. And family life cannot survive without love that gives and serves and blesses. The members of Isaac's family sought their own gain. They were divided: the father sided with the older son, the mother with the younger. Cheating and hatred were the result, and in the end tragedy was their lot.

The cause of it all is not hard to discern. The coming of the Messiah, the redemption of the world, was no longer a burning concern in Isaac's family. In such an atmosphere, small human concerns and petty likes and dislikes begin to count heavily. Family health is directly connected with spiritual health.

Come, Lord Jesus, redeem our families. Help us to be unselfish and loving to each other as children and parents. Give us spiritual vision. Amen.

In Trouble

Now Dinah the daughter of Leah, whom she had borne to Jacob, went out to visit the women of the land (Gen. 34:1).

Our text sounds innocent enough. Dinah, the youngest member of Jacob's large family, sought the company of the girls of Shechem, a city to which they had moved shortly before.

But everything went wrong for Dinah in Shechem: immorality, cheating, hatred, and ultimately murder.

Dinah, however, was only partly to blame. Her fall was part of a much larger family failure. Years before, Jacob had fled from his parental home to his uncle Laban's place in Paddan-aram. In great fear and loneliness he had stopped at a place later called *Bethel*. There Jacob had promised God that he would return to that place to show his thankfulness if God would bless him. Well, God did bless Jacob richly, but, as often happens, the promise was forgotten. Instead of returning to Bethel to pay his vow to God, Jacob bought some land in the prosperous but worldly area of Shechem and lived there comfortably. Like his father Isaac, Jacob didn't long very much for the Messiah. Small wonder that the children were weak morally and spiritually. When temptation struck, Dinah was no match for the powers of sin.

So to the young people we say today: God holds you personally responsible for what you do. Walk in His ways, seek His power for your life through Jesus Christ, be much in prayer, and read your Bible so that you will become more and more attuned to the high standards of His Kingdom.

But to parents we say: your lack of positive Christian living will be visited in your children. Your lack of spiritual investment will show up in lack of return. While it is still possible, then, repent and bear fruit.

Holy Spirit, cleanse us from sin—fathers, mothers, sons, and daughters. Fill our hearts with a deep love for Your cause among men so that there is no place for idols among us. Amen.

Christian Education

And you shall teach [God's words] diligently to your children, and shall talk of them when you sit in your house, and when you walk by the way, and when you lie down, and when you rise (Deut. 6:7).

The Bible was written in a day that differed vastly from ours. Through the centuries, simple community life developed into our complex, specialized society. But that does not mean that the Bible, the Word of God, doesn't shed light on the fullness of life today. Every part of modern life must be directed by the will of God as revealed in the Scriptures. The text quoted above emphasizes that it is the parents' task to show their children this full-orbed Christian lifestyle.

In our specialized age it is not possible for parents to educate their children personally. Qualified teachers have taken over this task. But that does not mean that the parents have no responsibility in the education of their children. Parents must see to it that the total program of their children's school is in harmony with the will of God. The atmosphere and the curriculum of the school our children attend must stem from the same spiritual roots on which our Christian families draw. Children are whole persons: the religious sensitivity at home should never differ from that of the school. Remember that the school years of the children are the most impressionable ones of their lives.

Education is never neutral and objective. It always promotes a way of life; it always instills values and ideals in the hearts of the students. All education is guided by a philosophy of life. Christian parents must see to it that their children attend schools where the entire educational process is guided by the Biblical world-and-life-view. Christians must help each other to make such schools possible.

Lord Jesus, help us to express Your power and redemption in the education of our youth. Give us the love and the means to maintain Christian schools everywhere in our land. Amen.

Love's Unique Concern

Love is patient and kind; love is not jealous or boastful; it is not arrogant or rude. Love does not insist on its own way . . . Love bears all things, believes all things, hopes all things, endures all things (I Cor. 13:4-7).

Throughout the ages, people have tried to unravel the mystery of love.

The ancient Greeks were aware of love's many aspects. They coined three words for love—one that associated love with passion and desire, another one for quiet affection and mutual care, and still another to denote the delights of friendship and companionship.

But it took the Christian gospel to reveal the real nature of love.

Christ, the Son of God, came to this earth to express that love among men. The secret of Christ's love was that He sought and saved those *totally unworthy* of His love. He loved those who were *unlovable!*

That love is still the heart of Christian life today. Christian believers love those who *don't deserve it.* Their love sets no conditions, seeks no rewards, and harbors no fear of being repelled. That's the unique thing about godly love. Human forms of love apart from God have always contained the element of "What gain does it bring me?" To be sure, the exercise of Christian love is not easy. The history of Christianity is replete with painful instances of Christians seeking themselves, Christians denying their Master. It is in the way of humble dependence on Christ that we can grow in expressing Christ's love in our attitude and actions.

Western civilization's only hope for survival lies in the homes and families where this Christian love is practiced.

Christianity was once known for this strong, quiet concern for love. This is no longer so. Unless Christians learn again to demonstrate this love, they do not have much to offer the world.

Dear Savior, teach us the meaning of love. Liberate us from selfishness, arrogance and pretense. Help us to deny ourselves and to serve our fellow men. Amen.

Quarrels Obstruct Love's Progress

But if you bite and devour one another take heed that you are not consumed by one another (Gal. 5:15).

In this chapter Paul sums up the believer's task in one word—*love*. In verse 13 he states, "Through love be servants of one another." In verse 14 he adds, "For the whole law is fulfilled in one word, 'You shall love your neighbor as yourself.' "

Now in verse 15 Paul points out one terrible barrier to the march of love—*quarreling*. Love cannot flourish in an atmosphere poisoned by bitterness and resentment. In his book *The Screwtape Letters*, C. S. Lewis tells of an experienced devil who emphasizes to his nephew the frightful possibilities of family squabbles. With family life becoming increasingly hectic, any little offense provides a skillful demon with a spark to set off another explosion.

Family life has exciting possibilities. Many readers of these meditations wish they could do it over again. Paul says that in family life, too, we are called to be co-laborers with the risen Christ. What a challenge for the home!

Galatians 5:15 says that our quarrels may lead to the dreadful reality of consuming one another. There is something painfully ironic about all this. Here we talk in lofty terms about love—that it is truly unique in Christ, and that it is the heart of the Christian faith. And then we say that love can be threatened by something as ridiculous as a family quarrel. Yet, that's how it is. Love and love's relationship are extremely strong, but at the same time they are delicate and frail. That's why the Bible sounds the same refrain: surrender to Christ, depend on your Heavenly Father, and be constantly filled with the power of the Spirit.

Holy Spirit, keep our eyes directed to our calling of love. Help us to cherish the love others lavish upon us. Help us to love those not worthy of it. Give us the wisdom not to make big issues out of trivial matters. Amen.

The Cause of Conflict

Cain said to Abel his brother, "Let us go out to the field." And when they were in the field, Cain rose up against his brother Abel, and killed him (Gen. 4:8).

Yesterday's meditation may have left us with a question: How can it be that conflict has such devastating power? From the dawn of history comes an example of its ruinous effect. We read here of the family of Adam and Eve. One day the older son, Cain, invited the younger one, Abel, to go to the field. There, in cold blood, he killed him.

How could such a tragedy take place?

Note some background facts. Just before the murder took place, the two boys had brought a sacrifice. Abel's had been accepted, Cain's had been rejected. That was not just an incidental thing. The two sons embodied two kingdoms, the kingdom of satan and the Kingdom of God. Those two kingdoms were at war in the one family of Adam and Eve. Cain allowed himself to be an instrument of satan's kingdom, which explains the violent power of his deed.

The warfare between these two kingdoms continues to this day and will last till the end of history, when Christ will return and destroy the kingdom of satan.

Not a single family can avoid that conflict. For, you see, the battle between Christ and satan rages right in our own heart. In the very depth of our being, we must embrace Christ as Savior and Lord, and in His power fight against everything that is unholy.

Our families will stand strong against satan's attacks only when we personally have Christ in our hearts. Satan knows very well that if he could destroy our homes, he could destroy our civilization. So let us be prepared and put on the whole armor of God (Eph. 6).

Lord Jesus, You have won the victory over satan and death. Thank You for having overcome evil in us. Fill us now with Your love so that we can accept others and live with them peaceably. Amen.

A Permissive Home

On that day I will fulfil against Eli all that I have spoken concerning his house . . . for the iniquity which he knew, because his sons were blaspheming God, and he did not restrain them (I Sam. 3:12-13).

We have all known the domineering father type who imposes his will on his family. Cocksure, confident that he is right, he orders his son out of the house or locks the door at midnight so that his daughter, late from a date, cannot get in. Such abuses of parental authority are very detrimental.

But the opposite is equally disastrous. Today the *permissive* home abounds. It is nothing new. The Bible tells of Eli, a pious man of high position. He was a high priest in Israel. Eli's sons were guilty of scandalous behavior. It bothered Eli a great deal. He *talked* to his sons about it (I Sam. 2:22-5), but he did not *do* anything to stop them.

The consequences were awesome. God took the high priestly office away from Eli's family. The service around the tabernacle came to a standstill for a long time. War also resulted, with thousands of people dying in battle, among them the sons of Eli. Years of darkness followed. And all this happened because "he restrained them not," according to I Samuel 3.

If we withhold discipline from our children, we deny them emotional security, fail to equip them with standards of good and bad, leave them without goals and ideals in life, and fail to bless them with the strong family ties of love and concern they need.

Finally, note one other implication. Eli avoided a showdown with his sons because he dreaded the possibility of a total break; he spared his sons because he was afraid of losing them. Yet, that's exactly what happened—he lost them. Many of our parental shortcomings stem from good intentions, but we pay the price in the end.

Lord, give much wisdom and firmness to parents everywhere. May a new generation become equipped to cope with life's problems in moral excellence. For the coming of Your Kingdom. Amen.

The Busy Housekeeper

But Martha was distracted with much serving; and she went to [Jesus] and said, "Lord, do you not care that my sister has left me to serve alone? Tell her then to help me" (Luke 10:40).

The little family crisis described in this part of Luke 10 has puzzled many Bible readers.

Martha and Mary suddenly received thirteen people for dinner. While Martha toiled away at all the chores, she noticed Mary comfortably sitting with the company, letting her do the work alone. When she finally told Jesus how she felt about that, Jesus defended Mary.

But read this Bible passage again, carefully. Martha said to Christ, "Mary has left me to serve alone." So Mary had been helping. But her work was a tribute to Christ, the honored Guest. And since Christ was greater than any work she could do for Him, she could afford to sit down with Christ for a while. Martha, however, was so busy that she didn't see Jesus in her work anymore. We read, "But Martha was distracted with much serving . . ." And when she lost sight of Jesus in her work, her work became a tyrant.

How ironic some of these situations can indeed become, also among us! We make preparations to honor someone and become so involved that the preparations become more prominent than the honoree. I have attended weddings where the photographer nearly took over; the pictures of the bridal couple became more important than the bridal couple. And isn't it strange that with our homes full of labor-saving devices, we have become busier than those who have only few? Even in church life we have not escaped the Martha syndrome: so much of our energy is devoted to keeping the organizational machinery going. Let's repent, then, and do the one thing needful.

Lord, free us from worrying about things. May we hear Your promises clearly again. You will care for us. Amen.

Materialism as a Way of Life

And Jesus . . . said to him, "You lack one thing; go, sell what you have, and give to the poor, and you will have treasure in heaven; and come follow me" (Mark 10:21).

The "rich young ruler" wasn't a bad fellow. He went to Jesus to inquire about how to get eternal life, and he kept God's commandments diligently.

But he didn't make the grade with Jesus. Imagine that!

Why not?

His life was split right down the middle. He agreed to go through all sorts of religious services for God, but his real security lay in his great wealth.

Jesus put this choice before him: either you rest in God or you rest in your money. Pitifully enough, he chose money.

Many Christian homes are caught in the same web. The twin gods, Production and Consumption, demand our full loyalty. Their prophets tell us on T.V. that without the blessing of these gods, our modern technological society will grind to a halt.

And this material way of life has become the actual religion of many homes. Though they still cling to Christian customs and slogans, many parents nurture their children in that controlling vision of life. The line between materialism and Christian virtue can sometimes be alarmingly thin. We urge our children to do their homework, to learn a skill, and to do well on the job. But from what motive? That they may be more useful to the Lord, or that they will be better off in life?

Heed the urgent call of Christ, who says: "Therefore do not be anxious, saying, 'What shall we eat?' or 'What shall we drink?' . . . But seek first his kingdom and his righteousness, and all these things shall be yours as well" (Matt. 6:31, 33).

Lord, we confess that we are on this earth to live as citizens of the Kingdom and not to make and spend money. Holy Spirit, remove our idols and lead us on the way everlasting. Amen.

Living Alone

And there was a prophetess, Anna . . . and as a widow till she was eighty-four. She did not depart from the temple, worshiping with fasting and prayer night and day (Luke 2:36-7).

Many people go through life single. Some of them don't mind, but many have known bitter sorrow, regret, rejection, and disappointment. Few of these people consider themselves understood by their fellow men. Few of them have hope that they will ever find happiness and fulfillment again. Indeed, there is much affliction that will not be removed in the present age, in spite of all the easy-solution manuals that have flooded the market.

But there is one thing the Lord leaves no doubt about: those of us who live alone can and should know meaning and purpose. God often trusted single people with special mandates. The great apostle Paul is an example. Dorcas, who helped the needy, is another (Acts 9). In fact, in the new creation, which Christ will usher in when He returns, there will be no marriage. Our whole life will be joyous service. We will be one big family, the household of faith, and we will be closer to each other than husbands and wives could ever be.

In today's Scripture passage we read of Anna, a widow for many, many years who has made the temple her home, praying her heart out that the Messiah Redeemer might come soon. She was one of the few vital prayer links left through which the Redeemer was born.

God responded generously. He gave Anna the great fulfillment of being introduced to the Christ-child. In the way of prayer and service, there is fulfillment for every one of God's children.

Holy Spirit, give vision and courage to all who live alone. Grant them a life of joy, meaning, fellowship, and service. For Jesus' sake. Amen.

People Who Deserve Our Appreciation

And Deborah, Rebekah's nurse, died, and she was buried under an oak below Bethel; so the name of it was called Allon-bacuth [oak of weeping] (Gen. 35:8).

We all depend on the good services of thousands of people around us. Since we fail to see this clearly, we fail to show our gratitude. The amazing thing is that we often show the least appreciation to those who are the closest to us and who mean the most to us. At this very moment, think hard about people in your life. Have you told your wife that you appreciate the selfless care she shows to the family? Have you told your husband that you are aware of the pressures in his life? And when the children stay out of trouble, you had better commend them for it.

The family of Jacob went through years of stress and turmoil. All that time faithful Deborah, Rebekah's nurse, remained part of the family, sharing the dangers, consoling in tragedies. Her name meant *bee*, symbol of industry and inexhaustible energy. Nothing was too much for Aunt Bee. Her life was spent in serving others, until the Lord relieved her from her duties and welcomed her into the rest which remains for the people of God.

Deborah probably didn't get all the appreciation she deserved. But when she died, Jacob and his family realized how much this woman had meant to them. They buried her with great honor. An oak tree, symbol of strength and dignity, marked her grave. They called the site "Oak of Weeping," as an expression of their feelings.

Appreciation means little when it is not expressed, or expressed too late. So, do it today! It will make for a special day.

Lord, we are grateful for the wonderful things so many people do for us. We are especially grateful for those who are close to us. Inspire us to serve others. For Jesus' sake. Amen.

A Godly Grandmother

I am reminded of your sincere faith, a faith that dwelt first in your grandmother Lois and your mother Eunice and now, I am sure, dwells in you (II Tim. 1:5).

We all feel discouraged at times. It's good, at such moments, to take stock of God's gifts to us.

Paul reminds his youthful helper Timothy of several such gifts. One of them is found in today's text: *remember the faith of your grandmother Lois!*

Actually, Paul points Timothy to their God, for God had shown His great faithfulness through grandmother Lois. By His grace, God had made Lois a believer. And He had used Lois to instill faith in the heart of Eunice, her daughter. The upbringing which Eunice in turn gave her son Timothy was blessed by God so that he grew up as a believer.

All this is a demonstration of God's *covenant faithfulness*. He uses the family lines to add to the number of believers.

If faith, then, has such deep roots, it is also *worth fighting for*, Paul reminds Timothy. Because faith is of this sterling quality, Lois and Eunice must have worked hard at the Christian upbringing of their children.

Have you ever noticed that we make problems of things which in the Bible are quite simple? The Bible tells us that salvation is a free gift of God and that children may freely claim this gift together with godly parents. The Bible also tells us that salvation results in *good works*. So the more we treasure our salvation, just because it is a gift from God, the harder we will work for Him! That, of course, is what Paul has in mind for Timothy: there is so much work to be done, Timothy, there are so many people to be converted! Covenant trust and hard work go together.

Thank You, Lord, for all Your covenant mercies. May the assurance of faith lead us to diligence and concern. Make us evangelists. Amen.

A Death in the Family

And as her soul was departing (for she died), she called his name Benoni; but his father called his name Benjamin (Gen. 35:18).

Every family knows—or will know—sorrow.

Today's Scripture passage tells of the tragic death of a young mother, Jacob's wife, Rachel. While camping in the vicinity of Bethlehem Ephratha, she died in childbirth. The midwife spoke words of encouragement, but Rachel's strength ebbed away. She put all her anguish into the boy's name—*Benoni*, son of sorrows. And then she died.

Death and suffering have always been the lot of the human race. Many readers of these meditations feel the weight of sorrow and affliction right this moment.

But for God's people death is not the end. Jacob looked upon that newborn child and changed his name to *Benjamin*—son of my right hand, son of my hope.

That hope was not put to shame!

Near the place where Rachel died, another Child was born years later. In Bethlehem-Ephratha, Mary gave birth to the Christ-child. Though fully God, He was also fully human. He bore all our griefs and carried all our sorrows. He understands what we experience. He is very close to His followers. He comforts them. He fills the void in their hearts with His presence. He knows your pain and the empty place in your family.

The Letter to the Hebrews was directed to believers who had suffered much. Some were widows who had witnessed their husbands being martyred. To them and to us the letter says: "For we have not a high priest who is unable to sympathize with our weaknesses, but one who in every respect has been tempted as we are, yet without sin" (4:15).

Lord, we pray now for those who grieve. Ease the pain of suffering. Thank You, Lord, for Your understanding. Amen.

Home Life as Investment for the Future

Train up a child in the way he should go, and when he is old he will not depart from it (Prov. 22:6).

This text comes with a bold promise. Instill in your children a Christian vision of life, Christian attitudes and ideals, and when they have become grownups they will continue in the Christian way.

The events recorded in II Kings 5 illustrate the point.

Once a cruel enemy attacked God's people. Among the many captives they carried away was a young girl who was ultimately sold as a slave to Naaman, the commander of the Syrian army.

In those very difficult conditions, that girl showed the worth of her godly upbringing.

We read two wonderful things about her. First, she sensed the presence of her God and clung to Him. And secondly, she was able to forgive her captors and show concern for her master. When she heard that Naaman had leprosy, she was convinced that her God could heal Naaman. Therefore she tactfully suggested that he go and see God's prophet in Israel.

Parents and youth leaders, how important it is that we demonstrate godly living to a new generation! Parents of little children, absorbed in busy concerns, often fail to realize that they have their children with them for only a few years. The boys and girls leave the nest, and parents can do nothing about their upbringing anymore.

The parents of the girl in Naaman's house had to pack her godly upbringing into a pitifully short time. So did Hannah, who brought the little Samuel to the temple for good. So, let's make the best of every day that we are together.

Holy Spirit, inspire this generation to godly living so that a new generation may walk in God's ways. We thank You, heavenly Father, for marriage, home and family. In Christ's name. Amen.

Remove Those Bushels

You are the light of the world. A city set on a hill cannot be hid. Nor do men light a lamp and put it under a bushel (Matt. 5:14-15).

These words of Christ seem logical enough. Hold high a blazing lamp, and everything lights up. So the Christian church is Christ's lamp in the world.

Ah, that sounds good, but is it true of the church you know?

What a strange contradiction! There are many who love Christ as Savior and Lord and who are the light of the world, and yet, somehow, the light doesn't get out. It shines so faintly that hardly anyone notices.

Christ tells us what the trouble is: we hide our light under a bushel. The problem lies with us, not with the light. We hide the light.

Let those who are Christians admit, then, that they are responsible for the darkness of the world. They are the only ones who possess the light, but they fail to make it available to others. Those who own the light of Christ must resolve that they are under a solemn obligation to share it with those who are in darkness.

This month let's consider the importance of the spread of the gospel. You may think that you have no gift for this work. "Everybody to his own," you say. It's not that simple and not that easy. Evangelism is not the hobby of a small band of church members.

Christ tells the entire community of the redeemed that they are the light of the world. If you will not share in some form of evangelism, you are hiding your light under a bushel. There is no other way to read the text at the top of this page. Scores of other Scripture passages tell the same thing. This month, let's pull a lot of bushels away. Then you will be surprised! Your light will shine!

Lord Jesus, You are the light of the world. Help us to be willing light-bearers. Use us to lead many from darkness into light. Amen.

Witnesses in a Great Controversy

But you shall receive power when the Holy Spirit has come upon you; and you shall be my witnesses in Jerusalem and in all Judea and Samaria and to the end of the earth (Acts 1:8).

Christians must witness.

The New Testament term *witnessing* refers to a *courtroom controversy*. The witness tells about the events which have taken place and which he has seen and heard. The purpose of his witnessing is the promotion of the cause of justice. Thus a witness is *for* the innocent and *against* those who violate the truth.

Sometimes it takes courage to assume the witness stand. But how can you live with yourself if you don't dare to testify to the truth you have seen and heard yourself? The innocent must be vindicated, and the guilty must be proved wrong.

Whether we like it or not, we are all part of a world-shaking controversy. God made the world in order to share it with His people. Satan invaded it and made many followers. Now God calls you to be His witnesses and to declare what you know about the rightful owner of this world. God gave His Son to restore fallen sinners to the Father. Do you know Jesus as your Savior and Lord? Well then, bear testimony to the person and work of Christ! God sent His Holy Spirit to fill His children with power. Well, state the facts! To do less would be immoral even by ordinary standards.

Such witnessing is more than slipping in a word or two about being saved in a take-it-or-leave-it manner. It is even more than rescuing someone from the misery of sin. Remember, the great controversy between God and satan involves all existence! Such witnessing cuts deeply. You do it at the risk of suffering. Many will be offended by you. That's why the word *witness* is so closely related to the word *martyr*.

Lord, give us the courage and vision to be worthy witnesses. Help us to testify fearlessly to the truth and justice of God. We thank You, Holy Spirit, that we may do all that in Your power. For Jesus' sake. Amen.

God Sets the Stage

And behold, an Ethiopian, a eunuch, a minister of Candace, queen of the Ethiopians, in charge of all her treasure, had come to Jerusalem to worship and was returning (Acts 8:27-8).

There once lived a man in Ethiopia who had everything a human heart could desire: money, influence, and a very important position. He was the queen's minister of finance. But in the course of time it happened that this man became restless and unhappy. He couldn't figure out the reason. He didn't know, you see, that God had begun to work with him.

At any rate, that man decided to get away from it all by taking a trip. Where to? Well, he decided to visit Jerusalem. *God* had planted that idea in his mind, but the man didn't realize that either at the time.

The trip to Jerusalem was a disappointment. He visited the temple, but the worshipers were quite uninspiring, and the temple officials appeared none too eager to welcome outsiders. That was sad, but it did prompt the man to pick up some reading material—a booklet called *The Prophecy of Isaiah*. And that also was God's mysterious doing. Isaiah, however, proved a difficult author, and it was quite a happy coincidence that a traveler whom he picked up on the lonely Gaza Road was able to explain the author's message.

It was only later that our man from Ethiopia understood that *God* had sent Philip to preach Christ to him. Then he also understood that *God* had given him the faith to accept Christ, and that *God* had filled his heart with joy.

All of which goes to show that *God* does it all. But in the process He led the convert from Ethiopia through quite a bit of trouble, and the evangelist Philip had to do an awful lot of work. May those two lessons not be lost on you.

Lord, You lead people via puzzling detours to heights of salvation. Make us trust in You, and give us diligence to do the job. Amen.

Broad Horizons

First of all, then, I urge that supplications . . . be made for all men, for kings and all who are in high positions, that we may lead a quiet and peaceable life (I Tim. 2:1-2).

Evangelism has broad goals. Those who "accept Christ" must be led to dedicate their whole lives to Christ.

That's why we must be very careful when we talk about evangelism as "saving souls." The Bible uses the word *soul* sparingly, and then usually to refer to a person's total life. The goal of evangelism must always be the restoration of the whole person to the Lord.

Today's text is an example of the far-reaching claims of the gospel call. The apostle Paul, who wrote these words, knew from experience the ungodly ways of people in authority. The state had become very corrupt. Paul also knew the tendency of believers to isolate themselves from society and government and to live only for "spiritual things" and the hereafter. Therefore he advises—no, he *exhorts*—Christians to become deeply interested in the affairs of "all men" and government. He urges them to beg the Lord earnestly to remember the world at large, but especially those who rule the nation.

The wider goal of evangelism is nothing less than to bring the Kingdom of God to bear upon the totality of human affairs.

Believers must understand that they are in the company of King Jesus in all their daily concerns. When we speak of the Christian life as being "spiritual," we mean that this whole down-to-earth daily life of toil, finances, friendships, entertainment, body, and soul, must be lived in a Christian way. Christ's redemption is that complete.

Pray, therefore, with Paul, that government may do its God-given duty in maintaining freedom and justice so that life can flourish to God's glory and the well-being of all.

Lord Jesus, as missionaries of the cross we know ourselves sent by the King of kings and the Lord of lords. Give us the vision and the courage to present the gospel in all its greatness and healing power. Amen.

Christ Gives an Open Door

I know your works. Behold, I have set before you an open door . . . (Rev. 3:8).

For many churches, evangelism is a sideline. All sorts of other activities enjoy a greater priority.

Christ never intended it that way. Consider the letter to the Christian church at Philadelphia, which Christ dictated directly from heaven. Christ indicated that He was aware of the many problems which that church faced. It was not a strong church (Rev. 3:8), it suffered trials (vs. 10), and it was open to satan's attacks (vs. 9). But Christ didn't suggest solutions to those problems. He devoted most of His letter to spelling out the evangelism mission for that church.

He promises the believers of Philadelphia an *open door*. They will reach many people with the Master's voice. People will give them an ear. Even those who were under satan's spell will come and acknowledge that Jesus is Lord. To be sure, more hardships will come, but Christ will protect them so that they can do more evangelism. And in the end, God will give them special rewards: He will write His name on them, and they will be a pillar in the temple of God.

Looking back at it, we realize that Christ actually did give them solutions to their problems—in fact, *the only solution*. He told them to *hold His Word fast*. God's Word is a living cable that connects His children with Him. That Word is the source of their life, their protection, and they can depend on it always.

Evangelism is the church simply displaying her inner reality! If evangelism runs a poor fifth on a church's activity calendar, that church has not understood what it means to hold fast the Word and to walk in the Word. That church has problems!

Jesus, Savior, bring the power of Your Word to bear upon us. Help us to experience its power in our lives. Help us to display Your redeeming power. May the power of that Word bring many to life. Amen.

Witnesses of a Big Christ

Raised . . . from the dead . . . at [God's] right hand . . . far above all rule and authority and power and dominion, and above every name . . . all things under his feet . . . (Eph. 1:20-1).

So much has gone wrong in evangelism because we tend to bring a small Christ. We so often picture Christ as far removed from the daily affairs of society, a Christ interested in mystical, spiritual things. We think of "religion" as a vague, separate dimension of life. And for many , evangelism has become the somewhat embarrassing business of peddling "religion."

But the Bible tells of the immense greatness of Christ. He is both God and man. He paid for our guilt. He arose from the dead. Though He remained fully human, He showed Himself in a glorified body and appeared to many. He ascended into heaven, where the Father gave Him all glory and power. He rules everything that exists. He upholds the universe. This is His world. He controls every situation. His commands apply to every area of society. Everyone is responsible to Him. People who ignore Him may seem to carry on perfectly well on their own, but they are like cut flowers severed from the life-sustaining stem.

Evangelism is the proud and urgent business of proclaiming Christ the King and glorious Savior in whom mankind may find total renewal.

When *Time* magazine stationed its first correspondent in Berlin, Editor Henry R. Luce sent him a brief note: "When you get there, remember, you are second only to the American ambassador."

We had better remember that too. We represent *Christ Jesus*, Lord of lords, King of kings, who will come soon to judge the nations. Don't apologize for your church membership. You are second only to Christ.

> *Lord Jesus, can it ever be,*
> *A mortal man ashamed of Thee?*
> *Ashamed of Thee, whom angels praise,*
> *Whose glories shine through endless days? Amen.*

Witnesses of a Big Salvation

Therefore, my beloved . . . work out your own salvation with fear and trembling; for God is at work in you, both to will and to work for his good pleasure (Phil. 2:12-13).

Yesterday we saw that we are witnesses of a big Christ, the glorious Ruler of all that exists.

If Christ is so big, then the salvation He offers is also big. Many people think that salvation is limited to the soul. Webster's *New World Dictionary* defines salvation as "saving of the soul." Mr. Webster should have known better. The Bible proclaims a far richer gift than that when it speaks of salvation.

Read all of chapter 2 of Paul's letter to the Philippians, the chapter from which today's text is taken. It begins by outlining Christian day-to-day conduct—love, affection, sympathy, unity, generosity, humility, and helpfulness. It then points out the great source of power that enables believers to perform such conduct—Jesus Christ, "the name which is above every name." And now our text follows: "Work out your own salvation in fear and trembling."

All this couldn't be any clearer. Salvation begins by becoming a child of God through faith in Christ. But that is only the beginning. That salvation must now take shape in the rest of life. All your relationships must be saved—all your activities, all your involvements, all your ways. Because this takes hard work, we are told to *work out* our salvation. Our whole lives must be directed to the Lord. That is not easy; it takes "fear and trembling." You struggle, you fail, you start all over again. It is a slow process, just as healing, growth, and fruitbearing are slow as well.

But with this work, salvation is made real and concrete. Others will see it and be drawn to Christ.

Evangelism comes in word and deed.

Lord, capture our whole being with Your power. May we announce it and live it with clarity. For Jesus' sake. Amen.

Since the Word Became Scarce

And the Word of the Lord was rare in those days; there was no frequent vision (I Sam. 3:1).

Our text tells us a terrible thing: the Word of God had disappeared from the land. Everything went wrong: immorality (I Sam. 2:22), poverty (2:36) and abuse by the enemy (4:10). Those were days of deep despair.

The Word of God is scarce in our day, too. True, it is preached on radio and TV, and copies of the Bible are available to everybody. But in spite of this, the Word of God is carefully kept from life itself. People don't know the Word of God for marriage, and so our homes are being destroyed. Scholars reject the Word of God for learning, and now despair has paralyzed our universities and schools. Citizens don't search the Word of God for government and politics, and now no one knows in which direction public affairs are headed. The Word of God is scarce in the world of trade unionism and economic enterprise, and the result is hatred, waste, greed, and exploitation. The baffling thing, then, is this: never before was the Word of God so abundantly available as today, and yet never has society been so utterly isolated from that Word. We grope in deep darkness, seeking solutions for the bitter problems that plague our age. But the nations don't humble themselves before God. We are estranged from our youth, from God's good earth, and from each other.

Does all this make us sad and hopeless? It well might, but the text above implies that we see again how big and rich the Word of the Lord is. And that entitles us to all the hope in the world. That Word, through us, can reach hearts, and from there it can reach homes, schools, offices, bargaining rooms, and council chambers.

Lord, forgive us if we have not grieved that Your Word was so scarce in our day. Speak again to the people. Amen.

Testimony That Hurts

But take heed to yourselves; for they will deliver you up to councils . . . and you will stand before governors and kings for my sake, to bear testimony before them . . . do not be anxious beforehand what you are to say . . . for it is not you who speak, but the Holy Spirit (Mark 13:9, 11).

Yesterday the apostle Paul told us to bring a gospel that embraces our whole life. Today the evangelist Mark, Paul's assistant, warns us that such big-style evangelism is dangerous. It may cost us our livelihood, our freedom, even our life.

This may seem unlikely to some. Isn't the gospel tolerated in most countries? Yes, but that is probably due to the fact that so many Christians have limited their Christian profession to a vague "religious" area of life. They have never penetrated life itself with the gospel. So, who would get angry?

But today's Bible verses speak of a more powerful testimony. It is the kind of testimony that gets you into trouble with powerful people in society.

Here's how it may work in your situation: you witness to your neighbors about Christ. That's evangelism. But evangelism doesn't stop there. You meet those neighbors again at the caucus of the political party, and there you stand up and express the will of Christ in specific political matters. Again: you witness to your fellow workers at the job. But at the union meeting you reveal your allegiance to Christ, propose Christian ideals for union policies, and expose greed. Or again: you tell your colleagues how to be saved, but when you observe immoral business practices, you have to warn against such evil. And they won't like it.

In short, your testimony will cause reactions because the Word of God hurts people. Be prepared. But don't be afraid, for that's also how the Word heals. Leave the outcome to the Holy Spirit.

Almighty Savior, give us courage and endurance in showing people how to be saved, and how to live salvation in the workaday world. Amen.

The Spirit: Mastermind

Who has directed the Spirit of the Lord? . . . Behold, the nations are like a drop from a bucket . . . (Is. 40:13, 15).

There are times when the church feels lost in the world. Situations change constantly, and problems have become very complex.

We must learn again to rely on the Holy Spirit. He controls all events, shapes every opportunity, and ultimately directs all human affairs.

How wrong our human predictions have often been. Over thirty years ago, all Christian missionaries were forced to leave Indonesia. From that darkness the Holy Spirit worked a revival which brought millions to Christ. It was predicted that Islamic forces in Africa would push back Christianity, but somehow those forces suddenly weakened, and Christianity is now growing rapidly. Similarly, the Spirit, contrary to human expectations broke the alliance between Russia and Red China, a development which completely changed the balance of power and will have far-reaching consequences for the spread of the gospel. The student protest movement filled our hearts with concern, but who could have foreseen that in its wake would follow a widespread yearning for Christian certainty and joy? There are signs of revival everywhere: Central and South America, eastern Europe, India, and we now hear reports of Christian congregations in Russia and China. Praise be to God! Not a single church can take credit for it. The church must discern the strategy of the Spirit and be ready to minister where the Spirit began.

The Spirit, then, delivers us from both nervousness and laziness. Don't put it past the Spirit to turn revolutionaries into prophets and materialists into priests. Be ready to minister to them all.

Holy Spirit, help us to remember that You are in control. Open the hearts of many for a great revival. Send us out with the good news. For Jesus' sake. Amen.

The Holy Spirit Through You

*. . . how much more shall the blood of Christ, who through the eternal
Spirit offered himself without blemish to God, purify your conscience from
dead works to serve the living God (Heb. 9:14).*

Evangelism work will be fruitful only when the Holy Spirit
lives in the heart of the evangelism worker.

But be careful. Don't try to manipulate the Spirit. Many
people do that. They frantically search for a shortcut to the Spirit,
and they work up inner feelings as sure signs of the Spirit's
operation in them.

When we read the Bible as a whole, however, a different picture of the Holy Spirit emerges. *God the Spirit* always shares in the
great works of *God the Father* and *God the Son*. The Spirit completed God's work of creation (Gen. 1:2; 2:7; Ps. 104:30). He also
completed Christ's work of redemption. When John baptized Jesus
at the river Jordan, the Holy Spirit descended upon Him (John
1:32). Today's text tells us that Christ did His work in the power of
the Holy Spirit. It is the Spirit who unites believers with Christ and
fills them with Christ's power and holiness. The text adds that the
blood of Christ, in the Spirit, purifies the believer's conscience
from dead works. Ephesians 4:13 sums it up: the Holy Spirit
restores us to "mature manhood, to the measure of the stature of
the fullness of Christ."

And there you have the great condition for evangelism. The
rest is a chain reaction. The Holy Spirit blesses our Bible reading
and uses it to bring us closer to Jesus Christ. The Spirit fills us with
Christ's grace and leads us in victorious Christian living. And
believers share this with those whom the Spirit leads to meet them.
Evangelism programs will be fruitful only when they find their
place within this rich pattern.

*Holy Spirit, fill us more and more with Christ. Make our life a testimony to
His victory over death. Help us to bring the gospel in Your power. Amen.*

The Speech of the Spirit

Parthians and Medes . . . Cretans and Arabians, we hear them telling in our own tongues the mighty works of God (Acts 2:9, 11).

Idealists have claimed that language differences have created strife and conflict in the world. They proposed one world-language such as *Interlingua* or *Esperanto* as the answer, the way to gain understanding and peace. It has become clear through the years, however, that human conflicts have a deeper source, and that hatred has a heyday even among people of the same tongue.

In Genesis 11 the Bible gives us the reason. Mankind had become very arrogant and decided to build a tower as the symbol of its might. God, in return, confused the language so that men no longer understood each other, with the result that their community was entirely broken up and scattered across the earth.

It is the beauty of Pentecost—the day of the Holy Spirit's arrival—that God gave His own answer to the confusion of Babel's tower.

Picture the situation. Jerusalem is filled with foreigners from all over. Suddenly they hear themselves addressed with the gospel *in their own language*. The language barrier between them and the Pentecost Christians has broken down.

That was an amazing miracle. But underneath lay a greater miracle: since the Holy Spirit came to earth, *one man can reach the heart of another man*.

What a miracle! What possibilities!

Believers can talk heart to heart. Bible translators know that their toil is not in vain. Missionaries have new courage. At the office and in the workshop you can show a new sensitivity to your colleagues' problems. When the world had never heard the word *communication*, the Holy Spirit made Christ's followers master communicators.

Spirit of the living God, create in us the firm conviction that the gospel is its own success and that it will bridge the abyss of all human division. Amen.

More Power to You, Missionary!

. . . and lo, I am with you always, to the close of the age (Matt. 28:20).

It takes a lot of courage to bring the gospel. Consider the experience of John Gibson Paton. Paton was sent out by the Scottish Presbyterian Church in 1858 to the New Hebrides in the South Pacific. For four years he worked on the island of Tanna, where his life was in constant danger. When he was forced to leave, not a single convert had been made. He then worked for two years on the island of Aniwa. It never rained during that time, and the island's chief concluded that Paton's presence had angered the gods. Paton dug a well and prayed to God for water. God heard his prayer and thereby turned away the fear and hatred he had faced thus far.

But it was not until 1869 that the missionary baptized the first convert. Sailing back and forth with his ship *Dayspring*, Paton brought the gospel to Tanna and the other islands. Many became Christians and helped in the spread of the gospel. But danger kept lurking. Four of Paton's fellow missionaries were killed on the island of Erromanga.

Much later, when Paton lived in retirement in Australia, someone asked him, "Weren't you afraid all alone on those islands?" Paton answered, "Yes, I was, but I would say over and over to myself the words of Christ, 'Lo, I am with you always.' That kept me going."

Well, all that was a hundred years ago. The world has changed, and so have mission situations and methods. But one thing will never change: the gospel still evokes reactions of hostility. Those who present the good news today know the agony of fear and discouragement. Maybe you are discouraged. Repeat after Christ: "I am with you."

Lord, You are here, so give us the courage to bear the shame of the gospel. When results are few and when we face setbacks, give us endurance. Amen.

Busy Converts

And they devoted themselves to the apostles' teaching and fellowship, to the breaking of bread and the prayers (Acts 2:42).

Those who have been Christians most of their lives are sometimes jealous of those who have come to Christ recently. The new Christians are so excited, and they want to talk about their Lord and bring others to Him!

The second chapter of the book of Acts tells us the secret of their vitality. *Those new converts worked hard at it!* If Christians of long standing would display the same diligence, their faith, too, would burn more brightly. So let's all learn from the early Pentecost believers.

First, *they studied*. They studied the apostles' teaching. That's still the remedy for churches that are in a slump. Back to God's Word! God's Word is strong, and using it makes Christians strong.

Second, *they had fellowship*. These people had just become members of the spiritual body of Christ, and they couldn't help but express their unity with fellow believers in daily life. Thus their unity became stronger. And that made them all the more eager to tell outsiders about what they shared.

Third, *they ate bread together*. In the light of verse 46, it seems that this refers to their daily fellowship meals rather than to the Lord's supper. They shared their food. They were aware of each others' needs. That, too, brought them close together.

Fourth, *they prayed*. They "devoted" themselves to prayer. Their prayer drew power from God and accomplished great things. They were doers of their own prayers.

So, before you try to convert someone, consider the consequences. Both you and the one who is converted will be very busy. But you will both be very happy too.

Lord, we talk much, also in this book, but help us to do what we say. Lead us to both study and do things together. Through Jesus Christ. Amen.

Strengthening the Churches

And after some days Paul said to Barnabas, "Come, let us return and visit the brethren in every city where we proclaimed the word of the Lord, and see how they are" (Acts 15:36).

Strange as it may sound, it sometimes happens that evangelism brings discord to a local church. Part of the congregation is involved in some evangelistic activity, and another part seems to resent that.

One of the reasons could be misunderstanding and lack of communication.

Here's how a situation may develop. A number of members are engaged in a door-to-door calling program in the neighborhood of the church. That kind of work takes a lot of motivation and some training. Other members may feel left out and become suspicious of the program. The more the neighborhood callers report on their work, the more uncomfortable the non-callers feel. The neighborhood callers, in turn, now think that their work is not backed by the congregation. They develop a tiny beginning of a persecution complex.

What should be done to remedy this situation and unify the church?

The solution lies in pastoral care. The whole congregation must be built in the Word and must grow together. Paul and Barnabas were ardent evangelists, but they decided in our text to devote a lot of time to shepherding existing churches. This will result in mutual understanding. There will be a harmonious division of work. Some will lay initial contacts, some will welcome new converts, some will instruct, some will do youth work, some will care for the sick, but they will all pray for each other and hear one another's report gladly. Happiness, cooperation and esteem will grow.

Lord, Head of the Church, bless churches everywhere. Give vision to those who are called upon to be leaders, and make Your people truly alive. Holy Spirit, create unity among believers and a sense of appreciation for one another's talents and achievements. May unity and humility prevail always. Amen.

Identify Yourself

And the Lord said to Paul one night in a vision, "Do not be afraid, but speak and do not be silent; for I am with you, and no man shall attack you; for I have many people in this city" (Acts 18:9).

The apostle Paul faced a lot of problems in the city of Corinth. While boarding with his fellow tent-maker Aquila, he brought the gospel to the Hebrew community of the city. He ran into a lot of opposition, and it left him not a little discouraged. It was then that the Lord appeared to him in a vision one night and told him to keep speaking, for, said the Lord, "I have many people in this city." By these "people," the Lord meant those who were not yet converted but would be.

Now, we personally need that same encouragement. The Lord says to us all: "Keep speaking, because I have many people around here."

How must you practice this command of the Lord to you?

Suppose that you work in a place where you have come to know a fair number of your fellow employees. You find it very hard to start a conversation with them tomorrow during the coffee break and tell them about Jesus. Let me suggest an intermediate first step. Begin by telling your colleagues that you are a Christian, a member of the church. Evangelism starts by *identification:* this is what I am, a Christian. Then keep praying daily for those people. From there on, the Holy Spirit will do the rest. The people chosen by God to eternal life will in due time be troubled by the Holy Spirit. They will come to you for advice, or simply to cry on your shoulder. That's the moment when you listen, help, speak, and invite them to come to Christ. Remember, the Lord has many people around you.

Holy Spirit, incorporate me in Your master plan. Lead people into my life. Help me to listen and to speak to them. Amen.

Backed by the Whole Church

And they all wept and embraced Paul and kissed him . . . And they brought him to the ship (Acts 20:37-8).

Two days ago we saw that there is not always unity in the churches about the task of evangelism.

Yesterday we saw that the task of evangelism is not always an easy one.

Today we will see that there is a connection.

In your personal witnessing for Christ, you must always know that you are backed by the whole congregation. That's one of the wonderful implications of today's Bible chapter. As Paul takes leave of the elders of Ephesus, he covets their prayers, their sympathy, their involvement, their blessing. They are in this together. Read about Paul's missionary journeys in the book of Acts, and you will notice how often you read about his co-workers and the churches. Paul always knew he was a spokesman for the body of believers, the church, and through them for Christ Himself. That always gave him courage again, and comfort. He reported to them, and they prayed for him, backed him up, and assisted him. That was the deeper reason for Paul's courage to speak: he was not just a private person, he was commissioned. He was an ambassador.

Christian congregations must somehow create the setting in which members can share together how they fare in their witnessing. Prayers can be said, counsel given, assistance offered, but above all: the mandate renewed. That's how the whole congregation becomes involved.

Witnessing is very personal, but it is not private and individualistic.

Lord, Head of the Church, send us, and help us as your children to join hands and hearts. May our courage be ever renewed through the closeness of fellow believers. Amen.

Forgiveness Leads to Evangelism

Blessed is he whose transgression is forgiven, whose sin is covered . . . I will instruct you and teach you the way you should go (Ps. 32:1, 8).

The writer of Psalm 32 is extremely excited. The word *blessed* is the strongest one available in his language to express the feeling of great bliss. But in order to make it stronger, he puts the word in the plural. In Hebrew this expresses bigness, just as in some African languages one big elephant is called "elephant*s*."

What is the reason for the psalmist's overpowering joy?

Well, he experienced *forgiveness of sin.* That sin had been a barrier between God and him. To be separated from God is to experience a taste of hell itself, because hell is separation from God. But God removed that barrier of sin. In His goodness and grace He forgave the psalmist. This is the heart of the Christian gospel: God gave His Son, Jesus Christ, who paid for the sins of believers on the cross of Golgotha.

It is very important to notice that Psalm 32 links this forgiveness immediately with *evangelism.* Now that he had been forgiven, the psalmist happily announces that *he will instruct everybody in the ways of God!*

That is natural!

Forgiveness is the gateway to new life!

That life is so rich and powerful that you can't keep it to yourself. It must be shared!

The forgiven man feels deeply about God. He received everything from God, free, without any charge! He knows that he has been bought—with an enormous price!

But he also feels deeply about those who are still strangers to God. He understands something of the darkness of their life. He earnestly desires that they, too, may be brought to the Lord.

Personal forgiveness is a very powerful motive for evangelism.

Savior God, we thank You for Jesus Christ, who came to take away our sins. Holy Spirit, lead us all to confession of sin and forgiveness. Then send us out to tell others about this great salvation. Amen.

Compassion Sustains Evangelism

When he saw the crowds, he had compassion for them, because they were
harassed and helpless, like sheep without a shepherd (Matt. 9:36).

Evangelism competence may never become a technical skill.
Our society knows experts for every human need. But the thing that
keeps a man going in evangelism is not expertise but *compassion.*

You can't really explain what compassion is; you must possess
it as a quality of soul. Literally, compassion means: to suffer along
with someone. You enter into his life and you undergo his distress.
That's an important condition for evangelism.

Jesus saw the big crowds. He knew how helpless they were at
the hands of those who manipulated them: they were harassed, the
text tells us. He knew their sicknesses, their fears, their poverty,
and their pains—"sheep without a shepherd."

And Christ had compassion on them.

The secret of His compassion was this: He suffered wholly
with them, because He suffered wholly *for them.* He didn't say,
"Why don't you work harder, or live cleaner, or straighten out
your affairs?" He knew that the source of their woe wasn't that
shallow. Sin was the cause, and He took that sin upon Himself.

Jesus still looks upon people that way. If you have been saved,
you were saved by His compassion. Then you have everything
going for you. Then you can understand the despair of people
stacked away in sub-standard apartments, of people caught up in
the money-making race, of young people without a worthwhile
goal, of children without security, of the starving masses on large
continents.

Compassionate people don't come with much noise. They
claim little, they condemn none, and they bring the good news of
hope and healing. They just keep on going.

Lord, we were saved by Your compassion. Help us now to be extensions of
Your compassion. Make us a healing balm in this broken, suffering world.
For Jesus' sake. Amen.

Trials Lead to Expansion

And he lived there two whole years . . . and welcomed all who came to him, preaching the kingdom of God and teaching about the Lord Jesus Christ quite openly and unhindered (Acts 28:30-1).

The book of Acts, which describes the first great missionary outburst of the New Testament church, ends with Paul, the great missionary, being put behind bars.

That sounds like a sad ending, but it isn't!

Though a prisoner, Paul somehow managed to have his own quarters and to receive many visitors. To them he preached the gospel.

Perhaps your life has come to a halt. *Don't pity yourself.* There is a task for you. Paul *welcomed* his visitors. He saw to it that his visitors had a great time. He discussed with them the mighty acts of Christ and the well-being of the churches. You, too, must see to it that your contacts with others are a blessing to them. Enrich them in the Lord, and they will be back.

But it doesn't stop there.

Paul's prison became the headquarters of world missions. Paul's visitors fanned out all over the nations, spreading the gospel of Christ. Paul, like most ministers, had become increasingly burdened with many administrative details because of the churches that depended on him for leadership. God halted it all. In prison nothing distracted him from preaching and teaching. Thus, hundreds were educated to become missionaries themselves. And so, ultimately, much was accomplished.

Paul's generous response to his trials turned an attack of satan's into a resounding victory for Christ.

Have you seen those possibilities in your trials?

Somehow, evangelism always benefits the evangelist first.

Lord Jesus, we are amazed at Your strategy. Help us not to complain when You seem to close doors. Help us to believe that You can fit the whole world into a sick room or a prison cell. Help us to be a blessing to everyone who crosses our pathway. Amen.

Prejudice Obstructs Evangelism

And Peter opened his mouth and said: "Truly I perceive that God shows no partiality" (Acts 10:34).

The apostle Peter had been appointed by the Lord to bring many people to the Christian faith, but he first had to be cleansed of his prejudice. Peter had not fully moved from the Old Testament to the New. During Old Testament times, God had commanded the people of Israel to remain isolated from the world because the Messiah, Jesus Christ, was to be born from their nation. This Old Testament separation became a way of life for Peter. Even after Jesus had come, Peter wanted to keep the gospel confined to Israel. What once was a virtue, had become a crippling prejudice.

God cured Peter from his prejudice once and for all by using a spectacular dream (Acts 10). There was to be no more isolation from the world in preaching the news of salvation. The gospel had to be brought to all people regardless of racial origin.

Prejudice is a terrible barrier to the spread of the Christian faith. Do you think you are free from prejudice? Chances are that you keep it tucked away under a cover of noble virtues and traditions.

Gibson Winter, in his book *The Suburban Captivity of the Churches*, shows that through the years most churches have confined their membership to people of one social grouping. Social acceptance is apparently a big factor in a happy church membership. Those who show by dress and manners that they do not accept the going values in society will likely be unacceptable in many Protestant churches.

We must follow the Master. He goes to social misfits, to people of doubtful morals, to revolutionaries, to the distressed, to the poor, completely without regard to merit, race, or social status.

Holy Spirit, show us our hidden prejudice. Lead us to those who differ from us. Help us to accept them as they are, and help us to bring Christ—not ourselves. Amen.

Witnessing in Tears

A sower went out to sow his seed; and as he sowed, some fell along the path . . . some fell on the rock . . . and some fell among the thorns (Luke 8:5-7).

Spreading the good news of Christ is not always a joyful task; it also brings sadness. Many will reject the gospel. In fact, the gospel hardens them in their resolve not to yield. Then witnessing for Christ becomes very hard. The Greek word for *witness* is *martus* from which our English word *martyr* has been derived. Christ came to suffer for sinners. We who preach Christ must be prepared to suffer with Christ. A witness is a martyr.

The parable of the sower prepares us for this grief. As the sower casts the seed about, some falls on the road's hard surface, some falls in the shallow soil on the rock, and some is choked among the thorns.

The sad possibilities are endless.

Some people have hearts as hard as a highway. They neither groan nor glory when they hear the Word. Some offer more promise. They hear the Word, and it seems to grip them. They are moved to tears—but it doesn't last. When hardships come or the test of discipleship, they find a thousand excuses. And again, some really want to become Christians, but they are too busy and too involved with the things of this life. Soon the thistles of their many concerns choke the gospel seed.

Actually, it would have been better for such people if they had never heard the gospel. The biggest enemies of the Christian faith have often hailed from a halfhearted Christian background. Rousseau, Nietzsche, Darwin, Marx, and Lenin are but a few examples.

But evangelism is not only a matter of tears, it also involves great laughter. Some seed falls in good soil. And it bears precious seed!

Lord, today we pray for those who hear the gospel. May it be as seed in well-prepared soil. Comfort those who see little results on their toil. For Jesus' sake. Amen.

Accounting for Your Hope

Always be prepared to make a defense to any one who calls you to account for the hope that is in you, yet do it with gentleness and reverence (I Pet. 3:15).

Most Christians find it hard to talk about their faith.

One reason, perhaps, is this: our faith is not really part of our daily life. It seems as if we have everything in common with the un-believers, except our faith. So we talk about everything except our faith. But our faith should have everything to do with sweat, tears, paychecks, fun, taxes, lyrics, and voting booths.

The apostle Peter, in the passage above, sums up our commit-ment to Christ in one word—*hope*. Hope is the vision that whatever happens, Christ is in control. Hope goes very deep; it is in the marrow of our bones. It keeps a man going. It is the cork on which his life floats.

Now, what do you do with this hope?

You give account of it! That's what Peter says.

Easier said than done. Peter wrote to Christians who were hated in the community because of their faith. That faith excluded emperor worship and the Roman way of life. Christians were dragged before judges who demanded an account of their loyalties. That was the situation Peter was talking about. And he tells these Christians to answer the judges' questions with a full account of their hope!

That took a lot of courage.

It takes a lot of courage today. Only when your whole life is bound to Jesus Christ by hope can you do it. It means that your own life must be placed on a new Christian footing.

Now, that would be the best thing that ever happened to you. A heart full of hope would be better than a safe full of gold. You would be an inspiring person, you would be drawn to people, and you wouldn't find it hard to make conversation with them.

Cleanse us, Holy Spirit. Fill us with hope, and remove barriers among us. Bless the account we will give of our hope. For Jesus' sake. Amen.

Conflict Among Workers

*And Barnabas and Paul returned [to the mission field] bringing with them
John whose other name was Mark (Acts 12:25).*
And John [Mark] left them and returned to Jerusalem (Acts 13:13).
*And Barnabas wanted to take with them John called Mark. But Paul
thought best not to take with them one who had withdrawn . . . And there
arose a sharp contention, so that they separated from each other (Acts
15:37-9).*
*Get Mark and bring him with you; for he is very useful in serving me [a
request by Paul] (II Tim. 4:11).*

The four texts above this meditation sum up a painful chapter
in the mission history of the early Christian church. Paul and Barnabas, great missionaries of the Lord, had been to Jerusalem to
visit with the home church. They agreed to take a young man called
John Mark with them on their next journey as their helper. Young
Mark, however, couldn't take the rigors of mission life and soon
deserted the two missionaries. Back in Jerusalem, Mark felt remorse; in due time he set out once more for Asia Minor to offer his
services. But the damage had been done: Paul refused to give Mark
another chance. Barnabas—Mark's cousin—disagreed. Feelings
ran high, and the two missionaries, both unselfish men of God,
parted company and went their separate ways.

But satan didn't have the last word in this sad conflict. In the
course of time, Paul and Mark met again. Their hearts opened to
each other. They forgave each other. A beautiful cooperation
followed. When Paul was facing execution in a prison cell at Rome,
he requested that Mark be at his side to minister to him. This was
the triumph of grace in the lives of great, but strong-willed, men
who not only forgave but also built up a new fruitful cooperation.

To represent Christ is a beautiful task. It is also a difficult
task. You have to cooperate with others. There will be
disagreement sometimes—even conflict. But keep going. Personal
hurt may never be allowed to slow down the coming of the
Kingdom of Christ.

*Lord, as our Sender, preserve among us all good and harmonious relation-
ships. Keep our eyes on the goal of our mission. Amen.*

Evangelist on the Run

Now the word of the Lord came to Jonah . . . saying, "Arise, go to Nineveh, that great city, and cry against it; for their wickedness has come up before me." But Jonah rose to flee to Tarshish from the presence of the Lord (Jon. 1:1-3).

God had considered the wicked ways of Nineveh for some time and decided to put the people there before a choice: repent from their evil, or face destruction. God delegated a prophet from Israel named Jonah to announce the ultimatum.

Jonah wasn't very happy with his assignment. The reasons aren't spelled out clearly in this little Bible book. Jonah was a man of complicated character. But this much is certain: the Ninevites just were not Jonah's kind. The prospect of welcoming them into the family of heaven was repulsive to Jonah. They had sinned recklessly, so let them bear the consequences! Moreover, they were a hopeless case; people like the Ninevites never change.

God had to correct Jonah's thinking a great deal. Through horrible experiences, God forced Jonah back to his original task. Much to Jonah's embarrassment, God crowned his half-hearted efforts with dramatic success. God also impressed upon Jonah the importance of compassion and mercy. In short: *God evangelized the evangelist.*

It is humbling to realize how brazenly we actually ignore our Christ-given task to bring the Word to the world. And let's admit it: deep down we don't care all that much about the people around us, people on their way to death. At any rate, evangelism is a pretty hopeless undertaking. Who would expect mass conversions? So we do a bit of evangelism here and there for the record, but for the rest we board our ship to Tarshish.

Now, if we admit that we are our own evangelism problem, we are well on our way to Nineveh. God will do the rest.

God, fill us with deep care about people in their prisons of ignorance about You. Make us yearn for them, Holy Spirit. Amen.

Little Girl, A Word with You

*Now the Syrians on one of their raids had carried off a little maid from the
land of Israel, and she waited on Naaman's wife (II Kings 5:2).*

Dear little girl at Naaman's place, were you really scared when
those cruel soldiers carried you off to that foreign country? But
when you finally were put to work at Naaman's, you didn't hate
them, did you? Your kindness was contagious. You soon became
part of the family; you shared their happiness and sorrow. But you
could never forget Israel, could you?

You must have wondered often what had become of your
family in Israel after that terrible raid. But I think you knew all
along that the God of your fathers was still Master of the situation.
Your heart must have skipped a beat when suddenly the thought
occurred to you that Naaman should go to your God for healing.
Was it hard to go up to your mistress with the suggestion that
Naaman see the prophet of your God in Samaria? How excited you
must have felt when your master came home healthy. That was a
real happy ending, wasn't it?

But did you know that your witnessing to Naaman actually
had a happier ending still? You see, your people in Israel had all
felt sad for many years. They thought that God had forgotten
them, and that the Messiah would never be born among them.

But now all that has changed. When they saw the healing your
God gave to Naaman, they realized that God was in control and
that He would protect them. You should have seen their eyes when
your master came out of the river Jordan cleansed! Who knows
what God will do next? He has probably only just begun.

*Dear God, thank You for working through the little girl at Naaman's place.
You will bring it to pass through us too. Amen.*

Thank You for Showing Us, Dorcas

Now there was at Joppa a disciple named . . . Dorcas. She was full of good works and acts of charity. In those days she fell sick and died . . . All the widows stood beside Peter weeping, and showing tunics and other garments which Dorcas made (Acts 9:36-7, 39).

Dorcas, that wonderful lady mentioned in today's text, probably never studied evangelism methods or techniques. However, she would put most of us to shame when it comes to getting the job done. *Evangelism was a way of life for Dorcas.* She witnessed in word *and deed.* She was "full of good works." She displayed her love to Christ in her actions. She probably wasn't even aware of it. Fruits increased faith, and faith increased fruits. Though nothing in this world can be called perfect, the Bible calls her works "full."

Dorcas would be the first to admit that helping people in itself doesn't spread the gospel of Jesus Christ. The Word of Christ must be explained in *words.* People must be asked to accept and to believe. But it is equally true that our *message* does not ring true if our *works* are absent, if we have a bad reputation, if our trade policies ruin the economy of small nations, if we don't care about the needs of others. Our actions and our spoken testimony are two wheels on the same cart. If we let Christ rule our actions, our words will have substance and our deeds will confirm our words.

How hard we find it to speak freely and meaningfully about our Master to others! Sometimes it seems so artificial. But a generous Christian life of kindness and justice dispels artificiality. It is natural, then, to share the secret of our joy. We know by experience whereof we speak. No wonder this chapter ends by reporting that many believed in the Lord.

So, Dorcas, we thank the Lord for making you an example to us. Who knows how many doors it will open in our streets?

Holy Spirit, fill us with the love of Christ and make us obedient, ready for all kinds of loving service. But save us from pride. May others see Christ's redemption and humility in us. Amen.

Reaching the Family

And they said, "Believe in the Lord Jesus, and you will be saved, you and your household." . . . and he was baptized at once, with all his family (Acts 16:31, 33).

The Bible has a less individualistic view of man than we do today. This does not mean that the Bible is not *personal*. The Bible reveals that each person is responsible before God. Yet the Bible emphasizes the importance of the family.

This has deep Old Testament roots. God worked out His covenant with man through *families*. The family came together at the Passover feast and the father explained the mercies of the Lord. In the New Testament, the family retained its prominence. In his Pentecost sermon Peter stressed that the promises of the Lord are to the *children* (Acts 2:39), even though this does not destroy the need for personal repentance (vs. 38).

Time and again we read the word *house* in the New Testament. The Roman captain of Capernaum believed, and *all his house* with him (John 4:53). The centurion of Caesarea feared God with *all his house* (Acts 10:2). The writer of the Letter to the Hebrews speaks of the salvation of Noah by faith, and makes mention of *his house* (11:7). And here is the Philippian jailer, who is assured by Paul that if he believes in Christ he will be saved—he *and his house*. Consequently, he *and his household* are baptized.

The point is not that children can enter the Kingdom on their father's coattails. The point is that we must recognize that God structured the human race along family lines, and that He established salvation along family lines. He has therefore made parents responsible for bringing up their children in the Christian faith.

For evangelism it means that we must not neglect the child, but our main efforts should be directed to the parents.

Lord, restore many families to You. May parents and children turn to Christ and be saved. To the praise of Your name. Amen.

Reaching Out to the Lonely

When Jesus saw him and knew that he had been lying there a long time, he said to him, "Do you want to be healed?" The sick man answered him, "Sir, I have no man . . ." (John 5:6-7).

There was a festival in Jerusalem, and everybody went downtown to celebrate. But not Jesus. He went to a hospital called Bethesda, for you see, celebration for Jesus meant bringing festivity to *others*. There He found a man who had been paralyzed for 38 years. His loneliness had become a bigger problem than his illness. "Lord, I have no man . . ."

Jesus' ministry to this man is summed up in *four verbs*.

"Jesus *saw* him." Few people know how to see. Visit a sick person, and you will find yourself gazing out the window. You avoid the patient's eyes, lest you sense his distress. Jesus *saw* him, Jesus entered his empty world, Jesus made the initial contact, Jesus committed Himself to this man.

"Jesus *knew* that he had been lying there a long time." To *know* here means to *understand*. Think of it literally: Jesus "stood under"; He placed His shoulders under the man's burden. He took his place.

"Jesus *said* to him . . ." Jesus spoke words. His words brought life, for Jesus is the Word of God (John 1:14). By His speaking, Jesus gave Himself to this man.

"Do you want to be *healed?*" To be healed here means to be *made whole*, ready to live a full life as God had originally intended it. No wonder we find the man in the temple soon after (vs. 14): he wanted to express his oneness with God and his fellow men.

Later Jesus paid the price for this healing when He suffered the loneliness of hell on the cross.

Have you welcomed this Savior? If so, remember that you have thereby become His hand which reaches out to others *who have no one*.

Holy Spirit, open our eyes to see at least one person today to whom we can be a brother or a sister. Amen.

The Agony of Reaching Those Who Know

"King Agrippa, do you believe the prophets? I know that you believe."
And Agrippa said to Paul: "In a short time you think to make me a
Christian!" (Acts 26:27-8).

King Agrippa, mentioned in this passage, was the son of King
Herod Agrippa I. The latter had been king over all Palestine and
had, at least outwardly, accepted the Jewish religion. Thus young
Agrippa, his only son, was brought up in that religion.

Agrippa, however, as soon as he had some territory of his
own, quickly forgot his godly upbringing.

But God did not.

When Paul, God's ambassador, was asked to address a
gathering of government officials about the Christian faith, he
singled out Agrippa for a response: "King Agrippa, you know the
prophets; you know what I am saying is true . . . *King Agrippa, do*
you believe?"

The critical moment in Agrippa's life has come. The gospel is a
matter of life and death. He must now own up to his "Christian"
upbringing, or it will count against him forever. But King Agrippa
refuses to make the choice. Trying to save face with his officials, he
mutters, "You think you can make me a Christian that easily?"
Pitiful . . .

Agrippa never became a Christian. Oh, he wasn't a bad man.
Later he did his best to free Paul from jail. But all his goodness and
godly upbringing could not save him *because he refused to choose*
for Christ.

How hard it is to reach "good" people who have a Christian
background. They just don't feel the need for the Savior. God's
spokesmen agonize over them. They are so close, yet so far.

Let everyone who reads this earnestly consider whether he is
truly a believer in Christ.

Lord, there must be so many who know all about You but have never
broken down before You. Send them Your Holy Spirit to convince them of
sin. Lead them to true repentance and faith. Amen.

Reformation Leads to Glorification

[God] will wipe away every tear from their eyes (Rev. 21:4).

Today we reflect on the meaning of the great Reformation at the beginning of the sixteenth century.

The principles rediscovered by the Reformers can be summed up as follows: (1) God entered our darkness in Jesus Christ; (2) we accept Christ by faith; (3) we walk in His light; (4) we bring His light to the world around us.

By showing us this vision, the Reformers continued the great themes of faith which had marked the early Christian church. The members of the ancient church of Travangore would walk out of their evening service holding high a burning candle as a symbol of their task to be light-bearers in the world. That is still our task!

But the Reformers realized at the same time that total perfection cannot be reached in this age. Only when Christ returns from heaven to earth at the end of times will the ideal order of things be ushered in. Reformation now will lead to glorification then.

We can hardly imagine the depth of that bliss. Sorrow will be unknown, and failure will no longer mar our way. There will be no more farewells, no fear, no pain, no death. And all that because God will dwell among His people; He will wipe away every tear from their eyes.

What we must learn today from this Scripture passage is that our faithful witnessing for Christ blazes a trail toward the perfection of the new creation. The task of preaching Christ has never been easy. What kept the great mission going was the sure expectation that one day the final tomorrow would arrive, the never-ending day with laughter—laughter evermore.

Glorious, triune God, bless what we have read this month about evangelism. We confess our shortcomings and our lack of zeal. Holy Spirit, kindle our hearts to sense a new urgency in spreading the gospel. Remove every obstruction between God and us. Uphold missionaries and evangelists, here and in faraway places. Amen.

John the Baptizer

In those days came John the Baptist, preaching in the wilderness of Judea,
"Repent, for the kingdom of heaven is at hand" (Matt. 3:1).
"Bear fruit that befits repentance" (Matt. 3:8).

The month of March was devoted to a study of some Old Testament people. This month let us see what we can learn from God's dealings with some of the New Testament people.

First we consider John the Baptist. A lot could be said about him, for he was not just your average prophet. John was the last of the Old Testament prophets, who, on behalf of all his Old Testament colleagues, as it were, welcomed the Savior of the world, Jesus Christ. By preaching the gospel of repentance, he cleared the way for Christ's ministry. He longed for the coming of God's Kingdom.

When you read today's verses again, you will sense the immense courage of this great man. If anyone ever swam against the stream, it was John. He stood up to the most powerful religious leaders of the day. In terms of public relations he ruined it for himself: just imagine calling the Pharisees and Saduccees a "brood of vipers" to their faces!

John had good reason for his boldness. He saw clearly the overwhelming greatness of the coming Kingdom of Christ Jesus in the hearts of the believers. Every obstacle to that Kingdom had to be blasted away.

Notice that John began by taking some of his own medicine.

He denied himself all luxury and devoted himself totally to his mission. The secret of that zeal lay in his commitment to his Sender. That commitment he demanded from others, in the name of Christ.

Today that call comes to us all. It comes with great urgency. Christ wants to take possession of our hearts and thus of all our ways. The Kingdom of Christ is totalitarian. Ask His Spirit to remove all obstacles to the coming of that Kingdom in your life.

O my God, give me the courage to oppose what opposes You. Remove all Phariseeism from my heart. Help me to live a strong Christian life. Amen.

Peter

So Peter got out of the boat and walked on the water and came to Jesus; but when he saw the wind, he was afraid, and beginning to sink he cried out, "Lord, save me" (Matt. 14:29-30).

The disciple Peter was an outgoing man. He readily expressed his opinions, sometimes to his own hurt. But he was not only a man of words, he also knew real courage. Today's Scripture passage gives us an example.

The disciples were in a ship on the sea of Galilee. That night a severe storm arose. Jesus was not with them at the time, having gone off to the hills for prayer. Toward dawn, Jesus came walking on the waves to join them. As soon as the startled disciples recognized Him, Peter stepped overboard and walked on the waves to meet the Master.

Now, that was an act of courage which very few of us would care to match. But notice that this event was not recorded in the Bible to show us Peter's courage, but rather his *fear!* At a certain moment Peter took his eyes away from Jesus and panicked when he saw only the angry waves. Frightened to death, he cried, "Lord, save me!"

Have you known such moments of fear? More important, have you learned to cry to the Lord for help? Then you have very likely learned that such a moment of total dependence can be a moment of triumph, for that is a moment of surrender to the Lord. Don't bank on your own courage. It will fail you. Acknowledge your weakness and accept rescue from Christ.

Christianity is the religion of salvation by grace alone. We tend to think that grace leads us to Christ and that we take over from there. Not so. From the moment of our new birth in Christ to our last breath on earth, we live by grace and depend on grace. Thank God for that. There is no greater power.

Help us, Savior, in all our distress. Give us trust even in the darkest hour. And save us, Lord Jesus, from the terror of sin and guilt. For Christ's sake. Amen.

Peter's Mother-in-law

Now Simon's mother-in-law lay sick with a fever, and [Christ] came and took her by the hand and lifted her up and the fever left her; and she served them (Mark 1:30-31).

We visit Peter's mother-in-law at Capernaum in Galilee. The visit we make turns out to be a sick-visit, and a very instructive one at that.

First, note that Pastor Peter, who was a very busy man in the ministry for Christ, takes time to minister to his mother-in-law. Peter is an example to many busy pastors: don't neglect your loved ones! Maybe Peter's concern could inspire some to do something nice for their mother-in-law.

Secondly, note that Peter thinks immediately of Jesus Christ when his mother-in-law is sick. As soon as Christ has finished the service at the synagogue, Peter takes Him to his house and leads Him to the sick lady. That seems a logical thing to do, you say, but do we readily bring Christ into all our difficult situations with a believing heart? We are often too shy to mention His name.

Thirdly, see the wonderful miracle Christ works. He heals Peter's mother-in-law. Can you imagine the joy in Peter's house? Hallelujah, what a Savior! Our Lord heals, He restores, He makes us whole! The purpose behind this miracle of healing also is to show the power of the Word which Christ had preached. That Word brings us to life in God. Christ constantly demonstrated its power.

Finally, notice the mother-in-law herself: she is up and about, serving the guests. What a wonderful ending: healed in order to serve!

The Lord has done great things for us. Let us now serve Him with gladness. The restoration to service is the ultimate goal of Christ's mission.

Thank You, Lord Jesus, for bringing healing to us and for many gifts besides. Help us to serve in dignity. Because of Your resurrection. Amen.

The Samaritan Woman

There came a woman of Samaria to draw water. Jesus said to her, "Give me a drink." "Whoever drinks of the water that I shall give him will never thirst" (John 4:7, 14).

What would happen if Jesus stepped into your kitchen? He would probably make a remark about the dish you were cooking. And that would give you a good feeling. It would imply that He valued you as a person and the things you were doing.

That's the kind of thing that happened to the woman He met at the well near Samaria. She came equipped with a bucket for drawing water. He was thirsty, so He asked her for a drink. That made her feel appreciated. She was good for something.

Of course, that was only the beginning. Just because Christ values a person, He wants that person to have real well-being. In the case of the Samaritan woman, that took some doing. Talk about problems . . . ! Married five times, and now living common-law. Think of all the mistakes, the rejection, and all the complications. Yes, and think of all the sin and guilt. Could that woman ever have happiness and self-respect again?

Christ did some wonderful things for her. He told her that He was the Savior of the world and that He would give her living water so that she would not thirst for the thrills of sin anymore. That woman became a powerhouse of action. She ran back to the city and told the people to see Jesus. When they had heard Him they exclaimed, "We know that this is indeed the Savior of the world."

Perhaps you feel worse about yourself than the woman at the well. Why have you not come with your troubles to Jesus? Drink deeply from the living water and receive power to make a real go of it! With Jesus you can!

Thank You, Lord, that You are there in hopeless moments. Give me new courage and Your power to go on living. To Your honor. Amen.

Jairus

Then came one of the rulers of the synagogue, Jairus by name; and seeing him, he fell at his feet, and besought him, saying, "My little daughter is at the point of death. Come and lay your hands on her, so that she may be made well, and live" (Mark 5:22-3).

Community pressure can be very strong. It is found wherever people live together. The community affords security and acceptance, it also demands compliance with its customs and standards. The Jewish community had decided that Jesus was not the Messiah but an imposter, and a dangerous one besides. Therefore, He had to be eliminated. Jairus, the ruler of one of the synagogues, was under that same pressure, but one day God ordained that he would experience a power far greater than that of the community in which he was a leader.

Jairus and his wife had only one child, a girl of twelve (Luke 8:42). She was everything to them; they loved her more than words could express. But that precious little girl became critically ill, and the doctors gave up all hope. That is when the painful struggle began in the hearts of those parents. They had heard of the miracles Jesus had done. He had even raised people from the dead. Could He save their little girl? But He was their enemy; He upset their established order. Behind that struggle was God's Spirit. He gave these anguished parents the courage to break with community power and go to Christ with their distress. Publicly, before the crowd, Jairus made his request to Christ. Now everybody knew his faith, knew where he stood with Jesus, the Rabbi from Galilee. In response to that faith, Jesus went to Jairus's house and raised his daughter from the dead.

What joy for those happy parents!

But Jairus knew that he was part of a greater miracle. He had confessed before his parishioners that his hope was in Christ in matters of life and death. He had become free in Christ, free from community pressure.

We thank You, Lord Jesus, that we may know true freedom in confessing You not only as Healer but also as Ruler. Help us to be worthy of such freedom. Amen.

The Samaritan

But he, desiring to justify himself, said to Jesus, "And who is my neighbor?" He said, "The one who showed mercy on him." And Jesus said to him, "Go and do likewise" (Luke 10:29, 37).

The practice of mercy must become much more prominent in the churches than it has been. The Spirit of God will touch many hearts to see the tears of the refugees and the hungry around the globe.

Two guidelines come to us from today's Scripture lesson.

Jesus tells the parable of the Good Samaritan to a lawyer of the Jewish nation. The lawyer maintains, true to Pharisaic tradition, that not everybody is your neighbor. Only those who fear Jehovah qualify for that honor. So, in bestowing favors, you have to be selective. There are many who are unworthy of your goodness. Jesus, however, teaches that everyone who is in need is your neighbor, and you have to be a neighbor to him. The Jewish man who was robbed and beaten while traveling from Jerusalem to Jericho was helped by a *Samaritan*, and Samaritans and Jews thoroughly disliked each other. But the Samaritan proved to be a real neighbor. He did not set his own conditions; he was a neighbor to all who suffered.

A second mark of Christian mercy is *that it is done*. The priest and the Levite who saw the victim lying by the wayside were too busy to help. And it was very risky too, so they did nothing. The Samaritan sacrificed time and money and saved the poor man's life.

As the multitudes of sufferers grow, we must multiply our efforts. That will cost a lot of money and time. There is a danger that we will get bogged down in the discussion stages. But Christ will repeat the parable of the Good Samaritan. The Samaritan saw the victim. He knew his pain and realized that he had to be a neighbor, and so mercy flowed richly.

Lord, fill our hearts with Your compassion. You gave Yourself for unworthy sinners. May Your love prompt us to action. Amen.

The Prodigal

And the younger of them said to his father, "Father give me the share of property that falls to me" (Luke 15:12).

Christ did not give him a name in this parable, so we call him the Prodigal, although this name is not found in the passage. Perhaps we could fill in our own name. *We* are the Prodigal. The parable of Jesus is a description of our heart.

The Prodigal, we read, surveys the family estate and says to himself, "When father dies, I can do with my share as I please." He dreams about it. That would seem heaven on earth. The more he thinks about it, the harder he finds it to wait. Would it not be wonderful to have his share right now? You see what actually happened? He acted in his heart as if his father was already dead. That was his great sin. He disowned his father. The other sins of which we read were a result of that deeper sin.

The fall of Adam and Eve in Paradise was that kind of sin. They turned their backs on God and made common cause with the devil. All the other sins which the Bible mentions and which we see in and around us are the results of that sin.

Sins bother us. As parents we are upset about the wrongdoings of our children. We fight against our sins, and we instruct our children. But you know the saying: "One strike at the root is more than a thousand hackings at the branches." The parable of the Prodigal teaches us that. It pictures for us the father eagerly awaiting the return of the son. When he does return, the father embraces him, and restores him to the family. There is great joy and merrymaking. The son who was dead has come home. That's the heart of the gospel. Without that gospel, no one can be saved.

Father, we admit our sin of leaving You, but we confess Christ as our Savior, the Son of Your everlasting love. Take possession of us, Lord Jesus. Amen.

The Older Brother

But he was angry and refused to go in. His father came out and entreated him, but he . . . (Luke 15:28-9).

Have you ever had the feeling that things just were not right in your church, or maybe in your family, or even in your own life? Somehow it seemed that something was amiss. The joy you once knew has lost its luster, and no new warmth and initiative is generated.

One of the likely causes is that we have forgotten the price God paid for making us His people. Christ died for our sins; He bore hell for us. He even had to send the Holy Spirit to bring us hardened sinners to acceptance of His grace. If we see and experience that clearly, we become very humble people, very happy too, and very willing. We then accept each other, we bear with each other, and we become very concerned about one another's spiritual well-being.

When we read about the Prodigal Son's older brother, we get that feeling of meeting a very unhappy man. He just is not free. He has not seen the real nature of sin, so he never experienced deliverance. But he does not realize that he feels heavy-hearted. He does not know any better. He is quite content with himself, and why not? He has always lived an honest-to-goodness life. He finds that quite normal, and so he finds being a child of the father quite normal—nothing to get excited about. That's why he is disgusted with his brother who wasted his goods. That's why he will have none of the festivities.

When church members lose the sense of wonder about their salvation, the church community no longer radiates the warmth and understanding that make some churches so special.

Lord, move us from the dead center of our feelings of personal goodness. Make us weep over our sins, and bring us to the festal gathering of the saved. Amen.

The Greeks

Now among those who went up to worship at the feast were some Greeks.
So these came to Philip . . . and said to him, "Sir, we wish to see Jesus."
And Jesus [said], ". . . unless a grain of wheat falls into the earth and dies,
it remains alone; but if it dies, it bears much fruit" (John 12:20-1, 23-4).

The request of the Greeks seemed so commendable. They wished to see Jesus! What a promising prospect!

But Jesus' response is unexpectedly sad. He says, "Now is my soul troubled. And what shall I say?" (vs. 27).

What could be the reason?

The Greeks were always on the search for a higher kind of wisdom and excellence. They traveled far and wide to find the secret of a perfect life. In the course of time they heard of Jesus, the Rabbi of Galilee, so they thought they should have a conference with Him.

Now we see why Jesus' answer is so important for us. Jesus tells the Greeks that the good life is not the upward-bound course, but rather resembles the grain of wheat: it must fall in the soil and die, and only then can it produce fruit. Jesus thinks of His own death. He must suffer hell and God-forsakenness. He must pay for the sins of His people, and only then can He rise from death to a new life. Jesus also thinks of the believers. They must share in His death, they must die unto sins, they must let go of their own dead selves and surrender to Him. Then they will be raised with Him to a new life: Christ will live through them.

The Greek design is: up and up and up. But in the end, life trails off into nowhere.

Christ's design is: down through death and then up. That's eternal life!

Dear Savior, You died for our sins; may we live with You forever. Give us the victory through Your sacrifice, and help us to live Your perfection. Amen.

Dives

There was a rich man, who was clothed in purple and fine linen and who feasted sumptuously every day . . . and in Hades, being in torment he lifted up his eyes . . . (Luke 16:19, 23).

His name is not mentioned in the Bible; he is simply called "a rich man." In keeping with the Anglo-Saxon tradition, we will call him *Dives*, a Latin word for *rich person*.

This parable is part of a larger series of teachings of Jesus that deal with the sin of *self-seeking*. Right in the middle of these teachings we read: "The Pharisees, who were lovers of money, heard all this, and they scoffed at him" (vs. 14). Having warned against the *love* of money, Jesus continues His teaching by warning against the *wrong use* of money. Dives's sin was that he luxuriated in money. This pompous man reveled in his riches. He perfected merrymaking into an art, and made it a full-time occupation. He "feasted sumptuously every day."

Parables are meant to be applied. They cut into our souls because Christ had His eyes on *us* when He told parables. Few of us, of course, have the means to buy a fine linen purple suit and invite the neighborhood for another big bash at our place. Christ's concern, however, is our *mind*. What is our mind busy with? Does it dwell persistently on the things we want to buy, the business move we want to make, the redecorating job we have planned, or the career our children are getting into? There are some very challenging needs in church and society, and among the people who are our responsibility. Does our mind dwell on them? The sin of Dives is that his goods were heaven to him. Blessed the people who manage their goods responsibly for the well-being of their fellow men and who keep their minds clear for God and His cause.

You own all things, Lord, so help us to be good custodians for You. Keep us secure in Your love. Thank You for Your daily gifts to us. For Jesus' sake. Amen.

The One Leper

And as he entered a village, he was met by ten lepers . . . Then one of them, when he saw that he was healed, turned back, praising God with a loud voice (Luke 17:12, 15).

It has happened to you too. You did something special for someone, and he forgot to show appreciation. It has probably also happened to you that *you* forgot to show appreciation yourself. It crossed your mind, you put it off, and then you thought another opportunity would come along later.

Jesus healed ten lepers in a little town north of Samaria. When He entered the town, they had put themselves at His mercy. He was their last hope. Leprosy is a hideous illness, a living death. You cannot imagine how elated those people felt when they were healed. They rushed over to the priest's residence for a health certificate so that they could join their families and the community. What a reunion that must have been!

And we read that only one remembered Jesus, came back, thanked Him, and worshiped God.

Where were the nine?

The nine were not callous ingrates. Jesus did not say that. Jesus said that they had not returned to praise God.

Are you a believer? Then this event has special weight for you. Jesus tells us that the nine lepers were church members, and that the one who returned was a "foreigner." Church members can get so used to the treasures of salvation that they forget the joyous art of giving thanks. We must remind one another of the many blessings we have and then express our gratitude publicly in praise. And in a personal way too: it is not enough to feel appreciation, you must tell it, and show it! Others around you need that.

William James, not a professing Christian, said: "Refuse to express a passion and it dies." That holds also for the passion of thankfulness.

Lord, we often take Your goodness for granted. Forgive us; prompt us with Your love to praise Your name. Amen.

The Rich Young Ruler

One thing you still lack. Sell all that you have and distribute to the poor, and you will have treasure in heaven; and come, follow me (Luke 18:22).

One aspect about the parable of the rich young ruler has been overlooked at times. It has to do with our capacity to be happy. Enjoyment and happiness are mysterious things. We can own much, know much, but when we sit down and contemplate life, we feel empty and wonder how we can capture the feeling of real goodness.

Carlyle Marney wrote that modern man has sought his refuge in a new kind of padded cell, a world of locks, burglar alarms, wind insurance, bank vaults, credit ratings, retirement plans, bulging medicine cabinets, fear of cancer, slats under bedsprings, and worry about guest lists for dreadful parties.

The young ruler represents something that lives in all of us—the things we count as good fortune, the high expectations, the longing to know real joy. But we lay our head down at night and ask: What was good about this day? And when we do capture a moment of genuine joy, we worry how to hold on to it. Only one life, never to reappear, days slipping through our fingers like fleeting shadows.

Christ told the young ruler to sell his goods and hand the proceeds to the poor. Must we all sell out? Christ meant to say: Do not *lean* on money. But which mortal can hold money in his hand and not feel its magic tug in his heart? He who has eternal life in his heart, Jesus said. He told the young ruler: Follow Me. Christ sets the course and becomes our concern. His presence in our hearts is the beginning of freedom from self-centeredness; it lifts us up above the high and low tides of good and bad fortune.

Make us Your followers, Lord. Take possession of our inner being and guide all our feelings. Show us the way we must go. Give us Your Spirit, because of the open grave. Amen.

Zacchaeus

And there was a man called Zacchaeus; he was a chief tax collector, and rich. [Jesus] said to him, "Zacchaeus, make haste and come down; for I must stay at your house today" (Luke 19:2, 5).

Zacchaeus was a wee little man. He was also little in hope. That was his main problem. Jesus called him a *son of Abraham.* Abraham had lived in the great hope of the promised Messiah, the Savior of the world. As Abraham's son, Zacchaeus should have shared that hope, but he didn't. Zacchaeus put his hope in money. For the love of money, he defrauded people and became a servant of the hated Romans.

But this hard-nosed materialist was no match for the power of Christ. Note how Christ changed him. He *called* Zacchaeus; He *spoke* to him. It was the *Word* of Christ that saved Zacchaeus. That Word not only opened Zacchaeus's *house* for Jesus but also his *heart.* That Word was so miraculously powerful because it was backed by Christ Himself, the Word-become-flesh. The more we read the Scriptures, the more we realize that everything depends on its life-giving power. We just cannot continue without the Word. When we read it, embrace it and pray about it, there's no telling the great things it will do in our life.

Zacchaeus is an example of that too.

We read that he became a different person after Jesus touched his heart. He applied Christ's grace to the actual situation of his life. First he promised to make restitution to the victims of his greed. That's a mark of the converted man—*justice!* We also read that he offered to share much of his wealth with the poor. That's also a mark of the new life—*mercy!*

Christ invites us today to take Him at His Word. Read that Word prayerfully. Through it Christ will take possession of your sin-darkened heart. And with Jesus in control, your life will take a new direction.

Move into the house of our heart, Lord Jesus, and take possession of it forever. Help us to be a blessing to others. Amen.

Salome

And immediately he called them; and they left their father Zebedee in the boat with the hired servants (Mark 1:20).
There [was] also . . . Salome, who, when he was in Galilee . . . ministered to him (Mark 15:40).
Then he said to the disciple, "Behold your mother!" (John 19:27).
He killed James the brother of John with the sword (Acts 12:2).

Salome was the wife of Zebedee, who owned a fishery business near the Sea of Galilee. They had two sons, James and John, who were partners in the family business. They were able men; Jesus called them *Boanerges*—sons of thunder.

We further learn that Salome was a sister of Mary, the mother of Jesus, which made her boys cousins of Jesus. It was not so strange, therefore, that Jesus stopped by for a little visit one day while the brothers were working with other helpers, mending the nets. But this visit turned out differently: Jesus announced that they were to follow Him, and it appears that they left their home and business the same day.

That must have been quite a loss for the business, but Salome was a woman of spiritual bigness: we read that she kept contributing towards Christ's campaigns. Yet, this great woman also knew her weaker moments. One day, as we shall see tomorrow, she proposed to Jesus that her sons be promoted to chief assistants. But Jesus taught her that service never comes without pain. For Salome, that became a difficult lesson. When Jesus was crucified, she stood next to Mary near the cross. There Jesus spoke the unforgettable words that John must become Mary's son. But Salome still had her son James left. Yes, but it was only a few months later that James was taken prisoner by King Herod and, shortly afterward, executed. All her life Salome gave and gave. She did it in the power of the one who gave Himself.

Dear Lord Jesus, we also want to give of our love and goods for the up-building of the church. We want to minister to our fellow man. Holy Spirit, help us to do it in Christ's power. Amen.

James

Then he appeared to James, then to all the apostles (I Cor. 15:7).

The name *James* is a familiar one in the New Testament. Two of Jesus' disciples were called *James:* James, the brother of John (one of the sons of Zebedee), and James the Less, the son of Alphaeus.

The James mentioned in today's text was not a disciple of Jesus but His brother. In Mark 6, four younger brothers of Jesus are listed; James is just below Jesus in age.

What was it like to be a brother of Jesus?

Not easy.

In Mark 3 we learn that Jesus was surrounded by a very excited crowd and that His brothers were trying to bring Him home. But they misunderstood His mission. In John 7 we read that His brothers did not believe in Him. They proposed a strategy to Jesus based on political considerations which He could not accept.

When Jesus died, their hearts must have been filled with sorrow. For them it was the end of their hopes.

But the apostle Paul tells us, in just one line, that the risen Lord appeared to James. Christ explained to James the meaning of His resurrection from the dead. Jesus talked to James as the *risen Lord*, not as brother according to the flesh. And James saw and believed.

That became the turning point in his life.

When the apostle James was killed by Herod, James, the brother of Christ, became the leader of the church in Jerusalem. He helped the Synod of Jerusalem out of its deadlock by pointing to Christ's grace. He welcomed Paul to Jerusalem and ministered to him. He wrote a letter to the churches which the Holy Spirit made part of the Bible. His life embodied Christ's resurrection power. A profound secret, yet so simple.

How wonderful Your works with Your followers, Lord Jesus! How patiently You shape them unto conviction and service! For Your name's sake. Amen.

Mary

Mary took a pound of costly ointment of pure nard and anointed the feet of Jesus . . . (John 12:3).

Several Marys are mentioned in the New Testament. The Mary of our text is from Bethany, the sister of Martha and Lazarus. Some time before, Jesus had raised Lazarus from the dead, and He had also healed a man called Simon from his leprosy.

When these people heard that Jesus was about to travel through Bethany again, they decided to offer Him a festive banquet at Simon's place.

A wonderful thing happened at that banquet.

Mary took a bottle of expensive essence of nard and spread it over Jesus' feet. That's what the gospel of John tells us. Matthew adds that she also put it on his *head*. There must have been so much that she sprinkled Him from head to toe.

With this wonderful love-offering Mary expressed her gratitude for Simon's healing, Lazarus's resurrection, and her own salvation.

Gratitude is a wonderful virtue. It is a quality of the heart and must be expressed spontaneously. But in Mary's case she *planned* it, and made careful preparation.

We should remember that. What good are feelings of thankfulness and affection if they are not expressed concretely? There are probably people in your life who crave the actual expression of your love to them. Why don't you show them what you feel? In fact, feelings of appreciation will actually grow when they are given visible utterance. Mary knew that secret, and Christ declared that she would be remembered for it.

Dear Lord, help us to know the joy of thankfulness, and help us to show it. Bless all the wonderful people in our life. For Jesus' sake. Amen.

The Murderer on the Cross

And the robbers who were crucified with him also reviled him the same way (Matt. 27:44).
And he said, "Jesus, remember me when you come into your kingdom" (Luke 23:42).

The verses we just read display the remarkable power of Jesus' words.

Matthew tells us that *both* criminals hanging on either side of Christ mocked Him.

Luke, who describes a moment that came a bit later, tells us that only *one* criminal mocked Jesus, and that the other one defended Jesus and asked Christ to save him.

We can only conclude that the second criminal had changed. From a scorner he had become a disciple, a man saved at the last moment of his life.

That great miracle came about as a result of the words of Christ. While hanging on the cross, Jesus uttered a number of sayings that we usually call "the words on the cross." One of them was: "Father, forgive them, for they know not what they do." The criminals heard those words. They touched the heart of the one criminal. His heart opened to the Lord, and though he saw only dimly, he recognized eternal life. The grace of Christ in his heart prompted that all-important prayer, "Jesus, remember me when you come in your kingdom." Thus Jesus saved that man whose life had been wasted and who now died an ignoble death. Jesus had taken the death of shame over from him. "Truly, I say to you, today you will be with me in Paradise."

The Christian religion is a religion of *hope*. You need no longer see yourself as hopeless. Lay the fragments of failure before Christ. He will take them over from you. All your sin too. He will accept *you*. No, not after a period of probation. He saves *today*.

O Savior Lord, save also me. Rescue me from death, and make my life a paradise of hope. Amen.

Thomas

Now Thomas, one of the twelve, called the Twin, was not with them when Jesus came. But he said to them, "Unless I see in his hands the print of the nails, and place my finger in the mark of the nails, and place my hand in his side, I will not believe" (John 20:24, 25).

It just cannot be! We are tempted to say that about so many glorious things which the Lord in His power has done. The victory of Christ over death, His majestic resurrection from the dead—it just cannot be. We all would have said that. Christ appeared to the disciples, so they *had* to believe that it was the Lord. They ran to Thomas and shouted, "We have seen the Lord!" "It just cannot be," Thomas said. So he set his own conditions: "Unless I see in his hands the print of the nails . . ."

There is one detail in John's account of this meeting of the disciples with Thomas that we must carefully note. Jesus appeared to the disciples on *the Lord's day*, as they were assembled for worship as the Lord had commanded them. Thomas was not with them, so he did not see the Lord or hear His Word. That's why he was left with his own sorrow over Jesus' death. The implication seems too obvious, yet it should be mentioned. Heaviness of heart stays when we avoid the ministry of the Word. There is much spiritual weakness in the world that stems directly from haphazard church attendance.

In today's passage we read that Christ only appeared to Thomas eight days later (vs. 26), which was the following Lord's day, and only then invited Thomas to touch the nail marks in His hands. Christ could have appeared to Thomas sooner, but why should He? Christ could speak to you in spectacular miracles, but why should He? He ordained the ministry of His Word for the strengthening of your faith. Those who seek His Word will be blessed.

Lord, we are grateful for the congregation to which we belong. Bless its ministry and fellowship. Help us to contribute. Amen.

Stephen

And as they were stoning Stephen, he prayed, "Lord Jesus, receive my spirit . . . Lord, do not hold this against them" (Acts 7:59-60).

Several of Stephen's experiences resembled those of Christ.

First there was the trial. His enemies rounded up evil men who testified falsely against him. They accused him of blaspheming God, of destroying the law of Moses, and of telling the people that Jesus would break down the temple. Similar things were said at Christ's trial. Stephen must have recognized that readily. That became one source of his power. He followed in the pattern of Christ; he would be close to his Master.

When Stephen was about to die the death of a martyr, he continued in the Master's pathway, and his enemies could not stop him. He prayed for his persecutors: "Lord, do not hold this sin against them." It was from a heart filled with Christ's grace that this great believer could pray for his executioners. In his final moment he seemed to see His Savior nearby. Again he modeled his words after his Savior's words: "Lord Jesus, receive my spirit." No wonder we read that "his face was like the face of an angel."

Christ will be that close to us. We need not doubt that. A creed of the Reformation era asks: "What is your only comfort in life and death?" The answer given is, "That I, with body and soul, both in life and death, am not my own, but belong unto my faithful Savior Jesus Christ; who with His precious blood has fully satisfied for all my sins, and delivered me from all the power of the devil; and so preserves me that without the will of my heavenly Father not a hair can fall from my head . . ."

Holy Spirit, fill me with the love and grace of Christ. Help me to dedicate my life to Him. Amen.

Cornelius

At Caesarea there was a man named Cornelius, a centurion of what was known as the Italian Cohort, a devout man who feared God with all his household, gave alms liberally to the people, and prayed constantly to God (Acts 10:1-2).

The Roman officer Cornelius had done an unusual thing: he had adopted the religion of a conquered nation. He had accepted the God of Israel as his God.

What was even more noteworthy was the quality with which he served his newfound God. We read a number of outstanding things about that. He was a *devout* man—our word *vow* is related to this word—someone who keeps his promise of love. He *feared* God, we are told; he saw God's holiness and stood in awe before his Creator. Next we read that he *prayed* much, a sign of personal intimacy with and dependence on his God. He also was a doer of *mercy*; the Lord had opened the eyes of this tough Roman soldier to the suffering around him. As if all this was not enough, we also learn that he *witnessed* openly for God, with the result that a group of people in his immediate environment had also become believers. And you know yourself that witnessing to people you know well is often the hardest.

In today's Bible passage, we read how God rewarded Cornelius's faithfulness: He gave this wonderful man an even larger portion of His grace. Cornelius knew God only from the revelation of the Old Testament. Now the Lord also opened to him the riches of the New Testament. The apostle Peter came to Cornelius and preached Jesus and the Holy Spirit to him. All of this led Cornelius to a deeper experience of faith.

God still deals with His children that way. He rewards faithfulness with a fresh new challenge, and He rewards godliness with another outpouring of grace.

Lord, make us faithful in our Christian service. Multiply God's grace in our hearts. For Christ's sake. Amen.

Ananias

But Ananias answered, "Lord, I have heard from many about this man, how much evil he has done to thy saints at Jerusalem . . ." (Acts 9:13).

How hard it is to always accept Christ's ways with us! We set out our own policies, we make our plans, and we have our own ideas about what course to take. And when Christ rules otherwise, we tend to resist His will.

Ananias was a good man. The cause of Christ was everything to him, but when Christ gave him that one mandate from heaven to minister to a certain man called Saul of Tarsus, he was taken aback. He quickly informed the Lord of Saul's terrible past, hoping that the Lord would see it his way. Ananias, in effect, said, "Lord, let's be careful with this man; let's not admit him into the church so easily."

To be sure, no one should trifle with church membership. But at the same time, let's not forget that the church itself is the assembly of people who did not deserve salvation, people with a past as dark as death, people saved by grace.

What a blessing for the church that Christ persuaded Ananias to obey the order and minister to Saul! Sacred history now records Ananias as the disciple who ushered Saul into the church. And Saul became the apostle Paul, the church's greatest missionary.

Through the years, Ananias must have followed Paul's mission. The more Paul accomplished, the more humble Ananias felt. Good for him! Honor and glory belong to Christ! Time and again Ananias had reason to say to Christ: "Thank You, Lord, for overruling me with regard to Paul."

Can you look back upon some wonderful thing you did for your Lord, for His church? Let not you, but Christ, be praised!

Lord, receive our thanks for all that is good and true and holy in the church today. Bring in many to share the tidings of good news. For Christ's sake. Amen.

Paul (I)

. . . nor did I go up to Jerusalem to those who were apostles before me, but I went away into Arabia; and again I returned to Damascus. Then after three years I went up to Jerusalem . . . (Gal. 1:17-18).

Our life's course is highly unpredictable. Older people especially will tell us of the many unexpected turns their journey took. Behind all those turns is God's hand. He works His design through all our experiences.

The conversion of the apostle Paul was a very dramatic turn in his life. The persecutor of the church was called to become its chief apostle. It meant a 180-degree turn for Paul, an overwhelming experience. The Lord had to mold his heart and will in order to prepare him for this demanding calling.

Today's text tells us of a chapter in God's dealings with Paul. After his conversion Paul spent three years in Arabia and Damascus, and only then could he begin his missionary work. The Bible does not tell us what Paul did during those three years, but we see some implications. The churches urgently needed Paul's services; there was much work to be done, much leadership to be given to scattered Christians. But the Lord ruled that there was work to be done in Paul first. Before Paul could give leadership, the leadership in his heart had to yield to the Lord bit by bit. This man with a tempestuous disposition for works-righteousness had to come to rest and peace. His mind and ways had to be cleansed, his patience had to be seasoned, and he had to learn the art of dwelling on the Lord in devout meditation. The Lord took three years for it.

Perhaps you have known disappointments, or even suffering and sorrow. Sometimes you think of how things could have been if those setbacks had not come. But ask the Lord to show you that He was at work in you.

You know, Lord, what is good for us. But give us grace and faith to accept Your ruling. Make us happy with what we are. Amen.

Paul (II)

But whatever gain I had, I counted as loss for the sake of Christ . . . but one thing I do, forgetting what lies behind and straining forward . . . the upward call . . . in Christ Jesus (Phil. 3:7, 13-14).

Someone pointed out that the secret of Paul's unflagging devotion to the spread of the gospel rested on four principles. Consider them and see whether they are true for your life.

Consecration. Paul threw away the baggage of his old life when he was converted in Christ. He tells us: "But whatever gain I had, I counted as loss for the sake of Christ." We have to check our life constantly and see whether there are concerns that weigh us down, keeping us from running the race.

Concentration. "But one thing I do," Paul tells us. *One* thing. Paul knew Christ as his only source of power and his only goal. George Campbell Morgan said, "We have one goal: storm the citadel of man's soul and capture it for Christ." A variety of callings come to God's people. Whatever you set out to do, do it with total concentration!

Cancellation. "Forgetting what lies behind." If ever there was anyone who could feel the burden of past sins and its results, it must have been Paul. Sometimes he preached in churches where there were women in the pew whose husbands had been killed because of him. But by the grace of Christ, that sinful past bothered him no more! All the remorse was cast overboard. That made him ready for the battle for Christ.

Continuation. "Straining forward to what lies ahead, I press toward the goal . . ." That can be so hard, to *continue* on the path of service, to stick with a goal. We must help each other to do that. We daily need Christ's power to persevere. On his last birthday David Livingstone made this entry in his diary: "Lord Jesus, I rededicate to you my life, my all, for you, my Saviour, my King."

Holy Spirit, establish me in Christ, and help me to live for Him, totally, always. Amen.

Epaphroditus

I have thought it necessary to send to you Epaphroditus my brother and fellow worker . . . Indeed he was ill . . . So receive him in the Lord with all joy (Phil. 2:25, 27, 29).

A Bible commentary lists some facts about a co-worker of Paul, called Epaphroditus, which enables us to reconstruct his life.

Epaphroditus was a pastor in the church of Philippi, a congregation with a fine reputation. He did his work with joy and felt at home.

One day the congregation of Philippi decided to send a gift to Paul, who was then working in the city of Rome. That was a sign of concern not only for the person of Paul but also for the work in Rome. Then someone suggested that it might be a wonderful gesture, and heartening for Paul, if Pastor Epaphroditus would deliver the money personally, and it was so decided.

When Epaphroditus arrived in Rome, he found Paul in prison, and he felt it his duty to stay so that he could minister to Paul and also look after the congregation, which was going through hard times.

That was a wonderful gesture, undoubtedly prompted by a keen sense of calling, but it turned out to be too much for Epaphroditus. He became seriously ill, and though he recuperated, he never regained his earlier vigor. The ministry in Rome now weighed even heavier on him. Robbed of his resilience, he became homesick for Philippi.

When Paul noticed this development, he persuaded Epaphroditus to return to Philippi. He gave him a letter to take back to the congregation, praising Epaphroditus for what he had done and suggesting that they install him again as their pastor.

All this goes to show that preachers can have their share of personal problems. Sound judgment, understanding, and compassion are needed to find solutions to these personal problems.

Lord Jesus, King of the church, we pray for pastors everywhere. Give them wisdom and the power of grace to do their work with joy. Amen.

Paul's Nephew

Now the son of Paul's sister heard of their ambush; so he went and entered the barracks and told Paul (Acts 23:16).

Some think that young people are worse than a generation ago; some think they are better. Some think young people get too much attention, some think not enough. The truth is that young people are as human as we all are. They share in the responsibilities of life, and they make their share of mistakes.

The fact remains that without an alert youth, the church faces a dark future. Paul should testify to that: his nephew saved his life.

Paul's nephew had probably not seen much of him through the years, for Paul had been away a lot on missionary journeys. But when Paul returned to Jerusalem, the youngster shared in the excitement as Paul, then a Roman prisoner, made a brilliant defense of the faith before a huge crowd of people. From there on the boy stayed around, keeping his eyes and ears open. And it was he who picked up the secret that a group of Jews had made a plot to kill Paul the next day when he was led before the Jewish Council. The boy managed to get into the barracks of the Roman military where Paul was being held. He informed Paul of the danger and later explained the details to the commanding officer, all of which led to proper safety measures and Paul's survival.

Should this story have a moral?

No, why?

God has always treasured children as members of His covenant together with their parents. Believers have always known that. That is why they have told their children of the boy Joseph in Egypt, young Samuel at the temple, and the little Jewish girl at Naaman's place. For that reason, too, we have always treasured our children and young people, and expect much from them.

Thank You, almighty God, that You are also the Father of our children. Make them grow in wisdom and spiritual stature. Give them a spirit of willingness and enterprise. For Christ's sake. Amen.

Apollos

Now a Jew named Apollos . . . came to Ephesus. He was an eloquent man, well versed in the scriptures. [Priscilla and Aquila] expounded to him the way of God more accurately (Acts 18:24, 26).

Christ mobilizes people for His church-building program in special ways. Acts 18 gives us an example.

We meet a man called Apollos, a Jew who had grown up in Alexandria. Thus he had seen a lot of the world and probably knew Latin and Greek in addition to his father's tongue. He was well versed in the Old Testament and had also taken note of the teachings of John the Baptizer, from whom he had learned about Jesus Christ. Armed with that knowledge and being "fervent in spirit," he freely preached the gospel in synagogues wherever he traveled.

One day Apollos preached in Ephesus, where a godly couple, Aquila and Priscilla, who had just fled from persecution in Rome, happened to be in the audience. They were overjoyed with preacher Apollos, but they also noticed that Apollos was not up-to-date with the later developments in Jesus' ministry. They offered to teach Apollos, and he gratefully accepted.

That shows us something of Apollos's character. This great preacher was humble enough to let others teach him. It also shows that he loved Christ and therefore was delighted to discover even greater riches in his Savior.

All that had further blessed implications. Apollos decided to join the team of workers around Paul. In fact, he became one of Paul's closest associates. They complimented each other. "I planted, Apollos watered . . ." Paul used to say.

That was the secret of the missionary power of the early Christian church: people feeling free to teach, people humble and eager to accept teaching, people ready to cooperate, workers mobilizing workers. The gospel multiplies and the churches grow.

And isn't that the way Christ's work continues today?

Lord, there are so many people to be reached with the gospel, so much in-struction to be given! Help us help each other to be willing workers. For Jesus' sake. Amen.

Onesiphorus

May the Lord grant mercy to the household of Onesiphorus, for he often refreshed me; he was not ashamed of my chains, but when he arrived in Rome he searched for me eagerly and found me (II Timothy 1:16-17).

Sometimes you meet these thoroughly good people. You see it in their eyes, you hear it in their voice, you read it from their bearing, you trust them, you feel drawn to them, you want to remain in their company. But they themselves seem to have no inkling of their own goodness.

Such a man was Onesiphorus.

He became a balm to Paul's soul.

When Paul was in prison in Rome, Onesiphorus traveled to the city, searched for Paul with eagerness, found him, and ministered to him. He kept coming back. Paul said, "He often refreshed me." Paul needed that. For years he had given himself to others in need. Now the Lord provided someone who gave to him.

There is something touching about this. Onesiphorus was an unknown man: he is not listed among Paul's co-workers, and he does not seem to have been an office-bearer of the churches. So we conclude that when Paul needed spiritual care while going through trying times, God sent a very humble servant to minister to this greatest of all apostles of the gospel.

In this letter to Timothy, Paul does two things in return. He reminds his readers of the fine reputation Onesiphorus already enjoyed before in Ephesus, and he expresses the wish that Onesiphorus may be given special mercy in the day of judgment—"That Day." For Onesiphorus that meant a joyful deathbed, meeting the Christ he willingly served.

Ultimately no one will be remembered for his money or his learning but only for his service of love. It's that simple.

Holy Spirit, keep us close to our Savior as He ministers to the lonely and the sick, and as we minister through Him. May we do that in humility. For His name's sake. Amen.

Demas

For Demas, in love with this present world, has deserted me and gone to Thessalonica (II Tim. 4:10).

What a sad experience for Paul! There he was in a Roman jail, knowing that his life would soon be ended, and it was then that his fellow worker Demas forsook him.

There were two reasons.

The times were bad. Persecution raged in many areas, and it had become dangerous to be a Christian, especially for the ministers. Mind you, Demas was no coward. In his letters to the Colossians and to Philemon, Paul lists him among other courageous workers. But there came a point when it was too much for Demas, and so he left.

There was a more pressing reason! Paul says that Demas was "in love with this present world." Oh, the charm of a free-wheeling life! Demas had turned his back on paganism when he embraced Christianity, but the memory of that life remained. Imagine: no more pressures, no more problems, no more fears—just being on your own! That memory grew until it became too big for his soul: it grabbed the reins of his will and told him to get out and go home.

Poor Demas! The freedom he sought was not real. No one is his own man if he is not Christ's man. What would we have done in Demas's situation? Paul knew the answer. He had committed himself to Christ. When Pastor Niemöller was put in a Nazi jail, he wrote: "In the bottom of my heart, thy name and cross alone shine forth at all times and in all hours. I can therefore be glad."

Keep us Lord, in the trying hour. Fill us with Your courage and vision when temptations strike. Make us willing to endure hardship with our Master. To His glory. Amen.

The Elect Lady

The elder to the elect lady and her children, whom I love in the truth . . . (II John, vs. 1).

Christians know the joy of warm personal relationships. They meet one another, get to know each other, appreciate each other, are introduced to other believers, perform tasks together, and later treasure the good memories of it all.

Every once in a while the Bible affords us a glimpse of such practical Christian living. Read the second letter of John carefully. One day John met some visitors in church whose mother, it turned out, he had known well in another place (vs. 4). These visitors were staying with their cousins, their mothers being sisters (vs. 13). Of course, there was a lot of news to be exchanged, and memories of the past were discussed with relish. John was happy with the good tidings, but especially with the fact that her children had turned out to be fine Christians. And so he decided to write the mother of his visitors a letter for old times' sake, but above all for the Lord's sake. Though the letter is brief, it is full of solid substance. He urged the elect lady to remain vigorous in faith, to be alert against false teachings, and to stay close to Christ. John added a greeting from the nephews and nieces there, and then he put his pen down and felt happy that their friendship in the Lord had been strengthened again.

Thus we are reminded that our faith is not only a matter of conviction of the heart but that it flourishes in actual situations, in common tasks, in circles of people with names, in relationships of love, appreciation, understanding, and concern. They are the strands that form the fabric of life. And as the years go by, we treasure it all as God's gift to us. In his letter to the elect lady, John gives the honor to Christ, in whose grace all life is sacred.

Open our eyes, dear Lord, that every moment of life can be lived in goodness and charity. Bless our ways; help us to discover precious gifts in each other. Amen.

Gaius

Beloved, it is a loyal thing you do when you render any service to the brethren, especially to strangers . . . But Diotrephes, who likes to put himself first, does not acknowledge my authority (III John, vs. 5, 9).

Life can be complicated. If only all people would love each other and do good, what a wonderful world this would be! But alas, there is error, and even bad intent. Such ill will sometimes creeps into the church too. Special provisions must then be made to bring correction and harmony.

John's third letter gives us an example. It is addressed to his young friend Gaius, who probably lived in another city. Gaius filled a special role in the church there. When traveling preachers came to minister to the church for some time, they would stay at Gaius's place, and he would care for them. This ministry had expanded into caring for other travelers as well. All in all, it kept Gaius quite busy.

In fact, it may have occupied him to such an extent that he was unaware of some disturbing situations in his own church. There were members in that congregation who opposed John's apostolic authority—yes, they had even put faithful members out of the church when they stood up for the truth. Now John had to teach Gaius a painful lesson: when you are loyal to Christ, you cannot be loyal to His enemies.

John added that he would soon come over himself and bring the whole thing out into the open. This was not easy for John, for he, too, was a man of peace. But he would not hesitate to do it, since the survival of the church and the honor of Christ was at stake.

For us there is an added personal implication. To love our neighbor means that we honestly show him his mistakes. But the other way around it is equally valid: treasure those who correct you. They show true love!

Lord, in these days of widespread confusion, keep the church pure. Give us love and vision that we may guard against all error. For Your name's sake. Amen.

Advent Beginnings

The Lord God said . . . , "I will put enmity between you and the woman, and between your seed and her seed; he shall bruise your head, and you shall bruise his heel" (Gen. 3:14-15).

This month let us meditate on Christmas and the many events that led up to it. We look at the Old Testament first, where it all began—the many centuries of preparation, the period of *Advent*.

We will also consider the beginnings of the New Testament in which the actual event of Christ's coming in human flesh is described—*Christmas* itself.

Today's text shows the remarkable beginning of Advent—an act of *war!* God instigated that war. Without that Advent war, there could be no Christmas peace.

Have you understood why?

When Adam and Eve broke away from God, they automatically became the henchmen of satan. This unholy alliance with satan was the cause of mankind's terrible predicament. Adam and Eve were totally at satan's mercy, and since he knew no mercy they were children of death.

Only God knows mercy. He broke up the fatal alliance between man and satan: He put enmity between them. That enmity would extend through the generations of the godly and the ungodly, the seed of the woman and the seed of satan.

There, right after the fall in Paradise, God wrote the first chapter of Advent history. The whole Old Testament is really a continuation of that chapter. It tells us of the generations of people who loved God and from whom Christ would be born. It also tells of cruel opposition by satan's followers. That long, drawn-out battle came to a head when Christ came to earth. In His death for our sins, Christ gained the victory!

Teach us, Lord, how to read Advent and Christmas history. May we recognize ourselves in the Advent struggle through the generations. For Christ's sake. Amen.

Advent Hope

And Adam knew his wife again, and she bore a son and called his name Seth, for she said, "God has appointed for me another child instead of Abel, for Cain slew him" (Gen. 4:25).

In 1931 President Hoover of the United States made a visit to Europe. Upon his return he told the American people, "I have met fear everywhere in Europe, but in the name of the American people I have offered the courage and ingenuity of this great nation."

Half a century later those words sound sad to us because as it turned out, the people of Europe—in fact, the whole world—had plenty to be afraid of. A terrible depression and a great world war followed Hoover's statement.

Broken hopes have always been mankind's lot. Eve had hopes when Cain, her first child, was born, because God had promised that there would be relief after the fall in Paradise *through her children*. But Cain grew up to be a man of anger. Her hopes revived when her second son was born—Abel. He was a godly man; would deliverance come through him? But one day Cain killed Abel. Was there no hope left? Adam was then 130 years old. Yes, God visited His people again, and another son was born, whom they called *Seth*. This time Eve knew that through him redemption would come, and she sang for joy: "God has appointed me for another child instead of Abel."

Advent joy came in a painful, roundabout way to Adam and Eve. But it did come. Christ was born of Seth's generations. In Christ lies our hope. Remember, Christ could have called up all the powers of the universe to shield Himself from suffering, but for our sake He did not. We may suffer for a short season, but with Adam and Eve we shall learn the deeper joy of having His love in our hearts.

Thank You, Almighty God, that You did clear the way for Christ's coming, and that we, too, may belong to Him. May that be mankind's new hope. Amen.

Advent Expectation

"I wait for thy salvation, O Lord" (Gen. 49:18).

In 1973 a man called Victor D. Solov died of a heart attack—at least, that's what the doctors thought. Twenty-three minutes after his heart stopped, an electric shock, administered by a determined intern, revived his heart and the man lived. That made medical history. But what made even more history was Mr. Solov's account of the experience. He said that he had felt deep peace and tranquility—a "vibrant luminosity," as if he walked through a tunnel of living light. His story gave rise to detailed studies of other death experiences, and books were published on the subject. It appeared that many people gave accounts similar to Mr. Solov's.

The question remains, of course, were those people really dead?

In today's chapter we read of Jacob on his deathbed. He was of a very clear mind. He called his sons together and then blessed them. But the things he had to tell his sons were not all so happy. Their sins were exposed in those words of farewell. And those sins were not isolated events. Jacob recognized himself in the sins of his children. What a sad deathbed for Jacob! Ah, but wait, suddenly God gave him a brief vision, right in the middle of all his words: "I wait for thy salvation, O Lord." Wonderful! God provided His salvation for His dying child. From Jacob's generations would come Christ, and because of hope in Him, Jacob could die in peace. No, not as in a tunnel full of luminous vibration, but in the arms of Christ, who would make all his deceit undone.

The years of our life know the zest of youth and the confidence of manhood and womanhood. But there are the sudden moments when the foundation seems to give way and the threats of darkness close in upon us. Those who love Christ as Savior will then experience the certainty of eternal life.

Dear God, may our security be in the love of Christ for us sinners, the love in which we are washed clean of a lifetime of sin. Amen.

Advent Renewal

Praise his people, O you nations; for he . . . makes expiation for the land of his people (Deut. 32:43).

Another deathbed. Moses, the great servant of God, bids the nation of Israel farewell.

Before he leaves, he writes a song and blesses Israel. Above this meditation you can read the concluding lines of that song. They are curious lines. Moses tells the nations of the world to praise the people of Israel. That's strange, because Israel had a bad record of disobedience and sinfulness. But Moses adds a line: God made *expiation* for His people: *He paid for their sins*. That payment not only covered their sin but also its awful results. So they deserved praise!

Wrongdoings have their consequences in our lives. Reject good advice, and you invite a lot of trouble. Make willful mistakes, and you produce injury somewhere. But in spite of all that, the Lord promises that He will not only forgive sin but also give us His grace in coping with its awful results. Moses saw a bedraggled nation not only as forgiven but as restored to glory—an attractive people, worthy of praise. Israel's Savior paid for you; He is also there to make repairs through you! You can know Advent reality!

A church in Milwaukee decided to build a service center for drug addicts. A committee went to a brickyard to select the bricks. One member pointed to a distant pile: "What about those?" "They are kiln rejects," said the yard steward. The committee looked around, but in the end decided to take the rejected bricks. "You may have them for the taking," said the steward. "They are of no value to us." From those bricks a graceful building arose, which daily serves a great purpose. Kiln rejects!

Thank You for Moses' vision of the Christ of God. May the forgiveness You brought, Lord Jesus, bring repair and glory to our lives. Amen.

Advent Setback

And of all your number, numbered from twenty years and upward, who have murmured against me, not one shall come into the land where I swore that I would make you dwell, except Caleb . . . and Joshua (Num. 14:29-30).

What a tragedy! The people in the desert had witnessed God's mighty acts time and again. But when they stood at the gate of the promised land, they became afraid and refused to conquer the country and take it away from the wicked Canaanites.

Note God's punishment.

He took the challenge away from the older generation. None of them would enter the land; they would all die in the wilderness. After that the younger generation would enter.

What a painful judgment! God had given His people a great challenge, and with that challenge great promises. The Savior of the world would be born through their faithfulness and God's grace. But they grew blind and murmured against God. So the Lord mobilized a new generation to work out His Advent program.

God has repeated that way of dealing with His people many times. He deals with us that way too. We have seen the fulfillment of the Advent hope of Israel, and we share in the riches of Christ, who became man for us. Now we must live for Him. That's a blessed challenge. If we neglect that challenge, God may punish us by taking it away. It could happen in small matters. You wanted to write that letter to someone who needed it, but you put it off, and then it wasn't necessary anymore. You postponed that sick visit, and then it was too late.

Around us a civilization is dying because it has disowned God. As members of the Kingdom community, we must hold high the light of Christ's banner. But if we are too busy in selfish pursuits, God's judgment may be that it is too late for Christianity to call the nations back to God.

Holy Spirit, wake us up to the urgency of doing the Master's bidding. Send us forth with the gospel of reconciliation. Help us to bring relief to the suffering. In Christ we pray. Amen.

Advent Reliance

The Lord spoke to me again, "Because this people have refused the waters of Shiloh that flow gently . . . it will overflow and . . . will fill the breadth of your land, O Immanuel" (Is. 8:5-6, 8).

Does God actually interfere in daily life? Does He arrange things for us, or must we manage our own affairs with Him watching from a distance? Is God for real?

The people of Isaiah's day struggled with that problem. It had to do with what our text calls *the gentle waters of Shiloh*. Shiloh was a natural spring not too far from the temple hill. During Hezekiah's days a covered conduit had been constructed, leading the water as a tiny river into the city itself. The people saw it as a symbol of God's ever-flowing grace, but they also realized its strategic importance in case of siege. Thus it became a symbol of God's protective care. For these reasons they called their little stream *Shiloh*, the name of the promised Messiah.

Now it happened at that time that the Syrian armies had surrounded Jerusalem. The question "Will God now actually show His presence?" became very real. Then the people saw how small Shiloh was, and they began to doubt. In their fear they made a treaty with Babylon. It was then that Isaiah rebuked the people. He announced that God would increase Shiloh so that it would fill the valley and wash all the enemies away, but at the same time it would frighten the people themselves since the waters would reach up to their necks. And then he added one line: he called those waters *Immanuel*, which is the Christmas name for Christ.

Are God's doings real in our lives? In Christ Jesus He is right on the scene! Seeing this great Immanuel, we shall no longer question His rule but in humble faith tremble before His majesty.

Lord, we confess that without Your will, not a hair can fall from our heads. For Jesus' sake. Amen.

Advent Urgency

"We have made a covenant with death, and with Sheol we have an agreement" (Is. 28:15).

As I was reading this chapter of Isaiah, a scene of a TV play I saw years ago came to mind. It pictured someone driving on a dark, rainy night, approaching a bridge. Suddenly his headlights pick up a man who runs up to his car, waving at him frantically. Our driver is overtaken by fear as he sees the man's flying hair and torn clothes. He tries to swerve around him but the man jumps aside, yanks the door and yells, "The bridge is out! A steamer collided with the pillars." Together they wave unwilling motorists down, risking their safety.

Something of that urgency marks the words of Isaiah. The people have become so blind spiritually that they brazenly mock Isaiah and say to his face, "We have made a covenant with hell." They did not care any more; they were speeding headlong into eternal damnation.

As Christians we look at the world and say: "We have seen it all. The same old story—nothing but unbelief, and therefore nothing but problems. There is so much of it, so what can we do?" We go our way, mind our business, and make the best of it.

Sluggishness is a great danger to Christianity. May God's Spirit open our eyes to the crisis of our age. The darkness deepens daily. Hatred and violence claim their victims everywhere. Corruption reaches into the highest circles. And everywhere around us, people die without Christ, facing eternity alone. If *we* do not wave them down, who will? Pray to God that a new urgency will grip our souls so that we will join the Savior's forces.

O Lord, show us the real plight mankind is in, and use us to save people everywhere. Give us the courage to present You to the wayward and the dying. Help us never to think little of Your power, O most High God. May Your name be honored by all mankind. Amen.

Advent Judgment

For the bed is too short to stretch oneself on it, and the covering too narrow to wrap oneself in it. Behold I am laying in Zion for a foundation a stone . . . (Is. 28:20, 16).

Some people never learn. They just keep running into trouble but never become the wiser for it.

In Isaiah 28 we read about such people. The prophet had warned the nation against their sinfulness. He had threatened that God would carry them away into exile, but they had just laughed and said, "Go away, Isaiah. You tire us. We are busy; we have a lot of things to do."

It was at that point that Isaiah spoke the words above this meditation. They are words of judgment. Isaiah said, "Your work and your riches will get you nowhere. Your life will be as a bed: you stretch out, but you find it too short—a terrible feeling, your feet are sticking out at the end. And you pull the blanket up to your chin, but it turns out to be too small. Your feet remain uncovered, also an annoying feeling. And you can do nothing about it. Your riches will not bring any satisfaction or happiness. The Lord will see to that. The more money you make, the shorter the bed and the narrower the blankets."

Can you imagine that? A no-win proposition. The things you cherished so much and worked for so hard become a source of frustration. A maddening situation. And it happens all around us. We have experienced it ourselves. In fact, let us pray God that we did, because that was the way God opened the eyes of the people for something better. Isaiah pointed the people to a stone, a *foundation stone* in Zion. That was the Advent promise. Do you know that promise? The Christ of that Advent will give you a new heart, and from that new heart the capacity to be happy and to enjoy whatever gifts He affords you.

Almighty God, how wise Your leadership in our lives. We seek ourselves, but You will lead us on to richer fulfillment in Christ our Lord. Your name be praised. Amen.

Advent Empathy

A bruised reed he will not break, and a dimly burning wick he will not quench. Hear, you deaf; and look, you blind . . . Who is blind but my servant, or deaf as my messenger whom I send? (Is. 42:3, 18-19).

In our day we see great problems, but also great solutions. The strong arm of technology and science has brought relief in thousands of ways. And more and more people have access to the benefits of a modern age.

For all that we are grateful.

But we also realize that many painful needs are not met. There are so many people who are afflicted with crippling illness, or feel lonely and betrayed, or are in the grip of mental distress, or struggle with financial shortages. They all keep searching for solutions and relief. Where will they find them? Must they keep hoping for a new drug, the right therapy, some special person, some new source of income? What can the Christian faith do for them? Will Christ bring relief? Yes, He does! The Bible is full of that. He promised to be with us till the end of the earth, and He is keeping His word. He is there in every step we take, every sentence we speak, every dollar we spend, every friend we meet. He provides daily. Don't ever think that He is the ever-absent help in trouble.

But Isaiah tells us that He is with us in even richer ways. The prophet tells us of the unfortunates of his day: "the bruised reeds" and the "dimly burning wicks," the deaf and the blind. He tells them of the coming Savior. And what will the Savior do for them? Will He help and heal them? Yes, but more: He will become destitute and blind and deaf *with* them and *for* them.

As New Testament Christians, we have seen that prophecy fulfilled in His empathy and His death for sinners. Therefore we freely go to Him with our needs. He will welcome us and prove to be a merciful High Priest to us, for He has been through it all before. For us! We will live with Him forever!

Dear Savior, thank You for living our life, and entering our death. You know our needs. Provide for us. For Your name's sake. Amen.

Advent Headway

But they rebelled . . . Like cattle that go down into the valley, the Spirit of the Lord gave them rest (Is. 63:10, 14).

Sheep and goats do not mind being led down from high grounds to low ones in search of new pastures. They balance easily and make quick progress. Not so with cattle and camels. They shy away from steep slopes and make the descent slowly, pausing stubbornly and moving only under constant prodding by the drivers.

That's Isaiah's picture of Israel. They are rebellious, they stray from God, they have no interest in God's plans, they want to be left alone to live life as they see fit. But God keeps visiting them. He leads them through trials because they must move to new areas of progress and service. There can be no Advent headway unless God's people move! God causes a lot of trouble!

We take note. Before we pray to God to take our trials away, we must ask: "Lord, bless these trials and accomplish Your purpose through them." That takes a lot of grace. But mark the outcome. Isaiah has something to say about that too. Once the cattle are down in the valley, they have already forgotten their ordeal and are enjoying rest, he tells us. Now, *rest* is a very interesting concept in the Bible. It is not idleness. When two parties agree to end a long conflict and perform a common task, they have *rest*, according to the Bible. Through trials God made His people partners in a common venture of redemption.

We have the privilege of knowing the outcome of Isaiah's prophecy. Christ completed His ministry, and the Holy Spirit came to earth to bring it home to the people. But we are slow to join Him in the great task. We like to go our own way. So God keeps troubling us, and bit by bit we are enlisted in His army. That's true *rest*.

Lord, overcome a lot of resistance in me. Don't give up on me, but lead me to abundant service through Your Holy Spirit. Through Christ my Lord. Amen.

Advent Pride

Now why do you cry aloud? Is there no king in you? (Mic. 4:9).

It is not easy to live according to high standards. The higher the standards, the higher the price to meet them. A good piece of art is produced at the cost of much training and effort. Good family life comes in the way of self-denial and sacrifice on the part of the parents.

In society, too, high standards come at a cost. Pollution controls bring a healthy environment, but they raise the cost of products. Standards tend to go down when costs go up. When there is not enough oil, industry must switch to coal; coal produces more pollution, so industry demands that pollution control standards be relaxed. But lower standards also come at a cost. The only way that the atmosphere can cope with the tons of sulphur compounds is to dump them in the form of acid rain, over such areas as the central lake district of Ontario. The more pressing our problems, the less we worry about the quality of solutions. Limitations beset us on all sides. When India used free shipments of Canadian grain for liquor production, Mitchell Sharp, then Minister of Foreign Affairs, told the press, "You must know that in our times we have learned that we cannot change situations; we only try to cope."

A lot of people experience all that in their personal lives. The Israelites did too; they chose the road of least resistance instead of the highway of excellence. But Micah came to the nation with the Advent gospel. He summed it up in one sentence: *"Is there no king in you?"* He was referring to the promised Messiah, to whom the nation would give birth. If they would live out of that Advent expectation, they would have strength from God to love His high standards. Then they would flourish.

Believers today know that. They have that King in their hearts. He demands perfection, but the wonderful secret is that He first gives Himself to them; He first supplies them with power. The demand becomes its own promise. There is a King in them!

Thank You, Lord Jesus, for coming with Your wholeness into this corrupt world. May Your Spirit dispel from our lives the spirit of compromise. Amen.

Advent Reassurance

. . . siege is laid against us; with a rod they strike upon the cheek . . . but you, O Bethlehem Ephrathah, who are little . . . from you shall come forth for me one who is to be ruler in Israel (Mic. 5:1-2).

Even radio stations wish that the news would not be so grim. A radio station in our area likes to refer to itself as the "Good News Station." After the regular news broadcast, another, more cheerful voice takes over and announces some happy cultural event. In the southern United States there is a radio station that follows the regular newscast with the recitation of some Scripture texts. Those are undoubtedly noble motives, but the problem is that the bad news just will not go away. This kind of "good news" has little effect on the bad news.

If anyone had his share of bad news, it was the prophet *Micah*. The nation went through terrible times. For years the people had suffered at the hands of cruel enemies. Their armies had surrounded the city. The king had been mocked. Bad tidings came in a steady stream. Was there no good news at all? Yes, Micah brought good news: Israel would have a new Ruler. He would be born in Bethlehem Ephrathah. The promise of His coming was God's answer to the bad news of the day.

Does that strike you as real?

We know of the birth of Him whom Micah foretold. But does that change the bad news? It does not seem so. Micah tells us two things about the Christ. He will feed His flock, and they shall dwell secure (vs. 4). Those are no empty words. This great Savior who died and rose for us pledges that He will provide for us and safeguard us. He does know all our needs and all our problems. We can totally depend on Him in all our everyday affairs. Yes, more: Micah's words also have a deep spiritual dimension. He will keep us close to God and preserve us unto eternal life. The Kingdom of this Ruler from Judah's tribe will stand forever.

Lord, how wonderful Your power and might! You are faithful to Your children through all generations. Help us to entrust ourselves to Your care. Amen.

Advent Awe

But who can endure the day of his coming . . . ? For he is like a refiner's fire and like fuller's soap (Mal. 3:2).

By now you have done some thinking about Christmas gifts and cards. Don't forget cousin Sally: she sent you a card last year. The busy-ness of the season weighs us down sometimes, doesn't it?

Norman Rockwell has a print of a salesgirl, at the end of the last shopping day, slumped over the counter, gasping: "Who can stand another Christmas?" And those were rather prophetic words, seeing that Malachi asked the same question ages before Christ was born: "Who can endure the day of his coming?"

Norman Rockwell had not thought of it that way, of course. Few of us do. We do not usually associate Christ's coming in the flesh with His holy majesty. But that was the mystery of Christ's coming: in Him God hid His holy presence so that He could come to us sinners in our fallen state. But that should never give us occasion to be casual about His coming to our world. His name is Immanuel—God with us. Our sins made His birth necessary. We were hopeless cases; God had to make a new start with the human race. That's why the gospels present Him as the man of sorrows in utter closeness to our hopeless condition. That was our salvation. But when John, on the island of Patmos, saw Him again, he fell on his face, for the eyes of Christ were like flames of fire and His voice like the sound of many waters. Before Him the nations trembled (Rev. 1:14).

The prophet Malachi saw all of this clearly in the Savior who walked among us on this earth. Our faith would be more vibrant and our convictions more fervent if we were more deeply impressed with the inexpressible holiness and greatness of our Savior. Come, stand in awe before Him.

We praise You, O Savior of the world, for Your perfections and power. Holy Spirit, open our eyes to Christ's greatness as You did with Malachi. Amen.

From a Bad Family

The book of the genealogy of Jesus Christ, [the descendant of] . . . Judah
. . . Tamar . . . Rahab . . . David . . . the wife of Uriah . . . Solomon . . .
Manasseh . . . (Matt. 1:1, 3, 5-6, 10).

Suppose your cousin were the president of Harvard University. Well, you might just be tempted to mention that fact on some occasion. But should your cousin be, let's say, a criminal, you would probably prefer to be discreet about it.

Consider the honesty of the Bible. Just before announcing the birth of God's Son, it tells us a few things about Jesus' ancestry. What a motley group! Judah committed adultery with his daughter-in-law, Tamar. Rahab, from pagan Jericho, was a harlot. David, in spite of the glory God had showered upon him, was guilty of the premeditated murder of a devoted general with whose wife David had engaged in a sordid affair. Solomon became wealthy at the expense of the people and wasted his life with imported courtesans. Manasseh introduced false gods to Israel, killed God's prophets, and sacrificed small children to pagan idols.

Those were some of the forefathers and foremothers of Jesus! Their reputation did not embarrass Him. He was not ashamed to pose with them all for a picture that would be spread on the front page of the New Testament.

And that's why there is so much hope for us in the Christmas event—at least if we realize that *we* are part of that picture. It was our sinful flesh that Christ took upon Himself when He consented to be born from the likes of David and Manasseh. He took their place, and our place. There is salvation for us, a new beginning!

Jesus Christ still goes out to seek and save the lost. There is hope for this desperate world. Jesus will liberate those who are imprisoned by their possessions. He will associate with the dropouts of society. He will move among the starving. And He will inspire the slaves of vice to a life of Christian joy.

Dear Lord Jesus, thank You for taking the shame of our misery upon Yourself. Let Your grace overwhelm us. We thank You that we may bring the good news to the proud, the arrogant, the desperate, and the dying. Amen.

The Name Is Jesus

... she will bear a son, and you shall call his name Jesus, for he will save his people from their sins (Matt. 1:21).

Most people feel pretty strongly about their name. The Bible, too, rates names highly. It refers to names over 500 times. A person's name is a symbol of his dignity and a guarantee of his acceptance in the community. To have a name is to have peace with yourself, with God, and with the brotherhood of believers. Names express friendship and concern. God told the first man, "Your name is Adam," and Adam promptly responded with "Father." People who have no God and no friends and no meaningful life are virtually nameless.

The world is full of nameless people, people who have no one and have nowhere to go. Impersonal forces expel many from the economic cycle, and they become jobless. Blind with greed, man oppresses his fellow man. People caught up in the rat race of material pursuits see no neighbor. Children wander away from the technological society.

To that world God came with the Christmas event. He began by announcing the new name—Jesus, Savior. That summed it all up, for He would save His people from their sins. He would restore them to God and would give them a new heart and make them good people.

We see the fulfillment of that gospel today.

Jesus goes out to the nameless millions. He saves them from their sins. He makes each one of them whole again. He brings them back to God. He gives them brothers and sisters. He tells them how to live. He fills their hearts with concern for those now in darkness. He helps His followers raise the banner of His name everywhere in society. He inspires them to tackle the terrible problems of modern life in His name. Actually, His people become extensions of His name. They want to save others from their sins, from their sorrow, and from their selfishness. "They shall see his face, and his name shall be on their foreheads," said John (Rev. 22:4).

Father, thank You for Your name among us—Jesus our Savior. Give us more faith in Jesus. Help us to introduce many to Your name, Lord Jesus. May Your name be written all over this world. We pray in Your name. Amen.

The Man Who Wrote the Christmas Account

It seemed good to me also, having followed all things closely for some time past, to write an orderly account for you, most excellent Theophilus . . . (Luke 1:3).

The Bible is the inspired book of God, but He used human writers with their talents and research. Luke, the writer of the third gospel, is an example.

Luke wrote his account for a man called *Theophilus*. Bible scholars think that the manuscript was completed in Rome and then sent by courier to Caesarea, the Roman capital for Palestine, where Theophilus lived. Luke called him "most excellent," a title used for Roman government officials.

Years before Luke had instructed this young civil servant in the faith. Both men were Greek and well-educated, and an enduring friendship had followed. Luke continued his travels for the spread of the gospel, frequently as Paul's companion, but off and on he would think of his friend Theophilus. Had he continued in the faith? An idea began to grow in Luke's mind. He would write Theophilus a letter and continue the earlier instruction by mail, so to speak. He worked at that letter regularly and with great care. He became engrossed in it as he went on.

When Luke first came to Jerusalem as a young man, Christ had already ascended into heaven. So Luke made it a special concern to consult and interview many people who had known Jesus. "Eyewitnesses," he called them. It became an "orderly account," written in beautiful prose, evidence of the learning of the writer. But Luke not only wrote with great excellence, he also wrote with deep compassion and love for people. Perhaps his profession as a medical doctor was a factor in his work. Half the materials in Luke's gospel are not found in the other three. They deal with people in their needs, their struggles, their pain.

The Holy Spirit blessed those painstaking efforts. When the "letter" to Theophilus was finished, the Holy Spirit made it part of the Bible, for millions to read. Thus one of Europe's early converts was chosen to write the account of Christ's birth.

Lord, we thank You that You used Luke's learning and love for people to prepare for us the wonderful gospel of Christ's coming. Help us to read it in faith. Amen.

Zechariah

. . . there was a priest named Zechariah . . . righteous before God, walking in all the commandments and ordinances of the Lord blameless (Luke 1:5-6).

His name was Zechariah, which means: "The Lord remembers His covenant." This is important to note: God would do special things through Zechariah. Zechariah points away from himself to some great things. He is a vessel of the Lord.

Zechariah was a very godly priest. "Weren't all priests godly?" you ask. No. The nation had come through 400 dark years. Instead of keeping the hope of the Messiah alive, the priests had made an agreement with Rome: they kept the people content, and Rome gave them quite a bit of authority. Zechariah was one of the few who did not share in the spiritual malaise; he walked blamelessly with the Lord. That was the Lord's doing. He preserved for Himself a faithful priest from Aaron's house who would make the final preparations for welcoming the Christ. It was ultimately the Lord Himself who knitted the Old Testament into the New. Even this godly priest stumbled in the process. He just could not believe the angel's promise that he, at his old age, would have a son who would become the herald of the Messiah. God took Zechariah's speech away till the child was born as a clear sign that His plan of redemption cannot be thwarted.

You hear it said these days: "There's nothing sacred anymore. Are there no standards of good and evil any longer? What do we know for sure?" But when we see again the craftsmanship with which God fashioned the Christmas events, the care with which He guided people to participate in them, the way in which He provided for and through those people, then we take heart again. His Word binds us to a straight course but supplies as we go along.

May Your children again see, Lord, how special Your great works of salvation in Christ are. May we reflect Your care for us in a life of obedience. For Christ's sake. Amen.

Elizabeth

And when Elizabeth heard the greeting of Mary, the babe leaped in her womb; and Elizabeth was filled with the Holy Spirit (Luke 1:41).

Elizabeth was the world's happiest woman. For years she and her husband had longed for a child, and then, by God's miracle, she became a mother. Who would have thought that at her age she would know such joy?

But her joy had a deeper dimension still.

Elizabeth knew that her new baby would play a very special role in the salvation which God had promised to Israel as a nation and to the world. One day she received a visit from her cousin Mary. As she opened the door and stood face to face with the mother of Christ, Elizabeth felt the child stirring within her. What unsurpassed joy! There was hope for the future. Her son John would prepare the coming of the Savior Jesus Christ. Together with her husband, the godly priest Zechariah, she would bring up this child in God's ways and prepare him for his calling. Thus God used people with all their gifts and devotion to make the ministry of Christ possible.

He still enlists godly people to bring Christ to the world. The need is so urgent! Everywhere families are under attack today. Parents are worried about their children. Children cannot understand their parents. Husbands and wives cannot get along. Anger fills many hearts. Nobody would deny that the causes are complex. But Elizabeth could teach us a lesson. What do we live for? Are we pleasure-seekers? Oh, if everywhere fathers and mothers and children would love each other and serve the Lord! There is so much work to be done for Christ! Let us join hands and hearts in that common task. No selfish concerns would then tear our families apart anymore.

Dear Lord Jesus, let us share a common hope and challenge. Help parents and children to walk one way, Christ's way. Amen.

Mary

And [the angel] came to [Mary] and said, "Hail, O favored one, the Lord is with you!" (Luke 1:28).
All these with one accord devoted themselves to prayer, together with the women and Mary the mother of Jesus (Acts 1:14).

God's idea of a favor is different from ours.

Take Mary, for instance.

The angel said to her, "Hail, o favored one, the Lord is with you!"

In what way was Mary "favored"? She was given the honor of being the mother of Christ; she bore Him under her heart and nurtured Him in godliness. Mary occupied a unique place in God's program of salvation. But for Mary that meant much suffering. Simeon said to her, "A sword will pierce through your own soul." Only in a deeper spiritual sense could Mary experience God's doings in her life as "favored one." How different from our idea of enjoyment and good fortune! We want to *take* and *consume*, but the godly believer wants to *give* and *bless*.

In Mary's life there was a second chapter.

We read about Mary again in the book of Acts. Jesus had risen from the dead and ascended into heaven. Humanly speaking, this would now be the period in Mary's life when she could relish the honor of having been the mother of the Lord. But Acts 1 does not give that impression. At that first worship service the names of the apostles are mentioned first, then "the women," and finally Mary. Her glory was not that she was Jesus' mother but that she was a *believer* in Christ. Her honor was not that He was her son but her *Savior*.

Our greatest honor is to be *redeemed*. You may have that honor. The gospel has to change our values. We harbor a deep longing for good fortune. That's our idea of being "highly favored." God's idea is that we are restored to Him as His children. And with Christ He will give us all things.

Father, help us to see happiness Your way. Keep us safe in the forgiveness of sins. Provide for us in all our troubles. For Jesus' sake. Amen.

Joseph

And her husband Joseph, being a just man and unwilling to put her to shame, resolved to divorce her quietly. But . . . an angel of the Lord appeared to him in a dream (Matt. 1:19-20).

Joseph was Mary's husband and Jesus' foster-father. When we read what the Bible tells us about him, we get the impression of a gentle and loving man. Without him seeking it, his life revolved around the birth and care of the child Jesus, who was to be the Savior of the world.

Those called upon to serve Christ will experience joy and trials at the same time. Joseph was no exception.

While Joseph was engaged to be married to Mary, she conceived by the power of the Holy Spirit. She did not feel free to share this with Joseph. Instead she left and visited her cousin Elizabeth in the southern part of the land. When she returned, she could not hide from Joseph that she was expecting a child. But even then she was unable to explain to him the hand of the Spirit.

Joseph could have felt bitter, but he didn't. Instead he made honorable provisions for Mary to spare her disgrace. It was then that an angel explained to him the wondrous works of God and turned his night into a joyous morning. Mary would be the mother of Christ!

But that was not the end of Joseph's problems. Great demands were made on him. He cared for Mary on the way to Bethlehem, he provided for her there when Jesus was born, and he had to flee with them to Egypt when Herod was out to kill the infants in Bethlehem. Later Joseph took his family to Galilee, where he instructed Jesus in the Scriptures. The last time the Bible mentions Joseph was at the temple, when he took his family to the Passover feast. Jesus was twelve years old then. It is generally thought that Joseph died soon after that.

We hold this humble man in grateful memory because of his loving faithful service around the coming of Christ. We thank our God for him.

Lord, we are grateful for being inspired by great people in the Bible who did so much in Your service, filled, as they were, with Your Spirit. Amen.

The Road to Bethlehem (I)

In those days a decree went out from Caesar Augustus that all the world should be enrolled (Luke 2:1).

We could think of four roads which led to Bethlehem: from Rome, from Nazareth, from heaven, and from our hearts. We will consider each one. Today let us look at the road from Rome.

Luke tells us that Caesar Augustus decreed that "all the world" should be enrolled. That was a big decision, but Caesar Augustus was a big man. His real name was *Octavianus*. He had adopted the name *Caesar* in keeping with his office, and, for good measure, had added the name *Augustus*—the *Exalted*.

The emperor had good reason for overhauling the administrative system of his empire, which reached from England to India, from southern Russia to North Africa. There had been many years of war, but peace had now been established, the *Pax Romana*, and consolidation was urgently needed. The enrollment in Judea was therefore a part of an empire-wide action.

Little did the emperor realize that not he, but God, had taken the initiative for the enrollment. God orchestrated all the events around the birth of Christ. God, ultimately, arranged for worldwide conditions that suited Him in the spread of the gospel of Christ after the outpouring of the Holy Spirit. When the emperor's officials traveled to Judea, they were among the first to make Christmas arrangements, though they had no inkling of it.

Remember that God has always ruled the world in keeping with His plan of salvation. He still does. He directs the nations and international developments along certain roads which all end up on the highway of His decree. There is nothing insignificant about the life of an individual Christian. His God is the great helmsman. Christianity may seem small, but it makes the world go around. Wonderful for us to know!

Wonderful, mighty God, we know that You are in charge. Remind us every time again of Your power and wisdom, also for our lives. Because of His birth. Amen.

The Road to Bethlehem (II)

And Joseph also went up from Galilee, from the city of Nazareth, to Judea, to the city of David, which is called Bethlehem (Luke 2:4).

The road from Nazareth is the second road to Bethlehem which we will consider.

Joseph and Mary, who traveled this road together, were ordinary people. They were not rich, but not terribly poor either, since Joseph was a good craftsman. They were from the house of David, which had lost its luster, but they had a good reputation. The Bible never makes mention of the donkey, with Joseph trudging alongside, as we usually assume. They probably traveled the way most people traveled. The enrollment was an extraordinary event, but everything about Joseph and Mary was rather ordinary.

We do not want to overlook this. The Lord Jesus Christ assumed human nature from ordinary people. He assumed *our* nature. *We* are those ordinary people. Christ did not come to earth to save us from the killer-instinct in us; no, our very ordinary heart had broken with God, and in our very ordinary daily affairs we rebelled against God.

That's the terror of the grip of sin. We—decent, respectable people—betrayed God and made common cause with satan.

Sin—what a treacherous thing!

Sin is when I look at the trees and the clouds without recognizing the Maker; when I build a house or sell a car without realizing that I touch His goods; when I talk with friends or greet people without seeing them as God's image-bearers; when I sing and dream without communing with Him; when I look at myself without feeling the need of a Savior. Sin is when life is not lived in close union with God. For such sin Christ came into the world. That's why we recognize in these ordinary travelers on the road to Bethlehem the love of God to save us in the fullness of daily life.

We expose our motives and ideals to You, Lord, for You see it all. We need salvation in Christ, and total healing. Thank You, Lord, that it is important to You what we do with our time and our goods, and how we deal with people. Amen.

The Road to Bethlehem (III)

And suddenly there was with the angel a multitude of the heavenly host praising God . . . (Luke 2:13).

Not many people are aware of this road to Bethlehem, the one from heaven. But for a while it was a very busy one: angels came down that road in amazing numbers. They represented heaven in greeting the new-born Savior of the world. This busy air-corridor is our guarantee that in Christ's coming, the harmony between heaven and earth has been restored. The angels felt perfectly at home over the fields of Bethlehem. No matter what evil might stalk mankind during the following years, heaven was not far but came to the rescue of the distressed. No matter what you may face now, remember that the distance between God and you has been bridged.

Note also what these visiting angels did. They sang praises to God in heaven: "Glory to God in the highest!" How wonderfully good God has been in sending His Son. But the song also implied how great that Son is—human for our sake, yes, but also fully God, worthy of heavenly praise. The angels were aware of the enormity of Christ's assignment in bringing the lost home. Only a Savior being both God and man could accomplish that. So, let the angels travel the sky-road from heaven in great numbers. Hallelujah, what a Savior!

Through the years, God's children have known much suffering for their faith. But they saw that road from heaven ever more clearly. That gave them great endurance. Did you know that if you descend into a very deep hole, right during the middle of the day, and look up from the darkness of the bottom, you will see stars overhead? Believers who went through deep valleys have seen heaven nearby; they could touch it in their soul. That was the secret of their courage and trust. The coming of Christ accomplished that, the angels demonstrated it, and you may experience it.

Thank You, Lord Jesus, for making God so real to us, for being such a perfect Savior—so holy, yet so close. Praise be to You forever. Amen.

The Road to Bethlehem (IV)

My Father gives you the true bread from heaven . . . and gives life to the world (John 6:32-3).

The fourth road to Bethlehem leads from our hearts. We have no share in the Christmas gospel if we do not travel to Bethlehem in faith and kneel down before our Savior.

Perhaps you know that the name *Bethlehem* means *house of bread*. The origin of that name is not clear, but Jesus frequently compared Himself to bread. In the verses we read today, He called Himself the "bread of life." In the previous chapter Christ miraculously multiplied bread and fed 5000 people in the wilderness. That really fascinated the people. They liked Him for it. Imagine, a leader who could solve all economic problems!

But Jesus rebuked the people. Their excitement made Him sad. He told them not to follow Him for the sake of bread that filled the stomach. Instead Christ offered food that would endure to eternal life. But the people did not understand. Uncertain of themselves, they said, "Show us that bread." Then Jesus said, "I am that bread." That disappointed the people greatly. They wanted bread on the table, and so they left Him.

Have you traveled to Bethlehem for the living bread? I would love to take your hand and lead you there, but I cannot. The only one who can is the Holy Spirit. That's why Christ sent Him. He can reach your heart. Do not resist Him.

The people who came to Jesus for bread are our cousins; we share a lot of family traits with them. We wonder how much benefit we get from our "religion." But when we eat the living bread, we become new people. Our hearts are right with God, we are His partners, we are what God intended us to be. And that, ultimately, is what happiness and fulfillment are all about. The secret of Christmas is the journey to Bethlehem in the heart.

We bow in deepest reverence before You, dear Savior, and ask You to give us a new purpose for life and a new source from which to live it. Because of Bethlehem. Amen.

For Our Sake

For you know the grace of our Lord Jesus Christ, that though he was rich, yet for your sake he became poor, so that by his poverty you might become rich (II Cor. 8:9).

Amid all the sentimentality, the hoopla and the bottles, this one question needs all our attention: What is Christmas all about? Paul summed it up in one statement: *Christ became poor, we became rich.*

In what way did Christ become *poor?*

The Son of God, eternal God Himself, took on human flesh—the Child Jesus (Phil. 2:6-8). The circumstances of His birth were humble: it brought hardship to people close to His birth. Church and state authorities opposed His coming, and, in general, people resented His presence (John 1:11). His poverty had even more painful sides. God's Son, the giver of the law, was "born of woman, born under the law" (Gal. 4:4), which meant that He not only fulfilled the law for us but also took the guilt of our sins upon Himself: "He humbled himself and became obedient unto death, even death on the cross" (Phil. 2:8).

But that poverty of Christ brought us *riches.*

How shall we enumerate those riches? The Bible is full of them. On this Christmas day, let us see some examples. "In Christ Jesus you are all sons of God" (Gal. 3:26). "And because you are sons, God has sent the Spirit of his Son into our hearts, crying 'Abba! Father!' " (Gal. 4:6). Imagine that: free children of God, filled with the Holy Spirit! What beautiful lives! "Sin will have no dominion over you, since you are not under law but under grace" (Rom. 6:14). Or look at this: "The free gift of God is eternal life in Christ Jesus our Lord" (Rom. 6:23).

When it comes to sizing up riches, don't be fooled. The physical eye sees a humble manger with a babe versus the grandeur of imperial Rome. But one thing: Could Caesar Augustus change one human heart? Could he put love there for God and fellow man? And without love, what good are earthly riches?

On this Christmas day we thank You, almighty Father, for having given Christ to be born among us. We thank You that we are Yours forever through Him. Amen.

Good for You, Shepherds!

The shepherds said to one another, "Let us go over to Bethlehem and see this thing that has happened, which the Lord has made known to us" (Luke 2:15).

Though shepherding had been an honorable profession during Old Testament days, it was not so much anymore during Jesus' time. Those who hired themselves out to tend the flocks were not considered the most dependable lot. Jewish law stipulated that their testimony would not stand up in a court of law. But the angels selected *shepherds* to hear the first Christmas announcement.

Their response was splendid, worthy of note.

The angels made a brief announcement of Christ's birth and added some sober details. But without being told to do so, the shepherds immediately decided to go and see for themselves. They ascribed the message of the angels to *the Lord:* they wanted to see the secret which the Lord had made known to them. That was the secret of their jubilant obedience: the *Word* of the Lord had changed their hearts. The spoken Word of the Lord led to the Word-become-flesh. Bible reading still does that; it leads to a personal meeting with Christ; it makes people really alive. We read that the shepherds went "with haste." The outcome was wonderful: "They found Mary and Joseph and the babe . . ." And they *believed*. No finer reception could have been afforded the Savior. Our lives may be confused and broken, but Christ welcomes anyone who comes and believes.

All that just filled the shepherds with joy. They spoke of it openly; they *made it known*, we read. Such personal witnessing was an unusual experience for them, but they did it! They also *glorified* and *praised* God, we are told. The Lord had given them so much happiness—what else could they do but express it with excitement?

Just note one little addition. It says: "They returned." They went back to their sheep and finished the night shift. Tomorrow we go back to work. That's where the gospel is experienced and expressed.

Give us the strength and courage, dear Lord, to go back to our tasks after these several days off, and to show in what we do and say that we love You. Amen.

Here Come the Wise Men

Now when Jesus was born in Bethlehem of Judea . . . behold, wise men from the East came . . . (Matt. 2:1).

We do not know exactly, where these wise men came from. Perhaps they lived in Mesopotamia, where once the Babylonian empire had been, the region of the Euphrates and Tigris rivers. What we do know is that the Lord spoke to them in special ways. First we read that the Lord showed them a star and bound it upon their hearts that this had something to do with the King of the Jews. That led them to Jerusalem, where the Lord spoke to them again when the scribes pointed them to the prophecy of Micah, from which they learned the birthplace of the Savior. But the most glorious thing God did was to lead them to His Son, Christ Jesus.

Isn't God good? He did it all. He led them step by step. Actually, when you come to think of it, He did even more for you. You have not just one verse from Micah's prophecy; you have all of Micah, all of the Scriptures! And the Christ of those Scriptures is always willing to receive you, to listen to you, to save you, and to help you! That's why He came to this earth.

Next, note how the wise men responded in a special way. They *rejoiced*. Those learned scholars were like happy children. And they *kneeled down*, we read. These independent men bowed before Christ, accepting Him as Ruler of their lives. Scholarship belongs to Him. And finally, they laid their *gifts* at His feet. Not just presents—no, the finest of all gifts: myrrh, frankincense, and gold. You must do that: give yourself, give your love, serve Him with your means and talents.

Christmas is a wonderful season. It dramatizes all of God's special dealings with us. He speaks to us with abundant clarity, and we respond with exuberance. Those two keep our Christian life fresh and fruitful.

You have invested so much in us, and now, heavenly Father, let all Your grace in Christ echo in our hearts and deeds. For Christ's sake. Amen.

There Go the Wise Men

Then Herod summoned the wise men secretly . . . And being warned in a dream not to return to Herod, they departed to their own country by another way (Matt. 2:7, 12).

The wise men from the East had to learn that Christianity is not all festive gatherings with presents all around. It also comes with conflicts and bitter opposition. Herod was afraid of the newborn King; he hated Him instantly and decided to kill Him. So the wise men became involved in the battle around the coming of the Lord. It would not be the last time. They had chosen for Christ, and that meant that they had chosen against His enemy, against Herod.

God spoke to them in a dream and told them not to go back to Jerusalem but to take another route. That involved considerable risk; the king's soldiers were all over. But the wise men readily obeyed. They had met Christ. That made them different people, and because they were different people they had to travel different roads. They had to take the roads of loyalty and obedience, roads that further the cause of Christ.

During this season we tend to eat a lot, go out a lot, and spend a lot. We become tired people. William Ward once said, "There are now so many weary Christians: they go to church and yawn in the presence of the Lord." The wise men *moved on.* They heeded God's directions. They had become part of God's unfolding Kingdom program.

What will revitalize us to get us moving by "another way," the way of risks for the Lord, the way of self-denial and sacrifice?

Let us learn again that we must not only *hear* God's Word but also *do* it. Worship and adoration are not ends in themselves. They replenish us to be stronger for the Lord, to oppose evil, and to do good. And the purpose of our earthly days is not material self-improvement but participation in God's program of salvation.

Inspire us, Lord, to be industrious for the church of Christ, and to help people walk in ways of godliness. Create in us a spirit of sacrificial service. Amen.

Simeon

Now there was a man in Jerusalem, whose name was Simeon . . . he took
[Jesus] up in his arms and blessed God and said, ". . . a light for revelation
to the Gentiles" (Luke 2:25, 28, 32).

Soon after Jesus was born, His parents took Him to the temple
"to present Him to the Lord." One of the people who welcomed
the Christ child there was a grand old man called Simeon. Simeon
had two outstanding qualities. He was a man of *deep feeling* and a
man of *broad vision*. We read that he broke forth in *praise* when he
held the Child, and he summed up the mission of Jesus by declaring
that it provided *light for the Gentiles*.

Those two gifts, *depth* and *breadth*, go together. Blessed the
person who feels deeply about the Lord, whose soul is on fire for
Him, who knows the spontaneous joy of praise, but who at the
same time has clear understanding, who is well-versed in the Scriptures and has tested the spirits of his age. If Christianity is all warmth
and emotions, it lacks endurance and direction, but if it is all
doctrine and teaching, it lacks the force of life.

The early Christians of Acts 2 loved their heavenly Father,
which is why they studied His Word daily. That was probably the
reason why the church grew so fast. They shared with their neighbors an urgent message wrapped in joy and love. They were not so
much out to make converts as to share their concern and goodness.

There lived in the second century a great defender of the
Christian faith, called Justin, who had earlier been a pagan Greek
philosopher. He died, ultimately, as a martyr for Christ, and hence
later became known as Justin Martyr. Justin had found his Savior
through a conversation with an old fisherman of gentle face and
manners when he walked along the seashore. That was evangelism
in the early church, and that is evangelism at its best—still today.

Dear Savior, bring many to the faith through our testimony of joy. May
our words be backed by a life of light. In Christ's name. Amen.

Jesus Grew Up

And the child grew and became strong, filled with wisdom . . .
And all who heard them were amazed at his understanding . . .
And Jesus increased in wisdom . . . (Luke 2:40, 47, 52).

Jesus was fully human, and so He went through stages of human growth. When He was twelve years old, His parents took Him to the Passover feast at Jerusalem. The study sessions at the temple added to His knowledge and wisdom, we read. That meant that He gained in Scriptural knowledge, but also that He began to understand His mission as Messiah more and more (vs. 49).

There is something moving about this visit to the temple. It added to Jesus' suffering. The young Jesus was without sin, but everything reminded Him of sin: the laws, the sacrifices, the people. Though at this stage of His life Jesus did not fully comprehend all the implications of His mission on earth, He began to see that those sins would be His suffering.

Now, normally a boy of twelve, when faced with such overwhelming experiences, would take refuge with his parents. But Jesus could not do that. His parents were upset that He had lingered at the temple, and they gave Him a mild scolding. That, in turn, deepened His loneliness. That's how the trip to Jerusalem prepared Him for a life of sin-bearing.

When we consider the further life of Christ, it amazes us how many sides there are to His suffering—a nearly endless variety of pain.

And that is so because our sins were of such dismal variety, yet each sufficient to isolate us from God.

He took all that over from us. What a Savior! Hallelujah! See and believe that He did that for you.

> Thus might I hide my blushing face
>   While His dear cross appears;
> Dissolve, my heart, in thankfulness!
>   And melt my eyes to tears.

How indeed, Lord, can we thank You for Your payment for our guilt? Make that gratitude a channel of Your power to us to live unto You in newness. Amen.

Goodness

Teach me thy way, O Lord . . . I believe that I shall see the goodness of the Lord in the land of the living! (Ps. 27:11, 13).

Do you feel good about the year that lies behind you?

I visited a man in the hospital who had suffered a heart attack. He said to me, "Looking back, there were the little warnings—a dizzy spell, a twinge of pain, shortness of breath, and the like. But I kept going! Now that I am lying here, I find myself wondering what I was doing with my life, what I have meant to people, what I have meant to the Lord . . ."

David knew those thoughts; he had known pressures and failures. Psalm 27 is a psalm with ups and downs, certainty and doubt, victory and defeat. There were so many things he felt so bad about, but they could not be undone. But then, suddenly, David turns the management of his life over to the Lord. He prays, "Teach me thy way, O Lord." And that sums it up for us—*teach me Thy way*. Do you think the Lord would not hear such a prayer?

On this last day of the year, we pause and ask the Lord to forgive our wrong way of living, the false goals, the disregard of others, the haste . . . We ask Him for a new heart and a new disposition.

When David had done that, he made a wonderful confession: "I believe that I shall see the goodness of the Lord in the land of the living!" He knew he could go on. Life would be good; he could live it to the full. *You* can make that confession too, and by Christ's grace *you* can live a wonderful life in the Lord's company. *You* can see the goodness of the Lord in the land of the living. This New Year's Eve is not the last hurrah for the mediocre; it is the gateway toward a new life with the Lord.

You are *on your way rejoicing!*

Father, I now lay this year, with all that I have made of it, before You. Purge all that was untrue and dishonest. Cover me with Your righteousness, Lord Jesus. Bless what was good, Holy Spirit. Amen.

Index